Dr. John Coleman

WE FIGHT FOR OIL:
A HISTORY OF U.S. PETROLEUM WARS

The American imperialism is a fatal product of economic evolution. It is useless trying to persuade our northern neighbor not to be imperialistic, they cannot help being so, no matter how excellent their intentions...

El Universal, Mexico City, October 1927

ⒺMNIA VERITAS®

John Coleman

John Coleman is a British author and former member of the Secret Intelligence Service. Coleman has produced various analyses of the Club of Rome, the Giorgio Cini Foundation, Forbes Global 2000, the Interreligious Peace Colloquium, the Tavistock Institute, the Black Nobility and other organisations with New World Order themes.

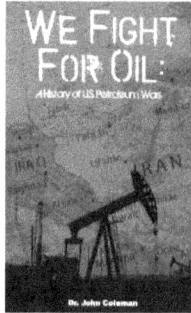

WE FIGHT FOR OIL
A history of US Petroleum Wars

© Omnia Veritas Ltd - 2023

ᴓMNIA VERITAS₀

www.omnia-veritas.com

A history of U.S. oil wars is a work-in-progress which began when President Wilson landed U.S. troops at Tampico. Future historians may very well have to fill in the blanks. The history of U.S. involvement in Persia (now Iran) and Mesopotamia (now Iraq) centered around the quest for oil and control of it as a vitally-needed natural resource. With this in mind, the reader may well come to the conclusion that news from U.S. (and British) sources has to be taken with a large grain of salt.

Oil diplomacy is governed by commercial and eventually, military considerations. Thus every U.S. President since Woodrow Wilson has formulated U.S. foreign policy to take care of oil interests. President McKinley said 'isolation is no longer possible,' and President Wilson echoed that sentiment when he said: 'We are participants whether we would or not in the life of the world. The interests of all nations are ours also. We are partners with the rest.'

Therefore this book affects or should affect every American, because modern international power is economic, just as all wars are economic in origin. Remember this the next time your sons and daughters are called to fight for the country. If Iraq did not contain huge oil resources, would the U.S. be bogged down in that country today? Fear of domestic shortages of oil seems to be the driving force at play. American strife over foreign resources has become the major factor in international affairs. These are issues examined in this book which should be read by every American interested in the future of their country.

CHAPTER 1

Petroleum industry's quest for oil

We surely need a clear, concise and easily understood guide to the long running 'conflict' with nations having crude oil deposits. On April 16, 1855 Benjamin Stillman of Yale University and George Bissell offered 'rock oil' to investors after reports reached them of a thick viscous black sludge in certain areas of Titusville, Pennsylvania. Russia had previously mentioned similar findings in Baku. Bissell immediately ordered Edwin ('Colonel') Drake to drill for oil in Titusville.

Nobody had any use for the 'sludge' except John D. Rockefeller who was the sole owner of the Cleveland trading firm that sold the product and was later joined by a partner, Henry Flagler in a produce company, who sold it as lamp oil, and packaged in another way, as a cure for cancer. The company was soon worth $450,000, an astronomical sum of money in those days. In fact it was John D. Rockefeller and his Standard Oil in all of its octopus-like variations that became a menace, not only in the U.S., but to the entire world. Standard Oil simply absorbed or destroyed much of its competition in Cleveland, Ohio and then the rest of the northeastern United States.

Rockefeller earned a nick-name, 'the Illumination Merchant' partly because his product called 'Brite' lit lamps in every household in the U.S., but also in a sly reference to his membership of the world's most secret society, the Illuminati, which consisted of the world's so-called "elite."

On August 27, 1859, Drake struck oil at his drilling site bolstered by financing emanating from Kuhn Loeb and the French Rothschild's Paribas banking giant, Standard Oil (1870-1911) either owned outright or had a controlling interest in 95% of all oil refineries in America by 1870, the year that Standard Oil was founded, and in 1879, Standard Oil owned and controlled 90 percent of U.S. refinery capacity.

In 1863 John D. Rockefeller met a chemist by the name of Samuel Andrews who had invented a shortcut to refining kerosene. Andrews was signed on as a partner and was later joined by Flagler in a partnership called Rockefeller, Andrews & Flagler.

In 1906 the U.S. Government tried to break up the Rockefeller Standard Oil Trust, because it was a monopoly of the strategic commodity of oil. The public saw it as a nefarious business and there were legal attacks by one State as well as a revelation by Ida Tarbell in 1904. (The History of Standard Oil) The Senate enlisted the aid of the U.S. Justice Department and in 1909 suit was filed in Federal Court claiming that Standard had engaged in the following methods which amounted to monopoly practices:

> Rebates, preferences, and other discriminatory practices in favor of the combination of railroad companies, restraint and monopolization by control of pipelines, unfair practices against competing pipelines, contracts with competitors in restraint of trade, methods of competition, such as local price-cutting at the points, where necessary to suppress competition, the operation of bogus independent companies and payment of rebates on oil with the like intent.

On May 5, 1911, the Supreme Court ordered the Standard Oil Trust monopoly dissolved. The justices said:

> Seven men and a corporate machine have conspired against their fellow citizens. For the safety of the Republic we now decree that this dangerous conspiracy must be ended by

November 15th.

The exposure of the octopus in their midst by Ida Tarbell's account of John D., published in 1904 in 24 issues of McClures Magazine, had alarmed too many people and at last it seemed that resolute action against the Rockefeller Trust was about to happen. But alas, it was only an illusion. Not fazed by such a mere trifle as a Supreme Court decree against him, Rockefeller merely split the giant into separate companies retaining a 25% majority in each of them. The break up actually enriched Rockefeller especially after William Burton of Standard devised a thermal cracking process that increased the yield of gasoline from crude oil.

The corporate state had arrived at the point where corporate fascism would henceforth be the controlling body behind all major foreign policy decisions, even the most important of all, war and peace. Mexico was the first to feel the lash of U.S. imperialism soon after the discovery in 1910 of major oil fields along the Gulf Coast, centered on Vera Cruz and Tampico.

It began when President Wilson, acting for Standard Oil interests, sent troops to Vera Cruz on the most transparent and flimsiest of pretexts. It was not the U.S. intention to take over Mexico, but to make sure that Mexico's oil would remain under U.S. corporate control.

Fomenting one revolution after another the U.S. kept Mexico in a state of turmoil while Standard and British interests looted its oil with impunity. John D. had once again thumbed his nose at those who feared his 'dangerous conspiracy.'

British interests were taken care of by Lord Cowdrey (Weetman Pearson), where a chance delayed stopover at Laredo in 1901 brought Mexican oil to his doorstep through Mexican Eagle Petroleum Ltd., which he founded in 1910. After the first Mexican 'revolution,' Weetman Pearson sold all of his oil holdings in Mexico to Royal Dutch Shell, a multinational company of Anglo-Dutch origin. Shell was destined to become a 'super-major' oil company.

The war in Europe gave Mexico a respite and allowed duly elected President Carranza to write a national Constitution approved in 1917. Contrary to the jackals of the U.S. media, General Venustiano Carranza was no wild-eyed revolutionary, but a well educated scholarly man from a wealthy family. He served as a state legislator and a deputy governor and was by all accounts a true patriot of Mexico. The black eye for Standard and the oil robber barons was paragraph 27 vesting the nation 'direct ownership of all minerals, petroleum and all hydro-carbons, solid, liquid or gaseous.' Henceforth, the only way foreigners could do business in Mexico was by signing an agreement to entirely respect and obey Mexican law. For defying the U.S. (Rockefeller), Carranza was assassinated in 1920.

There followed a campaign of vicious conduct that plumbed the depth of depravity, to wrest control of Mexico's oil away from its rightful owners. But when that failed, all the major Western oil companies boycotted Mexican oil for the next 40 years.

The Committee of 300 stepped into the picture when the French Rothschilds (Alphonse and Edmond) and the Swedish Nobel company in 1870 turned their attention to Russia by forming an oil company called The Far East Trading Company. But the Nobel brothers had beaten all competitors to the oil in Baku, having taken up residence there. Ludwig Nobel became known as 'the Oil King of Baku.'

The British House of Windsor and the Dutch Huis Oranje (House of Orange) joined hands to get into the business and in 1903 agreed with Shell Oil to form the Asiatic Petroleum Company. Efforts that were made to ease tensions in the Baku oil fields between Standard Oil, the Rothschilds-Nobel and some smaller Russian companies were unsuccessful.

The Royal Dutch Shell Petroleum Company was formed to exploit oil in Sumatra and Indonesia and elsewhere in the Far-East. Their membership of the '300' opened all doors.

The '300' placed the daily business in the hands of Marcus Samuel of Hill Samuel and in 1897-1898 prospector/oil driller Mark Abrahams, hired by Marcus Samuel, found oil in Borneo. The London merchant banking house and its affiliated trading company, Samuel Montague, combined with Edmond and Alphonse Rothschild and founded the Asiatic Petroleum Company. The Rothschilds did not stay in, selling their shares to Royal Dutch Shell and by 1892 Shell was shipping South Sea crude oil to European refineries via the Suez Canal.

There can be no doubt that the Royal Dutch Shell '300' company is one of the oldest and largest of all the oil companies operating in the world today. Its turnover in 2005 was $306.73 billion. The late Queen Juliana of the Netherlands, Lord Victor Rothschild, the Nasi prince of Africa Sir Ernest Oppenheimer, the Samuels of London and the House of Windsor are the largest stockholders in Royal Dutch Shell. On the death of Juliana her stocks were passed on to House of Orange (Netherlands).

The historical account of the petroleum industry takes us through the twists and turns of 'diplomacy' (lies, false promises, mendacity, double-dealing, political pressure, bullying and unfair robbery) of Iraq's lands and oil, coveted by all nations, but particularly by an industrialized oil-starved imperialistic Great Britain, that has busied itself in Iraq and Iran's internal affairs for almost a century, seducing, cajoling and wheedling concessions, one after another, based on promises never kept and threatened by an iron fist concealed in a velvet glove.

With the discovery of rich crude oil deposits in Iraq and Iran, a prolonged state of conflict with the U.S. and both countries has continued for the past 95 years.

CHAPTER 2

A vision of oil fired warships sir Edward grey foments WWI

Just before WWI, a chain reaction that spurred interest in oil was prompted through a report by a British Navy officer Captain Fisher, which said the Navy's future lay in oil-burning warships. He was later to become Lord Fisher, First Lord of the Admiralty, astute enough to see the possibilities for the heavy black, liquid discovered oozing through the rocks at Titusville, Pennsylvania and Baku, Russia in 1882. John D. Rockefeller had seen its possibilities as a new mineral for oil lamps and trade-marked it 'Brite.' He then formed the Standard Oil Company to exploit the new find.

Captain Fisher's vision in 1904 was for the British Navy to be converted from Welsh coal burning to oil burning warships. His idea was not new, most probably taken from the fact that since 1870, Russian ships on the Caspian Sea had been burning 'oil sludge' called 'mazut.' This development was also noticed by Baron Julius de Reuter (the patriarch of Reuter' s News Service) who had reported this development. In 1872, de Reuter was granted a fifty-year concession to explore and drill for oil in Iran. He called his company the Anglo- Persian Company and in 1914, on the advice of Admiral Fisher, it was renamed, British Petroleum Company (BP).

Control over the seas was vital to Britain to secure its long trade lines and Admiral Fisher put the case to the Lords of the Admiralty for oil-fired British warships, which he said, would have a great advantage over German naval power. By 1870 Germany was threatening to overtake British trade supremacy. This was considered a 'crime' by British leaders like Sir Edward Grey that would eventually lead to war. Captain Fisher pointed out that it would take far less time than the 4-9 hours for coal burning ships to reach full power; oil fired ships could reach the same readiness in 30 minutes and reach peak power in only 5 minutes. The big problem was that Britain had no known reserves of crude oil. It would have to import its oil from the U.S. and Russia, not a problem in peacetime, but in wartime it would perhaps be more hazardous.

In later years (1912) Churchill who succeeded Fisher as First Lord said:

> "... if we required it (oil) we must carry it in by sea in peace and war from distant countries."

Nevertheless, Fisher pushed his dream, pointing out that whereas it took 500 men 5 days to 'coal up' a battleship; using fuel oil would take 12 men only 12 hours to accomplish the task. Moreover, the reach of an oil-powered warship would be up to five times greater than a coal-fired ship. But their lordships of the Admiralty thought Fisher as a mere dreamer ~ that is until 1904 when Fisher was recognized and promoted to First Lord of the Admiralty after British Intelligence MI6 sent briefs to the government underscoring the importance of the new crude-oil fuel. Fisher was authorized to form and lead a Royal Commission in 1912 and form a committee to study and make recommendations as to how best for Britain to secure its future oil needs.

Lord Palmerston made his views known; Britain's longstanding intentions toward countries with crude oil resources would be based on a new creed: We no longer have permanent principles, but permanent interests which we pursue to the exclusion of all else. It was an attitude that would be supported one hundred percent by Winston Churchill, who added:

> "We must become the owners, or at any rate the controllers at the source of at least a proportion of the oil which we require."

'Jackie' Fisher who chaired the Royal Commission had risen to become First Lord of the Admiralty after a humble beginning. He was born in 1841 in Ceylon and christened John Arbuthnot Fisher. He joined the Royal Navy in 1854 and concentrated on technical developments. He was generally regarded as one of the Royal Navy's greatest admirals, astute enough to oversee the building of the super battleship 'Dreadnaught.' Fisher was viewed as very high-minded and with a superior attitude that did not sit well with his fellows. The Fisher committee recommended that MI6 play a leading role in Russia and the Balkans, and so it came about that Sydney Riley (Sigmund Georgjevich Rosenblum) one of its top operatives was sent to Baku to secure significant oil contracts for Britain. Riley was also commissioned to negotiate with a little-known British-born Australian by the name of William D'Arcy Cox, who appeared to have a significant share of the mineral resources of Persia under contract. William Knox D'Arcy (December 11, 1849-May 1, 1917) was born in Newton Abbott, a small English town. His father was a lawyer and in 1866 the family immigrated to Australia, settling in Rockhampton, Queensland. The D'Arcy family was directly related to Lord D'Arcy of Knayth, the Chief Justice and Chief Governor of Ireland in the 14th Century.

William began his career by joining his father's law practice, but switched to speculating in land. He entered into a partnership that had the good fortune of a gold strike. The partnership financed the gold strike, by started a mine called Mount Morgan Gold Mining Company. William Cox made a substantial fortune before moving back to England in 1889. In 1900 he decided to join Wolff, Kitabgi and Cotte and to proceed to Persia to search for oil. He began negotiating with the Shah of Iran, Reza Khan Pahlevi, in 1901.

D'Arcy secured a 'firman' (contract) from the Shah giving him

> "full powers to probe, pierce and drill at will on Persian soil in consequence of which all the sub-oil products sought without exception to remain his property."

A drilling team under George B. Reynolds was sent out to Persia and D'Arcy began his search. A company was formed with D'Arcy putting up $500,000 of his own money.

In consideration, D'Arcy paid the sum of $20,000 plus royalties of 16% to the Shah Reza Khan Pahlevi annually. But things did not go well and in 1904 D'Arcy was forced to bring in Burmah Oil Company that put up $100,000 to enable drilling to continue. In 1907 with no success, the drilling was switched to Masjid-I-Sulaiman, where drilling began in 1908. By April, with the venture close to collapse, oil was struck at 11,800 feet, the first discovery that was to eventually turn Persia (Iran) into the greatest oil producing country in the world. In 1909, a pipeline was run from the oilfield to a refinery that was built at Abadan. William Knox D'Arcy had pulled off a coup that rocked Standard Oil to its foundations.

With a lot of persistence Reilly located and met with D'Arcy, just as he was preparing to sign a contract with the French government arranged by the Paris Rothschilds. By whatever means (and they were considerable) Reilly somehow cajoled D'Arcy into signing a contract with the British government (on behalf of the House of Windsor) just as D'Arcy was about to sign with the French.

In 1909 a company was formed called the Anglo Persian Oil Company with the House of Windsor, the House of Orange and Baron de Reuter as the key shareholders with D'Arcy as the director. The British contract was a masterstroke pulled off by Reilly, and it earned him a special position of authority when the Bolshevik Revolution was launched. He was assigned to securing contracts from the Bolshevik Government for strategic minerals and metals. Before this momentous event (1902) it was certified by Queen Victoria's geologist that large oil pools existed in Mesopotamia (renamed Iraq by the British mandate), at that time part of the Turkish Ottoman Empire dating back to 1534.

Queen Victoria played her 'gunboat diplomacy' card by stationing British warships off the bottom end of the Shaat al Arab waterway under the rule of the corrupt Mubarak al-Sabah, who had come to power by murdering his two half-brothers in 1896, and advised Turkey that henceforth the territory (later called Kuwait) was a British Protectorate.

The next step in securing the area for the British Government came with Sheikh al Sabah signing an agreement with 'the Imperial English Government' for the oil concession. The arrangement was solidified by a 'Lease in Perpetuity.' This was followed by a second agreement signed with Sheikh al-Sabah that 'no person other than nominated by the British Government' would receive a concession. It seemed that oil supplies for the British Navy were now guaranteed. Forgotten in all of this was the indisputable fact that the land called 'Kuwait' belonged to Iraq as it had for the past four hundred years, and that Kuwait's northern 'border' ran right through the richest oil fields in the world at the time, the Rumalia Oil field that belonged to Iraq.

Thus was pirated a very substantial amount of oil from the ancient nation of Mesopotamia that became Iraq when the British coined the name for their new post WWI Mandate. That left the German Navy with no known means of oil supplies to bunker its warships, which conversion it had begun in 1909 ahead of the British 'Dreadnaught' oil-fired warships. Admiral Fisher's plans for the British Navy conversion were no longer the musings of a dreamer and the first of the new 'Dreadnaught' class were commissioned by Winston Churchill who succeeded Fisher as First Lord.

In 1911 Churchill urged his government to recognize that a strong presence in the Persian Gulf was essential if the British Navy was to continue to 'rule the waves.' The British Parliament set up a Royal Commission on Oil and the Oil Engine in 1912, chaired by Lord Fisher. It was recognized that oil would play a decisive role in the coming war. This was the beginning of treacherous conduct also called 'oil diplomacy' that was to continue to the present time. At the same time Britain set about securing oil for its Navy and entered the Mexican and Middle East oilfields in pursuit of the objective. Britain's imperial oil policy was described in a secret memo written by Sir Arthur Hirtzel:

> "What we want to have in existence, what we ought to have been creating in this time is some administration with Arab institutions which we can safely leave while pulling the strings ourselves; something that won't cost very much which the Labor Government can swallow consistent with its principles, but under which our economic and political interests will be secure.
>
> If the French remain in Syria we will have to avoid giving them the excuse to set up a protectorate. If they go, or if we appear to be reactionary in Mesopotamia, there is always the risk that King Faisal will encourage the Americans to take over both…"

This underhand imperial policy rubbed off on the United States which took up the running with great eagerness. There cannot be many people with any real knowledge of the imbroglio in Afghanistan and Iraq who do not know, that the one and only reason U.S. Armed Forces are in both countries is the holy grail of oil and other hydrocarbons. In top-secret conditions the British Government purchased a majority stockholding in the Anglo-Persian Oil Company, even though at that time it was close to bankruptcy due to lack of success in finding oil in Iran. Today the company is called 'British Petroleum' (BP) and is one of the flagship companies of the Committee of 300.

Alarmed by the growing industrial prowess and expanding international trade being enjoyed by Germany, on April 14, 1914 King George who succeeded Queen Victoria, made a highly unusual visit to Paris, accompanied by his Foreign Minister, Sir Edward Grey. The son of Lt. Colonel George Grey, Sir Edward was educated at Balliol College, Oxford and in 1892 was appointed Secretary for Foreign Affairs by William Gladstone. The purpose of the mission was to persuade France to join England in a secret military alliance against Germany and Austria.

The King did not tell the French Government that his country was Bankrupt otherwise no alliance would have come out of the visit. In fact, the state of bankruptcy was recorded in a memorandum from the British Treasury to Chancellor Lloyd George, dated May 12, 1914 setting out the fact in clear terms.

History reflects that there was no purpose in making a compact with France other than to use it as an excuse to 'come to the aid of an ally' in time of war. (The same subterfuge was to be used in 1939.) Grey made the defense of France against German commercial expansion the main plank of Britain's foreign policy. There was much concern that pledges to France were made in secret and this caused grave misgivings among opposition members of Parliament, notably Charles Trevelyn, who resigned in anger, George Cadbury, E.D. Morel, and Ramsay McDonald. Their misgivings proved well-founded when on the eve of the First World War, Grey told Parliament that he had 'no alternative but to fulfill Britain's obligations to France' by joining in France's war with Germany. This was 'diplomacy by deception' at its ugliest and was the direct cause of World War I with its hideous slaughter and huge loss of lives, and wanton destruction of property. History may one day show that without Edward Grey, World War I would not have taken place. The unforgivable sin of German trade expansion and its desire to create its own trading system and create its own exchange mechanism had to be curbed, at least in the opinion of Lord Grey.

The British-French Pact, based on the foreign policies of Sir Edward Grey alone, made in secret, set the stage for the First World War, the bloodiest war ever experienced. On July 28, 1914, a scant three months after the British-French military accord was signed, Archduke Francis Ferdinand of Austria was assassinated at Sarajevo. Grey's policy called for Germany to be virtually annihilated and for Britain to secure the natural resources it needed in quest of the goal of a New World Order. Germaine to the plan was the need to secure oil supplies at the very outset, the one detail that comes out in all of Sir Edward's papers.

In August 1914 Europe was engulfed by the searing flames of the First World War, the most brutal and horrifying war of our times with casualties in the scores of millions that defied human comprehension. The assassination of Archduke Ferdinand while visiting Sarajevo in Serbia was the second blatant use of many 'contrived situations' that were to be set up to provoke wars, and it was not 'uncivilized' Germany, but 'civilized' Britain, and later the United States, who were the authors and finishers of this terrible strategy. Throughout the First World War, oil was to play the key role in a continuation of British imperialism that began with the Chinese Opium Wars and continued with the Anglo-Boer War (1899-1903). By 1917 there was hardly a single industrialized nation not fully aware of the importance of oil, and we are reminded of President Clemenceau's urgent appeal to Wilson to send 'petrol' to France:

> *The safety of the Allies is in the balance. If the Allies do not wish to lose the war, then at the moment of the great German offensive, they must not let France lack the petrol which is as necessary as blood in the battles of tomorrow.*

On September 6, 1914, the London papers were full of accounts of French General Joseph Gallieni's armada of Paris taxi cabs pressed into service to ferry troops to the front lines. Without 'petrol' for the motorized armada of taxicabs and buses he had commandeered, France would have been defeated within a few months of hostilities breaking out. At this point in history it began to emerge why King George and Edward Grey had signed a pact with France.

It was to give Britain the excuse to 'come to the aid of France' as an indirect excuse to attack Germany. John D. was quick to answer Clemenceau's call for 'petrol' and shipped ample American supplies to the French forces at a time when Germany was cut off from its former Romanian source, which had been utterly destroyed in 1916 by Colonel 'Empire' Jack Norton to prevent Baku from falling into the hands of the Germans. As Lord Curzon, Britain's Foreign Minister said in a speech delivered at a November 21, 1918, Victory Dinner, ten days after the Armistice was signed:

> *The Allies were carried to victory on a flood of oil. Without oil, how could they have procured the mobility of the fleet, the transport of their troops, or the manufacture of explosives?*

As the nations who held oil beneath the surface of their soil were soon to find out, henceforth oil would not be an asset, but a curse thanks to the rapacious imperial powers. Unbeknown to the world, the League of Nations was but a thinly-disguised vehicle for massive land grabbing, one of its first victims being Palestine. Russia was not to be a partner, a fact that was discovered in November 1917, when the Bolsheviks found a cache of secret documents showing that Britain and the U.S. had formalized a plan to carve up the Ottoman Empire and split it between themselves and a select few 'Allied' powers. The secret agreement had been concluded in February 1916 in the middle of the war, the brunt of which had fallen upon the Russian Army.

The treacherous conduct of an Imperial Britain and the United States continued up to 2006, where the United States, led by a so-called conservative Republican Party President G.W. Bush claims that he, and he alone, could order a 'first strike' against a nation that had done the U.S. no harm, in total, willful disobedience of the U.S. Constitution and Vattel's 'Law of Nations,' plus all of the Geneva Conventions and the Protocols of Nuremberg. This book is an account of barely disguised imperial aggression by two of the most powerful nations, the U.S. and Great Britain, aided and abetted by accomplices, plumbing the depths of depravity and deceit in reaching for the rich prize of oil. 'Truth is stranger than fiction' and U.S. oil imperialism, which became rooted in official policy in 1917, has lived up to the truism. Harold Ickes was the Petroleum Coordinator for National Defense in December 1942 when the State Department posted the following:

> "It is our strong belief that the development of Saudi Arabian petroleum resources should be viewed in the light of the broad national interest."

It marked the first time that the national security of the U.S. was linked to a foreign nation far removed from its shores. It marked a big step up of imperialistic actions by the United States, from a passive to an active state. Iraq bears out the validity of this premise. The United States began to play the same role with respect to Iraq's oil that Britain had played during the last century. In the past ninety-five years we have seen Britain and its imperialist allies, never hesitating to stoop to base depravity to attain the top oil prize coveted and lusted after for so long.

Britain's history is an account of a rich and powerful nation conspiring to rob smaller poorer and weaker nations, and it makes for very distressful reading indeed. It is looking more and more like a replay of the British War against the Boers in 1899. Then, the conflict was over the Boer Nation's refusal to hand over their gold. Today, the 'conflict' is over Iraq's refusal to hand over its 'black gold.'

Iraq's oil development evolved against a backdrop of contrived situations; secret agreements, deceptions, political interference and then the last 'diplomacy' of them all which came from the barrel of the gun. Written from my perspective of a qualified economist and historian agent on location and backed by 25-years of research, this work confounds the crude propagandists who supported the oil barons. I assure you, the 'conflict' with Iraq would look very different, once you have read this informative work, based on secret historical records not available to the public, the private, personal papers of the rich and the infamous account of U.S. imperialistic wars of aggression to secure crude oil supplies.

One thing that we will quickly learn is that for the past 100 years, the United States has followed a policy of aggression against all nations that have oil as a natural resource, with intensive efforts to undermine them by instability and acts of downright interference in their domestic concerns, such as occurred in the case of Mexico, in total variance with international law and the U.S. Constitution. The Petroleum Industry has dictated U.S. foreign policy that has cost the American people billions upon billions of dollars dating as far back as intervention by U.S. Marines at Tampico by the order of President Wilson.

Just recently there has been an astonishing confirmation of this policy, which shows that the world has gone far beyond the 'conspiracy' stage to where it is now an 'open conspiracy.' In mid-2006, author John Perkins came out with an astonishing work entitled, Confessions of an Economic Hit man, which confirmed much of what I had already written about quite extensively since 1971, on how the U.S. moves to bring down governments it does not like, who will not bow to its demands. I quote excerpts from Perkins's book:

> "We economic hit men, during the past 30 to 40 years, have really created the world's first truly global empire (the United States), and we have done this primarily through economics, and the military coming in only when we've done this, and primarily coming in only as a last resort."

Therefore it has been done pretty much secretly. Most of the people of the United States have no idea that we've created this empire and, in fact, throughout the world it's been done very quietly, unlike the old empires, where the army marched in; it as obvious. So I think the significance of the thing, the fact that over 80% of the population of South America recently voted in an anti-U.S. President and what's going on at the World Trade Organization, and also. In fact, the transit strike here in New York, is that people are beginning to understand that the middle class and the lower classes around the world are being terribly, terribly exploited by what I call the corporate aristocracy, which really runs this empire, the United States.

Perkins then goes on to explain what it means to be an economic hit man:

> "What we've done… we use many techniques, but probably the most common is that we'll go in to a country that has resources that our corporations covet, like oil, and we'll arrange a huge loan to that country from an organization like the World Bank or one of its sisters, but almost all of the money goes to the U.S. corporations, not to the country itself corporations like Bechtel and Halliburton, General Motors, General Electric, these types of organizations, and they build huge infrastructure projects in that country; power plants, highways, ports, industrial parks and things that serve the very rich and selfdom ever reach the poor. In fact the poor suffer, because the loans have to be repaid, and they're huge loans, and the repayment of them means that the poor won't get education, health, and other social services, and the country is left holding a huge debt, by intention.

> We go back, we economic hit men, to this country, and we say to them: 'Look, you owe us a lot of money. You can't repay your debts, so give us a pound of flesh. Sell our oil companies your oil real cheap or vote with us at the next UN vote or send troops in support of ours to some place in the world, such as Iraq.' And in that way, we 've managed to

build a world empire with very few people actually knowing what we have done."

In explaining how the system works and how he came to be employed, Perkins revealed that he was first recruited by the National Security Agency (NSA).

But Perkins was rejected on the grounds that he had 'a number of weaknesses in my character' and so he was sent to work for a private corporation starting out at Charles T. Main, a big consulting firm in Boston, where he began as an economist with a staff of about twenty.

> "My job was to convince these countries to accept such very big loans, to get the banks to make the loans, to set up the deals so that the money went to U.S. corporations. The country was left holding a huge debt, and then I would go in with one of my people and say; "Look, you know you owe us this money. You can't pay your debts. Give us that pound of flesh."

> The other thing we do, and what is going on in South America right now is that as soon as one of these anti-American presidents is elected, like Evo Morales (of Bolivia) one of us goes in and says, "Hey, congratulations Mr. President. Now that you're president, I just want to tell you that I can make you very rich, you and your family. We have several hundred million dollars in this pocket if you play the game our way. If you decide not to, over in this pocket, I've got a gun with a bullet with your name on it, in case you decide to keep your campaign promises and throw us out."

> I can make sure that this man makes a great deal of money, he and his family, through contracts, through various quasi-legal means. If he does not accept this, the same thing is going to happen to him that happened to Jamie Roldos in Ecuador, or Omar Torrijos in Panama and Allende in Chile, and we tried to do it to Chavez in Venezuela and are still trying. We

will send in people who will overthrow him, as in fact we did recently with the President of Ecuador.

Back in the 1970s Torrijos was making a lot of noise and world headlines, because he was demanding that the Panama Canal be turned back over to the Panamanians. I was sent down to Panama to bring him around, and to convince him that he needed to play the game our way. And he invited me to a little bungalow outside of Panama City and he said: "Look, you know, I know this game and if I play it your way and I know if I play it your way, I'll become very rich, but that is not important to me. What is important is that I help my poor people." Now Torrijos wasn't an angel, but he was very committed to his poor people. So he said, "You can either play the game my way or you can leave this country."

I talked with my bosses and we all decided I should stay. But I knew the whole world was watching Torrijos because of the Panama Canal issue and that if he didn't come around, the jackals would be likely to come in. Not only would we lose Panama, but he would set an example that others might follow. So I was very concerned. I liked Torrijos, and one of the reasons I wanted to bring him around was not just because it was my job, but because I wanted to see him survive, and because he didn't come around, sure enough, he was assassinated.

There was a fiery airplane crash, and afterwards, there was no question that he had been handed a tape recorder as he got on the plane and it had a bomb in it. I know the people who did the investigation afterwards, and it is pretty well documented in many places, and I personally was aware of what went on. Our official, line was that, of course that wasn't what happened. The plane simply hit a mountain. But there was no question and we were expecting it to happen.

We also tried to do that to Saddam Hussein. When he didn't come around, the economic hit men tried to bring him around. We tried to assassinate him. But that was the interesting point, because he had pretty loyal security, and in addition, he had a lot of look-alike doubles, and what you don't want to be is a body guard to a look-alike double and you think it is the president and you accept a lot of money to assassinate him and you assassinate the look-alike, because if you do that, afterwards your life and your family's isn't worth very much, so we were unable to get through to Saddam Hussein, and that's why we sent the military in.

Saddam Hussein was in the pocket of the U.S. for many years-but we wanted that final deal, similar to the one we struck with Saudi Arabia. We wanted Saddam really to tie in with our system, and he refused to do that. He accepted our fighter jets and our tanks and our chemical plants that he used to produce chemical weapons... He accepted all that, but he wouldn't quite tie in with our system in such a big way that we could bring in the huge development organizations to rebuild his country, as the Saudis did in the Western image. And that's what we were trying to convince him to do and also to guarantee that he would always trade oil for U.S. dollars, instead of Euros, and that he would keep the price of oil within limits acceptable to us. He would not go along with these things. If he had, he would still be president."

Perkins explains many things as to how the 'empire' works, but I believe I have given you, the reader, enough to convince you as to how those pursuing the U.S. imperialist policy, deal with foreign countries. Another prime example that Perkins revealed was the Marshall Plan. After the close of WWII, the Marshall Plan was set in motion allegedly to speed the recovery of Europe, especially the recovery of Germany. What is not so well known is that the greater part of the Marshall Plan funding amounting to billions of dollars went to U.S. corporations to purchase and secure oil supplies for the United States that had nothing to do with helping a German recovery. State Department records show that as much as 10% of the Marshal Plan funding went to Standard Oil of New Jersey (EXXON) Soon-Vacuum (Mobil), Standard Oil of California, (Chevron) Texaco and Gulf Oil.

They were told to fan out into Ecuador, Venezuela, Baku, Peru, Iraq, Iran and the Philippines, all countries which have suffered onslaughts from an imperialist United States. In the wake of the Second World War an anti-colonial movement began in India and spread around the world as nations decided they would no longer tolerate the seizure of their natural resources for which they received a mere pittance. But it did little to stop the march of corporate fascism which has continued virtually unabated.

Today in 2008, what we are witnessing is the relentless hounding of Iraq, Iran and the Caspian Sea region ~ in pursuance of an imperial war to gain full control of crude oil resources. We have heard the false clarion calls by George Bush echoed by the sycophant Blair that Iran is a threat to world peace, whereas, a recent large-scale European Union poll showed that the Europeans regard President Bush and the United States as the real threat to world peace. So here was another set of politicians spreading their false messages over the airwaves. For the past seventeen years (since 1991) when former President Bush took this nation into an imperialist, unconstitutional and illegal war against Iraq, and did not succeed in his endeavors to gain control of the world's second largest producer of oil, the people of the United States have been subjected to a constant barrage of propaganda against Iraq. We are reminded of what Bolshevik leader Bakunin said in 1814 when he warned about the sort of outrageous propaganda directed toward the American people by the robber barons of the oil industry:

> "Lying by Diplomacy. Diplomacy has no other mission. Every time a State wants to declare war upon another State, it starts off by launching a manifesto addressed not only to its own subjects but also to the whole world.

> In this manifesto it declares that right and justice are on its side and it endeavors to prove that is actuated only by love of peace and humanity and that, imbued with generous and peaceful sentiments, it suffered for a long time in silence until the mounting iniquity of its enemy forced it to bare its sword.

At the same time it vows that, disdainful of all material conquest and not seeking any increase in territory, it will put an end to this war as soon as justice is reestablished. And its antagonists answer with a similar manifesto, in which naturally, right, justice and humanity and all the generous sentiments are to be found respectively on its side.

Those mutually opposed manifestos are written with the same eloquence, they breathe the same virtuous indignation, and one is just as sincere as the other, that is to say they are both brazen in their lies, and it is only fools who are deceived by them. Sensible persons, all those who have had some political experience do not even take the trouble of reading such manifestos."

One of the biggest and most often repeated lies in the Bush-Cheney oil junta manifesto is that Iraq 'gassed its own people.' This oft-repeated claim, which has been echoed many more times by Blair, refers to the gassing of the inhabitants of a Kurdish village. As it turned out, the rockets tipped with nerve gas that fell on the village, were fired by Iran, and the office of Naval Intelligence (ONI) subsequently confirmed this, pointing out that the type of poison gas used (Thickened Somane Nerve Gas), was not from the Iraq arsenal.

But that did not stop the lie of being repeated over and over again, in order to convince the people of the United States, that the Cheney oil junta war against Iraq was a 'just war instead of an imperialistic quest for control of Iraq's oil.' The following is taken from *World In Review* Insider Report of April 1991, Volume No I:

The truth is that the American and British governments betrayed the Kurds. Next to the Palestinians, the Kurds have had the most broken promises of solemn undertakings by London and Washington. Up to a short while ago, the American people had no idea who the Kurdish people were or where they lived. Like the nation of Iraq, the Kurds were an unknown quantity to Americans.

In 1991 there followed the imperial war against Iraq, which brought genocide upon the Iraqi nation and devastated their land. In the aftermath of that war, the British government, which has a long history of suppression of the Kurds, promised Bush would rearm the Kurdish guerillas to use as U.S. mercenaries to topple President Hussein. But the plot was prematurely executed, and did not succeed, causing Bush to hastily put distance between his administration and the betrayed Kurds. A short history of the Kurdish people might help to put matters in the correct perspective. Situated in the northwest corner of Iraq (and note it is IRAQ) Kurdistan was always the only semi-autonomous state in the region.

In 1900, following widespread British intervention in the affairs of Turkey and Persia, Britain assumed control of vast areas in the region which was fixed by a treaty signed in 1907. Persia was not satisfied with the arrangement and sent a delegation to the Paris Peace Conference held at Versailles to demand abrogation of the treaty of 1907 that gave Tarnscaspia, Merv, Khiva, Derbent, Erivan and Kurdistan to the British, but the British managed to block the abrogation demand. In 1919 the British invaded Baghdad. In 1922, the British concluded a military agreement with Iraq. In June of the same years, the Kurds rose in revolt and fought the British forces for a whole year. The British used extensive aerial bombardment and poison gas to quell the rebellion. Of the gassing, a report to the British prime minister said its effect 'was salutary.'

CHAPTER 3

Britain' acquires leverage in Persian oil G.H.W. bush pushes for wars in the Middle East

Oil was discovered in Iran in 1908 at the Masji-i-Suleman field. It was an event that was to completely alter the fate of the Middle East in much the same way as the discovery of gold in South Africa was to doom the Boer nation. More oil in Iran was discovered in the Mosul Province (District in Iraq) and in Basra. The British sent oil experts disguised as archeologists from the Palestine Exploration Society to spy on the developing oil fields. The spies arrived in Mosul and helped to establish the Turkish Petroleum Company in 1912 and which was recognized at a Foreign Office meeting in London in March 1914 of British and German delegates as well as representatives of German and Dutch banks. Although it sounded as if it were a company with participation by Turkey, in actual fact Turkey was not part of the company.

With the outbreak of war Churchill declared that oil was of paramount importance to Britain, which statement was reinforced by a memo from Sir Maurice Hankey, secretary of the British War Cabinet, to Arthur Balfour in which he declared that control of Iran and Iraq oil was a 'first class British war aim.' The British Army invaded Iraq in 1915 to carry out the 'first class British war aim' regardless of the sovereignty of Iraq securing the oil town of Basra, the capital of Baghdad and the Mosul by 1917. But then the British forces got bogged down and had to be rescued by an Indian Army Expeditionary Force. On August 9, 1919, Sir Percy Cox signed the Anglo Persian Agreement that gave Britain great leverage over Persian oil. Later, the majlis (Assembly) refused to ratify the agreement. In February of 1920, Reza Khan and 3000 Cossacks marched into Teheran. Reza Khan dropped the unified treaty, and on December signed a Treaty of Friendship with Turkey.

None of the minority groups (including the Kurds) were represented, nor were they consulted by either Persia or Turkey, and never by Britain. As a result, the Kurds felt betrayed, and thus they began a long series of revolts. From the foregoing it is clear that the Kurdish 'problem' started decades before the advent of President Hussein of Iraq. Britain's Prime Minister Blair who has repeatedly told the world that 'Saddam gasses his own people' conveniently said nothing about the proven role of the Royal Air Force in gassing Kurdish civilians. The Tavistock Institute is good at distorting the facts of history, and have successfully hidden this deed from sight as the British and Americans have gone on fighting for oil, just as they hid the concentration camps housing Boer women and children, who died in them like flies, in pursuance of the British Government's continued determination to steal gold that was the property of the Boer nation.

In Iraq, the object of the British Government was clear; use the Kurds to destabilize the entire area so that the vast oil regions could come under its total dominion. Britain was not satisfied with the strength of the oil concessions granted to D'Arcy in 1901. It also intended to weaken the Iraqi government, which was fully recognized as an independent state by Persia on August 11, 1929.

Oil was the target of British and American imperialists. The British and their American ally should have adopted the slogan 'We Fight for Oil' and had they been honest, they would have done so. Instead Lord Curzon flatly stated that His Majesty's

Government policy on Mosul was not related to oil; rather it was based on a sacred obligation to fulfill its mandatory obligations to protect the Kurdish people! In the light of British involvement up to its eye-brows in the Mosul oil struggles, Lord Curzon's words were the height of cynicism.

The British shamelessly and ruthlessly used the Kurds in 1921 and 1991 to further Britain's interests in the exact manner that Britain had done in 1899 in supposedly securing a 'franchise for foreigners' in the Boer Republics in South Africa, whereas control of the Boer's gold was their prime concern. Today, in 2008, the only difference is that the British are being upstaged by the United States. The United States has assumed the mantle of British imperialism.

At the Lausanne Conference (November 1922-February 1923) the Turks agreed to respect minority rights, especially of the Kurds, but they never did so. *The New York Journal of Commerce* editorial of July 1923 said:

> Lausanne was all that an International Conference ought not to be. It was the sacrifice of all human and humanitarian questions to expediency.

The Lausanne treaty that emerged from the conference has its place in history as a treaty that changed the course of events and set the stage for the 20th Century. The series of peace treaties concluded at the end of WWI and the establishment of the League of Nations was ostensibly to bring 'freedom' to the world, but far from bringing freedom, it brought a new wave of imperialism and the death of the Ottoman Empire. The Lausanne Treaty was signed on July 24, 1823 and came into effect on August 6, 1924 after being ratified by Britain, Italy, France and Turkey.

Of the conference, the *New York Times* editorialized:

Mosul and freedom give us all a chance in the scramble for oil that has been the object of all of the negotiations. But the United States might be better occupied today than looking after the interests of oil kings. Peace and civilization may be talked about in public, but in private there is talk of oil, because territories where the future concessionaires will be are at pains to insure their rights, are at stake.

Although not obvious at the conference, what was going on behind the scenes was a constant jockeying for positions by the major oil companies to get a foothold in the unexplored regions of Iraq where large vilayets (a large pool of oil) were known to exist. Such an area 150 miles long was north of Kirkuk in Iraq on land occupied by the Kurds. In October 1927, drillers at Baba Gurgur struck oil, and a huge uncontrolled gusher flooded the lands around with oil for nine days, while a thick pall of gas hung in the air. The Kirkuk field with reserves of 2150 million tons of crude oil has lived up to expectations, both in the size of the huge find and the damage it has done to the entire Middle East through the intransigent greed of British and American oil companies is still being felt to this very day. 'Dad' Joiner's surprising East Texas gusher three year later (October 1930) although a major find, was largely played down because the petroleum companies were heavily invested in Middle East oil and did not want U.S. oilfields to develop. Dad Joiner's 'Black Giant' was signed away to oil tycoon H.L. Hunt (1889-1974) in very questionable circumstances.

Following indecisive elections in May 1930, the Kurds thought they saw their chance, and revolted against the new Turkish government under their leader, Ali Fehti Bey. The uprising took place in the vicinity of Mt. Ararat and was brutally and bloodily put down by British forces.

On June 10, 1961, the Iraqi government took up Kurd leader al-Barzani's new challenge backed by the U.S. and Britain, and the Kurds found themselves once again under attack. In April 1965, they again took up arms against the Iraqi government. Their demands were for a 'clearly defined area and a Kurdish army.' In March of 1966, renewed fighting broke out again, and lasted for three months. A large contingent of British forces took part in the action. The rebellion ended when Iraq promised to give the Kurds regional autonomy, a promise that was never fully kept.

In March 1969 the rebellious Kurds once against took up arms, resulting in the heaviest fighting of the period. A covert plan of action using the Kurds was put into effect and for a while it looked as if President Bush's desire to topple President Hussein would come to pass. I might add that in terms of the cease-fire agreement (which the Iraqis adhered to, but which the U.S. did not) the Iraqi military was forbidden to fly any combat aircraft inside their own territory. In defiance of the cease fire terms, U.S. planes twice attacked and shot down Iraqi planes to prevent them from attacking the Kurdish guerillas. While the Bush administration pretended that it was acting in the interests of the Kurds, the real target was the oil that lay beneath the sands of the Mosul. The Bush administration was indeed acting under the imperialist banner, 'We Fight for Oil,' albeit under other pretexts, the real thrust of the Bush Gulf War being to get control of Iraq's huge oil reserves. Anything else may be safely dismissed as pure Emmanuel Kant philosophy.

The Kurds received the brunt of Iraq's attack helicopter gun ships. They held fast for a while. Having experienced one such incident during the Iraq-Iran war, the Kurds broke and ran. Mindless panic set in and sent them streaming towards the Iranian and Turkish borders. Prime Minister Ozul's worst fears were realized. After allowing a trickle of refugees to come in, Turkey then sealed its borders against the unwanted Kurds. Ozul then proposed that Western Europe accept the bulk of them, but the suggestion was declined. The Kurds remained in a sort of a no man's land and were caught in the crossfire of the Iran-Iraq war. About 50 Kurdish people were killed by chemical weapons, to whit, thickened Somane nerve gas of the type that Iraq was not known to possess, but which was definitely possessed by the Iranians.

Since all the Kurds who fell victim to the attack were killed by a particular nerve gas, it is most likely that it was the Iranian Army which is to blame for their deaths. Since the start of the sting operation organized by Bush against Iraq by April Glaspie, the number of Kurds killed by chemical weapons has risen from 50 to 50,000.

Just as shamelessly as the British used the Kurds to gain their own ends, just so shamelessly was the Bush administration using them to foment hatred for Iraq, and thus hoping to turn the whole Middle East into a quagmire of destabilized countries. It is easy in all of this to lose sight of the Bush objective, to go forward under the imperialist banner 'We Fight for Oil.' It was Mexico all over again.

This report, written and published in 1991 proved to be accurate, but here we are once again, with the Bush family plunging the world into another war against Iraq with the same 'promise' about a 'just Palestinian state' being dangled in front of the Arab world by Blair with the agreement of G.W. Bush. Americans who blindly supported genocide against Iraq in 1991 are finding out that their blind faith was entirely misplaced. They are finding out that the Gulf War is only the beginning, and not the end of the drama of which there is no end in sight. In sowing the seeds of war against Iraq, President Bush also sowed the seeds of future wars in the region, which could conceivably end up in a 30 Years War.

The aims of President Bush and his aides were crystal clear; destroy the nation of Iraq through economic strangulation that would bring on pestilence and disease and starvation. But that did not do the job, so genocide against Iraq took the form of a U.S. invasion. What we are witnessing now is merely a pause, a prelude of things to come.

Iraq will become a second Vietnam. Millions are slated to die at the hand of the Bush administration under the banner, 'We Fight for Oil.' Jordan, Syria, Lebanon and Libya will follow in the wake of the destruction of the nation of Iraq, fought for a just cause - 'We Fight for Oil.' Syria will be the first to go down. U.S. friends will find that the quickest way to lose their sovereignty is to become an ally of the U.S. Egypt has yet to learn this lesson which will come soon enough.

Although 'read my lips' Bush was at pains to deny it, stationing U.S. troops in Saudi Arabia on a permanent basis is very much the goal. Such an arrangement has already been in place for the past five years. The U.S. will keep a permanent force of 150,000 men in Saudi Arabia. What will be their role? Stamp on any Muslim nation that gets the least bit out of line. In short, the U.S. is going to be the new 'Foreign Legion' in the Middle East, an imperialistic goal to control all Middle East oil. Both of the oil-producing nations of Algeria and Libya have already been taken over by U.S. and British imperialists. The second invasion of Iraq by U.S. military forces took place in 2003. Iran is under virtual siege. One thing we can be certain of is that a 'kinder, gentler' George Bush will not be satisfied until all Middle East oil is under U.S. imperial control. Blame for the sad plight of the Kurds was laid at the door of President Saddam Hussein. Given the fate of the Diem brothers, General Somoza, Ferdinand Marcos, Torrijos, Noriega and the Shah of Iran, it would be absolutely out of character for the Bush administration not to invade Iraq for the second time. Press reports had already demolished the credibility of the former U.S. Ambassador to Iraq by explaining that April Glaspie would come up short if ever she were forced to undergo a really thorough cross examination at the hands of a competent prosecutor. Now, confirmation of the sting operation has come from another source. Dennis Kloske, a top administration official with the Commerce Department testified before a House subcommittee on April 8, 1991 to the effect that until the invasion of Kuwait, the Bush administration was bending over backwards to supply Iraq with 'high technology.'

Kloske charged that the State Department ignored his warnings and recommendations that the flow of American technology to

Iraq be halted. Neither the Commerce Department nor the State Department would listen, Kloske told the House Foreign Affairs Committee. For his pains, Kloske was fired by a 'kinder, gentler' George Bush. In the case of Iraq, 'truth won't be out' and will never be allowed to surface. What is that truth? We fight an imperialist war for possession of Iraq's oil.

That is why Bush and son have kept up the drumbeat of aggression against Iraq. If Iraq had no oil, our relations with it would be sweet. An imperial U.S. would have no quarrel with Iraq or Iran. We would not be violating international law and the United States Constitution, as we have done many thousands of times since 1991. The Bush family has led a campaign of violent abuse of the Constitution in its quest for oil.

When Bush left office after escaping impeachment efforts by Rep. Henry Gonzalez, he primed his son George to follow in his footsteps and pursue what ought to have been the family motto: 'We Fight for Oil.' By dint of some fancy footwork, the U.S. Supreme Court elected G.W. Bush by forcing Al Gore out of the election. It was an astonishing contravention of the U.S. Constitution, in that elections are state elections and do not come under Federal jurisdiction, but it did not provoke a constitutional crisis. Bush was no sooner in office than he took up the anti-Hussein refrain until it became a drumbeat of hate; the fight for oil was on with a vengeance! Bush, the younger, had wider support than his father, not from the American people, more than 160 million who did not vote at all or voted against him, but cleverly disguised so-called "conservative" figures who were able to fool the American public all of the time with their bogus sincerity. The leader of the remarkable propaganda coup was one, Irving Kristol. This man became the standard bearer in a new round of attacks on Iraq, as the chief representative for Richard Murdoch, the press mogul who has the American people fooled all of the time.

Murdoch, Kristol, Perle and Wolfowitz knew how to work the

circuits, drumming up support for the Bush/Cheney oil junta. Billing himself as a 'neo-conservative' was a masterstroke. Americans just love labels. Murdoch put up the money to finance a paper called The Weekly Standard. This publication is a front for the Rothschild-Rockefeller oil interests in which the desire to grab Iraq's oil is all - pervading. There is nothing like the lust for oil to get the blood pounding. Kristol now joined the U.S. imperialists, all the while posing as a 'conservative.'

The billionaire 'gang of four' swiftly moved into high gear to push for an imperial presidency. The United States was about to be transformed from a Republic into an empire, ruled over by an emperor. The transition, made possible by the 'big bang' of September 11, was remarkably swift. Overnight, the Constitution was trampled and relegated to a place of no importance. The 'gang of four' most to blame for the fall of the United States Constitution came from the ranks of the Trotskyites of which William Buckley was a member.

Watched over by the CIA, Kristol senior, a life-long Communist began to penetrate the ranks of conservatives and in the mid 1950s, spearheaded by 'conservative' William Buckley, had taken over almost all conservative institutions. The Trotskyites were ready for their bloodless coup and their big chance came when Richard Perle and Paul Wolfowitz were granted positions of vital importance within the Bush inner circle. The stage was now set for the big push, the big offensive in the ongoing drama for control of world oil. Digging deeper into the 'conservative' background of William Kristol, we uncovered the following: Former secretary of State Henry Kissinger was associated with Kristol and his publishing ventures, National Affairs and the National Interest. Later there was a third publication called The Public Interest. Where did funding for these 'journals' come from? It was supplied by the Lynde and Harry Bradley Foundation and it seems that this wealthy foundation also funded Kristol's American Enterprise Institute, yet another 'conservative' organization.

Other 'conservatives' in the game with Kristol were William Bennett, Jack Kemp and Vin Weber, all nominally 'conservative' Republicans, although we can be certain that men like the great Daniel Webster and Henry Clay, would have made short work of that claim. Unfortunately, we have no men of the caliber of Clay and Webster in politics today. Kristol and his men saw their task as the destruction of Iraq. That was their goal, and in their drive to bring it home to the American public, they enlisted some of the most fanatical so-called "televangelists" to their cause. One such individual was on television recently, claiming that 'the anti-Christ is alive and well in Germany, France and Russia.' With leaders like this person, no wonder so many American Christians are utterly confused.

With the advent of 9/11, the hour had arrived for Kritsol, Perle, Wolfowitz, Cheney and Rumsfeld. Now they had the cause célèbre, the 'big bang,' the 'Pearl Harbor' they needed to galvanize their plans into action. We may never know the full truth about 9/11, but one thing is true, our controllers are ruing the day they allowed public access to the Internet. Whereas absent any news media but the controlled media, Pearl Harbor remained a secret for almost three decades, already serious discussions about 9/11 are going on, and many doubts are being raised about the government's claim that it had no warning of what was going to happen. There is now open and growing doubt about this claim. David Broder, columnist for the Washington Post headlined his March 17 article, '9/77Changed Everything for Bush.' This is very profound, for it changed Bush from a quiet little man to one filled with sudden confidence to the point of being overbearing. In a word, 911 'transformed' George Bush. Here is some of what Broder wrote:

> It has been a long road to this moment of decision on Iraq but the inevitability of the destination has been clear. When historians have access to the memos and diaries of the Bush administration's insiders, they will find that President Bush set his sights on removing Saddam Hussein from power soon after the 9/11 terrorist attacks, if not before. Everything the

President has said publicly, everything that Vice President Cheney reiterated in his Sunday television interviews - confirms that the World Trade Center and the Pentagon attacks were to steel to Bush's determination to disarm any ruler who plausibly might collaborate in a similar or worse assault. And to him, disarming clearly meant dislodging that potential assailant from power. Last spring, the president announced and his new security team promptly amplified a new doctrine that replaced the Cold War policy of containment with a new policy of pre-emption.

Bush's West Point speech and the subsequent white paper declared that the United States with its allies would move forcefully against any nation or force assembling weapons of mass destruction that could threaten U.S. security - and not wait passively for the attack to occur. It quickly became clear that Iraq had been chosen as a test case of the new doctrine.

We wonder why? Let us suppose that Iraq did not have oil, would it have then been so vital to 'disarm' the nation? The case against North Korea was much stronger.

North Korea openly admitted that it had nuclear weapons - but as yet it remains untouched by the U.S. and Britain, because, as logic would seem to suggest, it has no oil! So what is this about with Iraq? Is it about 'disarming' Iraq or is about taking over its rich oil deposits? We venture to suggest that 90 percent of the world would opt for the latter as the true reason why Britain and the U.S. wanted to crush Iraq.

Subsequently, the president used the pending decisions of the United Nations to persuade most of the members of Congress to endorse the pre-emption doctrine as American policy and apply it to Iraq. And once backed by the Congress, he was able to persuade the UN Security Council to give Saddam Hussein what amounted to a unanimous ultimatum; disarm yourself, or be disarmed.

What is wrong with this?

What is wrong is that the whole scheme is 100 percent unconstitutional and yet, Bush was able to get away with it because the American people don't know their Constitution, and much less do their representatives in the House and Senate.

There has never been a Congress of the United States that has been so woefully ignorant of the Constitution. Hence, Bush was able to bluff his way through into going to war without a declaration of war, an impeachable offense. What we know is that the imminent prospect of pre-emptive war with Iraq has damaged America's relations with much of the world ~ opening rifts with major trading partners such as Germany, France and China. The fact that Bush has broken a lot of china even before the first shot has been fired. The after effects of neighboring Canada and Mexico and the Middle East cannot be gauged nor judged.

Thus we come now to one of the worst travesties of justice ever to befall this nation: We were going to attack Iraq without a just cause.

The U.S. Constitution says that the United States cannot go to war with any nation save and except that nation has committed verifiable acts of belligerency against it. Not even Perle and Wolfowitz could claim that Iraq has committed acts of belligerency against the United States. There were no constitutional grounds for a 'pre-emptive strike.' It was an illegal, unconstitutional act and has no place in the policy of a nation that has its Constitution as the highest law of the land.

CHAPTER 4

Imperial Britain and U.S. strong-arm diplomacy

How did the U.S. go from a legacy left to it by the Founding Fathers and the generation that followed, to the present, unconstitutional belief that it can attack any nation perceived as a threat? What has come about is the U.S. has changed to an imperialist power in the pursuit of oil Anglo-American trouble making in foreign affairs of nations. We might call the struggle 'oil diplomacy' for it is interwoven with commercial and military issues. These are not always revealed as sometimes secrecy is preferable. Modern economics is power. The nation that controls oil will rule the world. This was the imperialist policy adopted by the U.S. government.

Political separation from the America's legacy of wisdom left by the Founding Fathers was violated by the Spanish-American War. 'Isolation' as it was dubbed by those who sought to internationalize America, 'is no longer possible,' trumpeted McKinley, a refrain taken up with a vengeance by Woodrow Wilson:

> We are participants whether we would or not in the life of the world. The interest of all nations is ours also. We are partners with the rest. What affects the nations of Europe and Asia is our affairs as well.

Espousing International Socialism was the beginning of the end of the Founding Fathers America. It led to 'free trade' and

Wilson's removal of our trade barriers that had made the U.S. a great nation. Wilson completely ignored the warning of George Washington that the U.S. should not get involved and entangled in foreign intrigues. But in fighting imperial wars for oil, this would prove to be impossible. No nation can defy the imperialist demands of Washington and live, as Iraq is presently discovering. The people of the world largely despise what America has become under the Bush family, father and son. They have alienated the whole of the Muslim world by greedy grasping after oil.

Rear Admiral Plunkett remarked in January 1928:

> "The penalty of commercial and industrial efficiency inevitably is war; if I read history correctly, this country is nearer war than ever before, because its commercial position today places us in competition with other great commercial nations. If you substitute 'oil' where it is appropriate, we begin to get the picture."

As French Premiere Clemenceau stated:

> "Oil is as necessary as blood in the battles of tomorrow."

Henri Berringer, French diplomat and Clemenceau's deputy wrote a memorandum worth quoting:

> "He who owns the oil will own the world, for he will rule the seas by means of heavy oils, the air by means of ultra-refined oils, and the land by mans of petrol and illuminating oils. In addition to these he will rule his fellow-men in an economic sense, by reason of the fantastic wealth he will derive from oil - this wonderful substance which is more sought after and more precious than gold itself."

President McKinley stated:

> "Isolation is no longer possible or desirable."

President Wilson said:

> "We are participants whether we like it or not in the life of the world."

Spoken like true imperialists especially when we recall that at the time the United States had less than 12 percent of world reserves of oil. About 70 percent lay in countries whose weakness invited economic and political encroachment by major powers. And in Wilson's time this applied to the Middle East, the Caribbean-Mexican Gulf basin and Russia. Nations with large oil deposits defended their assets by passing laws vesting subsoil rights to their people and their government and passing restrictive barriers, regulations and high royalty rights. The major imperial powers of Britain and the United States classed such self-defense as 'defiance' and used diplomatic pressure to overturn such barriers. And when that failed, they reverted to armed intervention.

Just bear this in mind and ponder these words the next time you hear Bush and Cheney claim how necessary it was to 'disarm Saddam' and then it will begin to filter down into our understanding that we are in Iraq for its oil. 9/11 was a contrived situation like Pearl Harbor was, and 'weapons of mass destruction' was a mere red herring dragged across the oil trail.

Lord Curzon, after the terrible tragedy of WWI, spoke the truth when he said:

> "The Allies floated to victory on a wave of oil."

Every other reason advanced by Bush has less and less validity as we examine the issues. As I have stated, about 70 percent of oil in the world lies in countries that are economically and nationally weak. By their very weakness they invite U.S. and British interference in their national affairs. We see the example of Iraq in front of us now; Venezuela has just survived an onslaught by the United States acting from behind surrogates. Any nation that has worthwhile reserves of oil is today threatened by an imperial U.S. and Britain, and they will fall, one by one.

Self-defenses by these nations to protect their people and preserve their assets from the rapacious grasp of U.S. and British oil moguls is described as 'intransigence' or 'vindictiveness,' which is at first fought with 'diplomatic pressure' and then by force of arms. The Bush family has followed this dubious pathway and we saw their policy climaxing in a brutal attack on Iraq, a nation half the size of California.

Britain and the U.S. have already gained control of most of the world's oil reserves. What they are not able to win by diplomacy, they will win by waves of massed bombers, cruise missiles and rockets as the sham and pretense of being good, Christian nations is dropped. The struggle going on in the world today is between nations that do not have a great deal of oil or none at all, and the world's 'only superpower,' better yet, 'imperialist,' the United States. Russia is fighting to keep its place in the oil world, while Britain and the United States are seeking to topple it. Thus the struggle for oil will come to a great and cataclysmic battle between the U.S. and Russia, and that day is not so far off. In the near future, the sons and daughters of America will be called up to fight for oil in a total world war.

The United States State Department generally does the bidding of the major oil companies. This is backed up by an aggressive oil policy by the United States as A.C. Bedford, chairman of Standard Oil of New Jersey said in 1923. As a result of this fixed policy, U.S. consuls abroad always hew the oil line when it comes to matters of foreign policy. In 1923 the Federal Trade Commission aided this official U.S. Government policy. All U.S. embassies and diplomatic missions received the following memo on August 16, 1919:

Gentlemen: The vital importance of securing adequate

supplies of mineral oil, both for present and future needs of the United States has been forcibly been brought to the attention of the Department (the State Department.) Nationals of various countries and concession for mineral oil rights are being actively sought are aggressively conducting the development of proven fields of exploration of new areas in many parts of the world. It is desired to have the most complete and recent information regarding such activities either by United States citizens or by others.

Charles Evans Hughes testified before the U.S. Congress and the Coolidge Oil board:

... The foreign policy of the government, which is expressed in the phrase 'open door' consistently prosecuted by the Department of State, has made it possible for our American interests abroad to be intelligently fostered and the needs of our people to no slight extent, to be appropriately safeguarded.

The fight for oil in the Middle East began in earnest with the arrival of an Australian by the name of William K. D'Arcy and the American, Admiral Colby Mitchell Chester (1844-1932). In 1901 D'Arcy obtained a concession from the Shah of Persia covering five-sixths of the Persian Empire, to last for 60 years. D'Arcy paid $20,000 cash and agreed to pay a 16 percent royalty on all oil exploited. Admiral Chester got nothing and D'Arcy went back to London to organize the Anglo Persian Company. He returned to the Middle East in an attempt to grab the Mosul oilfield in Persia. In 1912 the Turkish Petroleum Company, consisting of the British-Dutch Shell oil and Deutsche Bank of Berlin was formed to exploit the Mosul.

Sir Henri Deterding , (known as the 'Napoleon' of the oil business) of the Royal Dutch Shell Company was a big player in the intrigue going on around the oil owning nations. The British government was active in the person of E. G. Prettyman, Civil Lord, who arranged for British capital to hold the line on the

Turkish Petroleum Company, which D'Arcy was threatening to sell to the French. In 1913, Deterding stated in the House of Lords, that he controlled oil in Romania, Russia, California, Trinidad and Mexico. He was, said Deterding, squeezing Persia, which was a practically untouched area of immense size reeking with oil.

Sir Thomas Browning said before the Lords that Royal Dutch Shell was far more aggressive about oil than the Standard Oil Trust of America. Deterding had sole control of the most powerful organization in the world for the production of a source of power. Enter the fight for oil, Winston Churchill, then First Lord of the Admiralty and fresh from his experiences in the Boer War. Churchill told the House of Lords that he believed… we must become the owners, or at any rate, the controllers at the source, of at least a proportion of the supply of natural oil which we require.

CHAPTER 5

Unheard-of new doctrine: Mexico under the gun

U S imperialist policies had now entered into a new phase, a 'preemptive strike' phase, to quote Bush terminology. The British Government now moved actively to get its hands on the Mosul oil held in what is today, northern Iraq. The British bought a quarter interest in the Turkish Petroleum Company with the Germans and Turks holding the other shares.

Within three months, by means of 'diplomacy by deception,' the British had control of three-quarters of the stock and the Turks were completely forced out of their own company. The Kurds, who owned the oil land over the Mosul, got not one red cent. Turkey, which controlled the land around the Mosul, also found itself out in the cold.

That was only the beginning. The British Government then bought, for $12 million, the controlling interest in Anglo Persian, which was to run for 48 years. It soon became apparent that not only did oil win wars, but that wars were waged because of oil.

Looking back over the history of WWI, this becomes starkly apparent, as Clemenceau was later to acknowledge. Wars did not end with WWI. Instead, Britain and the United States continued an aggressive imperialist policy against Persia (Iraq) and Turkey to try and shake the hold of nationalist elements. In May 1920, the State Department issued a note saying that Great Britain was quietly preparing to take over the whole of the Mosul oil fields.

Oil politics continued to grab the headlines in the U.S. with President Harding stating in a speech,

> "... next to agriculture and transportation, the petroleum industry has become the most important adjunct to our civilization and well-being."

The Wilson administration began to be embroiled in a struggle to gain control of oil in Mexico after it was announced that large oil reserves had been found on the Gulf of Mexico. When the Mexicans showed signs of resisting exploitation, U.S. warships were dispatched to Tampico. Wilson declared...

> "the United States is only intent on preserving democracy in Mexico."

The United States was busy in other areas too, negotiating with Britain to obtain a share in the Turkish Petroleum Company with the Mosul oil fields the glittering prize. Turkey was ousted entirely from its own company. But the U.S. main focus was on the Mexican fields, which Edward Doheny had secured at Hacienda del Tulillo through his friend President Diaz. Doheny soon got other fields going, notably the Potrero Del Llano and the Cerro Azul. But then Diaz double- crossed Doheny and allowed Weetman (Lord Cowdrey) to come onto the Mexican oil scene.

The fight for oil led to trouble between the 'Allies,' when the U.S. came to the decision to overthrow President Diaz who had been in power for 35 years.

As is usual in these matters, American intelligence operations and U.S. economic 'hit men' were sent in to foment trouble in the Diaz ranks. The U.S. directly caused the overthrow of Diaz as testimony before the U.S. Foreign Relations Committee was later to confirm.

Lawrence Converse, an American officer on the staff testified:

> "Mr. Madero himself told that as soon as the rebels made a good showing of strength, several leading bankers in El Paso stood to advance him - I believe the sum was $100,000; and these same men (Governor Gonzalez and Secretary of State Hernandez) told me also that Standard oil interests were backing them and had bought bonds of the provisional government of Mexico. They said that Standard Oil interests were backing them in their revolution."

Standard Oil was to have a high rate of interest and there was a tentative agreement as to an oil concession in the southern states of Mexico. Madero was deposed and executed, and General Huerta took over. When President Wilson came to power he openly opposed Huerta claiming that the U.S. could not... have any sympathy with those who seek to seize power of government to advance their own personal interests or ambitions. At the same time Wilson accorded recognition to a revolutionary government in Peru.

Oil interests in the person of Albert Fall began demanding that the United States send armed forces to Mexico to 'protect' American interests and to 'lend their assistance to the restoration of order and maintenance of peace in that unhappy country and the placing of the administrative functions in the hands of capable and patriotic citizens of Mexico.' When Wilson came to power he put matters to the Congress in this light:

> "The present situation in Mexico is incompatible with the fulfillment of international obligations on the part of Mexico, with the civilized development of Mexico itself, and with the maintenance of tolerable political and economic conditions in Central America."

Wilson was now preparing for armed intervention on the basis that Americans were being 'threatened' in Mexico. It was the sort of refrain we were to hear from George Bush in his never-ending complaints about President Hussein in later years, and like Wilson, they had the ring of insincerity resounding through them.

The American people so easily misled as to be a national and historic tragedy, were convinced that Mexico was a 'threat' to them, and that opened the way for Wilson to send a letter to U.S. consuls in Mexico with a directive that they should warn

> "the authorities that any intimidation or maltreatment of Americans is likely to raise the question to intervention."

Here we have a clear case of an imperial U.S. President looking for an excuse to interfere in the internal affairs of Mexico, which conduct was repeated by the imperial Bush family, father and son looking for an excuse to grab Iraq's oil and they hit upon the flimsy pretext that Iraq had 'weapons of mass destruction.' Strong in the knowledge that he had fooled the American people into believing their nationals were being badly treated in Mexico and that a 'horrible dictator was in power and had to be removed' (do you hear the 'Saddam Hussein refrain' here?), Wilson grew bolder:

> "It is my clear judgment that it is my immediate duty to require Huerta's retirement from the Mexican Government, and that the Government of the United States must now proceed to employ such means as may be necessary to secure this result."

Echoes of 'Saddam must step down or else the U.S. armed forces will make him,' that kept coining from the president as if he had the right to take act like a brigand and a bandit, any more than Wilson had that right. Wilson and Bush both got away with their naked aggression against the sovereign state of Mexico and Iraq respectively, because the American people do not know their Constitution. No one challenged the Bush administration in the courts to produce evidence from the U.S. Constitution proving where this amazing power had suddenly come from?

From whence did this amazing power usually reserved to the emperors of their empires come? It certainly did not from the U.S. Constitution or from international law. It came under the aegis of imperialism and apparently marching to that drum under that banner, made it legal for the U.S. to interfere in the sovereign affairs of a sovereign state!

As long as the American people do not know their Constitution, just for so long will tyrants get away with interference in the sovereign affairs of sovereign states (such as Mexico and Iraq) and until constitutional knowledge replaces rank ignorance, we shall continue to see American foreign policy creating havoc in the world. Because the American people do not know their Constitution, they no longer have a Constitution. The American people allowed Wilson to get away with further acts of imperialism in Mexico and the Bush administrations to ravage Iraq after their plans to assassinate Hussein could not be carried out.

In November 1912, Wilson gave the following astonishing order, astonishing because his military commanders should have known the Constitution by heart and known therefore, that what he was ordering was unconstitutional and they should have disobeyed the orders.

> Cut him (Huerta) off from foreign sympathy and aid and from domestic credit, whether moral or material and force him out... If General Huerta does not retire by force of circumstances, it will become the duty of the United States to use less peaceful means to put him out.

Wilson was now emboldened and continued along his pathway of imperial tyranny, interfering in the sovereign state of Mexico, threatening its leader and its people, and worse yet declaring it the 'duty' of the United States to throw out its elected leader if he did not step down! Not even Caesar in his most imperial majesty spoke thus.

Even now, all these years later, the audacity of Wilson, still causes astonishment. And what was the response from the American people to the threats from Wilson? Exactly nothing! If anything, the American people by their silence encouraged Wilson to do the wrong thing and to violate their Constitution. All of a sudden, under an imperial banner the United States assumed the right to pacify Mexico. In reply to a British proposal that Huerta be allowed to resign, Secretary Bryan penned another amazing missive:

> "The President intends to dispose of Huerta by giving American aid to the rebel chiefs. There is a more hopeful prospect of peace, of security of property and early payment of foreign obligations if Mexico is left to the forces now reckoning with one another there. He (Wilson) intends, therefore, almost immediately, to remove the inhibition of export of arms and ammunition from the United States."

This came just after Huerta had been re-elected in a peaceful and fair election. Decades later, the American people would once again stand aside and allow their government to inflict imperial political havoc in Iraq and Afghanistan, while pretending that it was all legal under the U.S. Constitution. The reality is that Bush, father and son, ought to have been impeached, removed from office and tried for treason. Yet, it seems it will never happen and the American people now deserve to lose their Constitution, because they have given assent to the leaders of the petroleum industry to trample it underfoot without so much of a murmur of protest.

No wonder the nation is in trouble when we allow a supposed 'commander in chief,' who has not been called into service to lead this nation into a war, which he does not have the right to wage, because the Congress has not declared war and to stay in office and bring about the criminal waste in human life and billions of dollars of our national treasure. We deserve all that we are going to get for our dreadful neglect of the Constitution.

The prospect of U.S. interference in Mexico greatly alarmed Chile, Argentina and Brazil and they moved to intervene to help Mexico by an offer to conciliate. When these three countries were moved by an offer to conciliate, Wilson tried to block the Argentina, Brazil, and Chile Conference when it met at Niagara Falls. Like the Bush family in 1991 and 2002, Wilson did not want peace; he wanted to expel Huerta with violence for standing in the way of those who were pressing forward under the banner oil imperialism. Wilson showed his true colors and his contempt for the U.S. Constitution by direct intervention in Mexico while he sabotaged efforts toward a peaceful settlement.

Wilson isolated the Huerta government through financial machinations and by a blockade of arms and ammunition for his government forces. At the same time he supplied the rebel leaders, Carranza and Villa, with arms and money. He concocted the flag incident at Tampico as an excuse for the occupation of Vera Cruz. When General Huerta apologized for the flag incident, Wilson like the fake gentleman from Princeton he was, false and treacherous to the core, refused to accept it.

In this deplorable conduct we see similar deeds and actions in the Bush family's handling of Saddam Hussein. In both instances, General Huerta and President Hussein, we find the oilmen scurrying around in the dark like cockroaches, refusing to pay their taxes to Mexico and helping Carranza every turn of the way. The American people never got to know just what an imperial president Wilson was, and they paid the price for their ignorance when in violation of the Dick Act, he sent their sons of the Militia to die on the battlefields of France, although he had been told, over and over again by his Attorney General Wickersham, that he had no constitutional authority to send the Militia to fight outside of the United States. Because the American people have allowed themselves to be so bereft of protection, their sons of the Militia are again on battlefields outside of the United States, in violation of the Constitution, and once again, the American people are allowing the lawbreakers, the Bush family, to trample the Constitution and escape the consequences of their violence, all in an imperial pursuit of oil that is the national property of other nations.

In front of a Senate Foreign Relations Committee in 1919, Doheny bragged that every American oil company had participated in helping to get rid of Huerta, just as in later years, every oil company executive was to be engaged in undermining the Shah of Iran and driving him out of office. The fight for oil goes on and on, the United States imperial army marches under the banner of the petroleum companies, while they sing their battle hymn:

> "Onward Christian soldiers, marching as to war, with the flag of the Petroleum Industry, going on before."

There were many nights of clinking champagne glasses over the ouster of Huerta in the corporate offices of Standard Oil. But the oil executives miscalculated. Carranza tried to pass off the revolution as something of the people and he reneged on the oil concessions he had given out to the American oil companies. When General Obregon came to power the whole of Mexico was plunged into unrest due to the machinations of the U.S. oil lobby, fully supported by the State Department and Secretary of State Hughes.

Hughes advanced the claim that Wilson's action in sending American troops and two warships to Tampico was 'morally justified.' These were baseless empty words, not found in the U.S. Constitution, and were meant to impress a world deeply concerned about U.S. imperialistic meddling in the internal affairs of its neighbor. In a statement to the Republican National Committee in 1924, Hughes kept up his 'moral' tone:

> "The Huerta revolt was not a revolution with the aspirations of an oppressed people. It was an effort to seize the Presidency: It meant subversion of all constitutional and orderly procedure. The refusal to aid the established Government would have thrown our moral influence on the

side of those who were challenging peace and order in Mexico..."

Years later, in 1991 and 2006, we were to hear the same refrains from the Bush family, father and son, that their attacks on Iraq were 'moral.'

In truth there was nothing 'moral' about it - it was plain open imperialist aggression against a smaller, weaker nation in pursuit of oil interests; Hughes and Wilson were not fighting to defend morals - they were marching under the banner of oil imperialism. American oilmen continued to interfere in Mexico through the Coolidge administration, and a correspondent of the New York World wrote an article from Mexico that encapsulated the situation:

> "It is an imperial fact, for example, that in recent past the personal association of United States officials was not with the Government to which they were accredited, but with that class of Mexicans, among who were to be found the rich, the cultivated, and sometimes charming people, who are financing and provoking the rebellion. It is no less a notorious fact that many of the lawyers and representatives of oil companies were not satisfied to argue their claims under international law, but openly, and persistently used all the influence they possessed to undermine the Mexican Government."

That notorious behavior was extended to Venezuela, Iraq and Iran, where every effort that was possible to make was made by U.S. agents, oilmen and their allies in the CIA, to bring down the governments of these nations and replace them with puppet regimes favorable to those operating under the banner We Fight for Oil. This notorious behavior extended for more than 90 years until today, where we have witnessed the perpetrators almost succeeding in overthrowing the elected leader of Venezuela, overthrowing the Shah of Iran and now, engaged in an all out war in Iraq in order to gain control of the long-coveted Mosul and

WE FIGHT FOR OIL

other Iraqi oilfields. The imperialistic tendencies of those holding unbridled power and who operated behind the scenes in Washington were well exposed by El Universal, the Mexico City newspaper:

> "American imperialism is a fatal product of economic evolution. It is useless trying to persuade our northern neighbor not to be imperialistic; they cannot help being so, no matter how excellent their intentions."

Let us study the natural laws of economic imperialism, in the hope off finding some method by which, instead of blindly opposing them, we can mitigate their actions and turn them to our advantage.

CHAPTER 6

Oil, not WMD's ignites invasion of Iraq

That fatal imperialism is running rampant throughout the United States today, having been given a free hand by the Bush family and their supporters, Richard Cheney, Kristol, Perle, Wolfowitz and the Christian fundamentalists is no longer deniable. This rampant Bush imperialism will not stop with Iraq, when we have overwhelmed that nation, it will continue until the Bush imperialists, in total defiance of the U.S. Constitution, have overwhelmed every oil-producing nation in the Middle East and dispossessed the Arabs of their natural resource heritage.

And in the process, Middle East nations are being robbed blind. Take the Anglo-Persian agreement purchased for $12 million dollars. Winston Churchill said that Britain had profited by $250 million out of the arrangement from 1921-1925. The fact is that the oil baron's greed to get their hands on Iraq's Mosul oil fields was what let to the First World War.

The unholy mess of the Middle East was caused directly by the meddling of British oilmen and U.S. imperialism. The treacherous Sykes-Picot arrangement led to nothing but discord and bloodshed in Palestine, which endures to this very day.

It is strange to read the history of the period and to realize that what passed as national politics at the time (1912-1930) was no more than dirty oil politics. It is indeed a sobering experience to read the history of the period - for which millions of lives on both sides of the combatants were needlessly laid down. After the British defeat of the Turks in 1916 (largely because of the Arabs under Lawrence of Arabia in exchange for promises to give them Palestine, which were never kept), the Sykes-Picot Agreement offered support to French claims to Syria and the Mosul in exchange for French help in the Near East. The British drive against Baghdad was successful in the spring of 1917. But the collapse of their Tsarist Russian allies prevented the British from reaching the Mosul.

The Armistice removed the Turkish-German army defending the Mosul. These were nothing but moves and counter-moves by Western nations, and especially by Britain and the United States to secure for themselves the coveted Mosul oilfields. The nations of the area were not even consulted. It was we fight for oil imperial diplomacy at it's ugliest.

To quiet the uproar occasioned by the rapacious oil companies, a conference was held in Lausanne, Switzerland in November 1922, but in advance of that event, British troops led a push into the Mosul while Secretary of State Hughes said the U.S. would not recognize British claim to Mosul as it lacked validity. The British thought they had Mosul 'in the bag' through occupation and the correspondent for the *London Times* could not conceal his pleasure:

> We British have the satisfaction of knowing that three enormous fields situated within close proximity of each other, capable of supplying the oil requirements of the Empire for many years to come are being almost entirely being developed by British enterprise. Turkish Petroleum geologists have confirmed the existence of three large pools within the Mosul concession. The northeast pool runs from Hammama Ali through Kirkuk and Tuz Kharmati to Kind-I-shrin. A second extends south to Mosul from Khaiyara through Kifri to Jebej Oniki Imam. Another pool starts southwest of Mosul, and runs toward Baghdad along the Tigris to Fet Haha Pass and Mandali.

It was to take this rich prize that George Bush Sr. attacked Iraq in 1991 after 'failing to bring Hussein around' to paraphrase John Perkins. We can ignore the political speech-making about the Iraqi people living under a dictator. We can forget the pious platitudes about bringing democracy to Iraq. We can forget the lies that flowed from the White House in 1991 and forget the lies flowing from the mouths of the oil junta in 2008. What one can seize on is the solid evidence that what the oil moguls are doing in Iraq today, and what they did, starting from 1914, is merely a continuation of their imperialist quest for oil. This imperial quest for oil has never been so nakedly exposed as it was by the cruise missile attack on Baghdad on March 20, 2003. In violation of every tenet of international law and without one shred of authority from the U.S. Constitution, not to mention that the U.N. did not give sanction to the Bush-Cheney oil junta to attack Iraq, a bombardment of Baghdad began.

The pious platitudes of George Bush, the son, may be safely consigned to the trash can of history, as the Bush imperial family does not represent the American people. G.W. Bush was voted into office by the U.S. Supreme Court. It is fair to say that had the Supreme Court not elected George Bush there would be no war for oil today, because it is a known fact that Al Gore had openly stated that if he won the election, there would be no attack on Iraq, nor would the American people be forced to pay sky-high prices for gasoline at the pumps.

The following ought to show how little the imperialists and their antecedents care about people, how hollow did the words of George Bush Jr. ring when he declared his love for the Iraqi people embodied in his desire to get rid of 'Saddam' who was oppressing them. The background to this account from the saga of oil wars is that the U.S. ruthlessly rejected the rights of the Armenians to the Mosul and acted as if the more than 1 million Armenians were not of the slightest consequence.

Vahan Cardashian, attorney for the Delegation of the Armenian republic, tried to take this oversight of Armenian rights in an application for a Senate hearing and investigation.

In his letter of March 14, 1928 to Senator Borah, he said if the Foreign Relations Committee failed to act favorably on his application, he would request President Coolidge to present the American-Armenian dispute to the Hague Tribunal for adjudication. Cardashian's letter to Senator Borah read:

> *"I charge that two members of the President's Cabinet bartered away the Armenian case at the Lausanne Conference and conspired to affect the expulsion of nearly 1,000,000 Armenians from their ancestral homes of their victims.*
>
> *I charge that these men and their confederates in this outrage have used and are using the Department of State as their willing tool to carry out their infamous design, and that the Department of State, in an effort to cover up the tracks of those who have dictated its policy in this respect, has resorted to misrepresentations, intrigues and even terrorism, and has flooded the land with shameless irresponsible propaganda.*
>
> *Under these circumstances, what then, is the motive, the purpose behind the Turkish policy of the Department of state? We charge that it is oil. An administration which has surrendered legitimate American rights and then has had the impudence to fill the air with irrelevancies, wild insinuation and falsehoods to divert attention from its disgraced policy; an Administration which has deliberately trampled upon the Constitution of the United Stets in its conduct of foreign relations - such an Administration, I charge, would not hesitate, and has not hesitated, to sell out the Armenian people and their homes for oil, in the interest of a privileged group.*
>
> *If for any reason the Senate Committee on Foreign Relations should be unable and unwilling to consider these wrongs*

> *inflicted upon a gallant people, I shall then request that the President of the United States to summit the point at issue between the administration and Armenia, to the Permanent Tribunal of Arbitration at the Hague for adjudication."*

It seems that if the charges leveled by Attorney Vahan Cardashian were redrafted today, and the names of the oil junta regime of the United States substituted with Cheney, Bush, Rumsfeld, Blair et al, and 'Armenians' substituted for 'Iraq' and the 'Iraqi people,' we would have a perfect indictment to lay before the World Court at the Hague and to press for punishment of these people, who hiding behind the mask of false 'correctness,' are actually promoting their imperial grab for oil belonging to Iraq. We should first address a petition of grievances to the President of the Senate and the Chairman of the House of Representatives with a bill of particulars, charging treason against the oil junta members asking the House to impeach and the Senate to find them guilty and force them from office. We should then present a petition that these men be tried in the courts of the land, as provided for by the U.S. Constitution.

And if these pleas and petitions fall on deaf ears, then we must address a charge to the World Court at The Hague and ask for the members of the imperialist oil junta to be brought to justice. Nothing less will do and nothing less with stop this oil junta from continuing to rampage through the world for they are now, as always, marching roughshod over all nations under their Petroleum Industry banner.

There was an attempt made in 1991 by Representative Henry Gonzalez to impeach G. W. H. Bush, but this was bottled up by politicians of both parties who had no regard for the U.S. Constitution. No doubt a similar resolution filed against George W. Bush would meet the same fate, for the politicians in the House and Senate today, have even less regard for the Constitution than those who were there in 1991. If the resolution meets with indifference or political posturing, then the people have the remedy of submitting it to the International Court of

Justice at The Hague. At least, let a move be made in the direction of restoring the Constitution to its rightful place, and not let the oil junta go on trampling it underfoot.

The imperialists fighting for oil did not confine their efforts to Iraq, Iran and Mexico. They branched out all over the world and even interfered with the sovereign rights of the Russian people, not to mention their intervention in Venezuela. One of the most extraordinary incidents occurred in Siberia, about which not much has been written.

In 1918, Japan tried to occupy the Siberian coast. Wilson tried to prevent it by diplomacy, but when that did not work, he sent an American army to Siberia without the authorization of Congress, not so much to help Russia, but to stop Japan from taking over valuable oil and coal deposits in Sakhalin because Wilson wanted it for Sinclair Oil, the U.S. company. Russia looked with favor upon Sinclair thinking that the Americans were dealing with 'clean hands.' But those who operate under the imperial banner of the Petroleum Industry do not play fair. They play dirty as has been their custom.

While the Russians were favoring Sinclair Oil, behind their backs the motley crew of oil moguls was scheming and plotting against Russia's control of the Caucasus with its valuable oil deposits. It was the Mexican story all over. The U.S. secretly backed dissident Georgian groups in the belief that if successful, the sought after oil concessions would come to the U.S. The U.S. thirsted for control of the Grosni-Baku oilfields, but Moscow put the rebellion down and captured documents that proved U.S. interference in Grosni-Baku.

The imperialists then went to Congress and tried to get recognition for a 'National Republic of Georgia' whose government was in exile in Paris. But the State Department, in cahoots with the Bolsheviks, opposed the scheme and it fell through. Undaunted, Rockefeller - Standard then obtained concessions to buy Russian oil cheaply, and the Anglo-American Oil Company bought 250,000 tons of Baku oil. Suddenly the anti-Bolshevik Rockefeller oil lobby stopped slandering Russia and began to praise it. Rockefeller then sought bigger and bigger contracts with Russian oil suppliers, and in 1927 purchased 500,000 tons.

Things began to go very well between Rockefeller and the Bolsheviks, in spite of the horror stories that were coming out of the Communist- controlled regime. In June 1927 Standard Oil ordered another 360,000 tons of oil and Vacuum-Standard signed a $12,000,000 a year with the Bolsheviks.

The imperialist oil junta, (Bush, Cheney and Rumsfeld) horror stories about Saddam Hussein (the beast) set the stage for an unprecedented attack on Iraq, a so-called "pre-emptive strike," that violated every tenet of the U.S. Constitution and trampled international law.

Yet their antecedents were very happy to do business with the Bolshevik beasts whose record of brutal murders and suppression of freedoms in Russian far surpassed by one hundred thousand times, anything that Saddam Hussein could possibly have done to his people. The Bush administration dares to speak in lofty tones about 'morality' being on their side, and then have the Christian fundamentalist television preachers tell the nation that this evil imperial oil junta is fighting a 'just war.'

The British journal *The Outlook*, summed up the situation with the oil trade with the Bolsheviks, and the viewpoint it expressed, would fit the oil junta of Bush, Cheney and Rumsfeld like a glove if we change the time frame from 1928 to 2003:

> "Both the British and American authorities regard business with Russian oil as legitimate… The point is simply that the various companies have been trying to do each other in the eye."

WE FIGHT FOR OIL

The sordid intrigue and competition is grim business enough; the attempts to explain it in terms of morality and ethics are sheer hypocrisy. It is indecent and disgusting.

We come now to the 'morality' of the imperial oil junta of Bush-Cheney running the United States. They attacked Iraq, without one scrap, one vestige of authority from the U.S. Constitution and international law, and dropped thousands of bombs and rained down cruise missiles on the open, undefended city of Baghdad, in violation of international law, and they confidently expect to escape punishment and judgment of the Nuremberg Protocols.

In addition, the imperialist junta picked up huge profits from 'reconstructing' Iraq after bombing it to the ground. Oil junta Vice President Richard Cheney's companies Halliburton and Bechtel, were awarded a lucrative contract worth $6 billion long before 'hostilities' began. If the American people stand for it, then they deserve the fate that awaits them.

For his valor, Bechtel was secretly awarded a CBE (Commander of British Empire) by Queen Elizabeth II. The success of the huge propaganda machine has shut out all reasonable discussion by the American people, who, we told at the start of the attack, supported the oil junta's war on Iraq by a margin of 75 percent. Therefore, the truth about the barbaric onslaught of March 20, 2003 is in the minds of relatively few people.

George Orwell would have understood the oil junta and its imperial march on Iraq. Born in 1903, the master technician schooled in the arts of propaganda and diplomacy by deception, would not have hesitated to take on the Bush-Cheney-Rumsfeld oil junta. But unfortunately for America, Orwell died in 1950 having left the world with his book '1984,' a profound understanding of how things work. The resume written by Paul Foot and published on January 1st 2003 is worth quoting:

"The year I suppose, for many of us will be the George

Orwell year. He was born in 1903 and died in 1950 and has loomed over the British literary scene ever since. This centenary year there is certain to be an entertaining re-run of the arguments on the left between his supporters, including me, and his detractors, who hail back to the good old days under comrade Stalin."

CHAPTER 7

Transition to barbarism

We start Orwell's year with a reminder that this famous satire '1984,' foresaw a horrific world divided into three power blocks, constantly changing sides in order to continue fighting each other.

The governments of all three keep the allegiance of their citizens by pretending there has always been one war, one enemy. The Party said that Oceania had never been in alliance with Eurasia. He, Winston Smith, knew that Oceania had been in alliance with Eurasia as a short time four years ago. But where did the knowledge exist? Only in his own conscience. All that was needed was an unending series over victories over your own memory. Reality control, they call it: Newspeak; 'doublethink.'

We have that 'double think' over Iraq and it exists in more places than just in our minds. There is the record of Margaret Thatcher of Oceania (the U.S. and Britain) and her treacherous plot to get the U.S. to fight a war against Iraq in 1991. And then we have the Doublespeak of April Glaspie, who led President Saddam Hussein into the trap, just another step in the long road littered with attempts by the U.S. imperialists to dispossess Iraq of its oil.

The American people, by their silence in 1991 and again in 2008, condoned imperialist acts of barbarism and wholesale destruction, with barely a murmur of protest. The American people have taken scant notice of the deliberate destruction of their Constitution by successive Bush administrations and they have not raised a murmur of protest. Why should Germany be held to the doctrine of 'Collective Responsibility' and the United States not held to this doctrine, following its deeds in Iraq? Where is the Collective Responsibility for the war crimes against Iraq at the behest of George Bush and Margaret Thatcher and their fellow imperialists? For twelve years the papers have lain unseen in British and American archives, papers detailing how 'Oceania' misled and lied to Iraq. Margaret Thatcher, before she turned to denouncing Hussein, spent over $1.5 billion, arming Iraq with 'weapons of mass destruction.' That was done because 'Oceania' had formed a bloc with Iraq, and Hussein was the blue-eyed boy of the regime of Oceania. In the mammoth Scott Enquiry held in Britain in 1996, some details of this giant duplicity leaked out.

In the 1980s the Thatcher government had supplied Iraq with most of the military hardware supposedly 'banned' by law. Chieftain tanks were smuggled to Jordan and from there shipped to Baghdad. Machine tool regulations were 'relaxed' to supply Iraqi arms manufacturers to get into business. Credits for the purchase of military hardware were disguised, as 'civil development' needs.

In the 1980s the 'bold strategy' as it was described in Whitehall files of guaranteeing loans to the bankrupt Iraqi dictator was agreed to by Mrs. Thatcher herself, her foreign secretary Douglas Hurd and her trade and industry secretary Nicholas Ridley. They in turn strenuously lobbied by officials from Whitehall's arms sales department — the defense export sales organization — who had close links with arms firms. The Iraqi guarantees were too risky to be genuine commercial propositions. They were made under section two of a special provision allegedly 'in the national interest.

The guarantees were supposed to cover only civil projects. But one firm RACAL, which under the chairmanship of Sir Ernie Harrison regularly donated $80,000 a year to the Tories, was then provided with a secret 'defense allocation' of $45 million of special ECGD insurance after getting a contract with Iraq in 1985. ECGD documents show civil servants protested that a single company was getting virtually all the benefit from this secret association. But they were overruled.

RACAL was building a factory in Iraq when the Gulf War broke out. Subsequently, the ECGD had to write RACAL's bankers an insurance check for $18 million. In 1987 Marconi Command and Control got a bank loan of $12 million backed by a taxpayer guarantee to sell AMERTS - the Artillery Meteorological System to the Iraqi Army. Crucial for accurate artillery fire, AMERTS uses weather balloons linked to radar to measure wind speeds.

It was two of these mobile units that the American WMD hunters announced with great fanfare as 'biological weapons' only to retreat with red faces when experts said they were used for filling artillery spotter balloons with hydrogen.

But ECGD's secret allocation had been used up on RACAL. So Ministry of Defense officials got the contract reclassified as civil. The murky deal led ECGD officials to protest privately that they had been misled by the MoD. ECGD ended up writing a check for $10 million when Marconi failed to get its money.

Another contract was also subjected to maneuvering, Tripod Engineering, backed by John Laing International, succeeded in getting a $20 million deal classified as civil, even though it was for a fighter pilot training complex for the Iraqi air force. Tripod got assistance in its negotiations from an air vice marshal, who shortly after retirement was paid by Tripod as a consultant, without seeking the consent of the MoD as the rules required. The Scott Report found that his behavior, however unintentional, was apt to give rise to suspicion.

The Scott Report goes on and on to cite one arms deal after another with Iraq that cost the nation $1.5 billion.

Members of the Conservative cabinet refused to stop lending guaranteed funds to President Saddam. The firms who benefited from this tender concern have since cashed in their chips. The Midland Bank has been sold to the Hong Kong Bank (HSBC) and Grenfell sold to the German Deutsche Bank.

Even if Britain now obtains reparations from President Saddam $1.5 billion loan defaults, this will go nowhere near meeting the cost of the war to Britain. This has been estimated at $4-6 billion depending on how much occupying and administering Britain has to do.

America will never know the cost of this war or the involvement of giant U.S. conglomerates Bechtel and Halliburton, for instance. But we do know that thus far, the cost of the war is estimated at $650 billion (mid 2008 figures.) The double-cross perpetrated by April Glaspie and George Bush has gone unpunished; the doublethink Newspeak of Oceania has been successful in deceiving the world.

That doublethink Newspeak was on a massive scale as Oceania (Britain and the U.S.) launched their war against Iraq. We, the Winston Smiths of today, know that 15 years ago the U.S. and Britain were in an alliance with Iraq. We know that the British Foreign Secretary sided with Saddam Hussein when he did all those terrible things to his own people listed in Jack Straw's recent doublethink dossier.

We know that our government changed their own guidelines in order to sell Saddam the ingredients of any weapons of mass destruction he may or may not have had. We also know that the key bases from which U.S. bombers took off to kill Iraqis are in Saudi Arabia, whose regime is even more dictatorial, savage and terrorist, than Saddam Hussein. (And, we hasten to add, Kuwait is ten times worse than Iraq and Saudi Arabia when it comes to a brutal dictatorship.) But where does that knowledge exist? It exists only in our consciousness.

Orwell's great novel was not only satire, but a terrible warning. He wanted to alert his readers to the dangers of acquiescence in the lies and contortions of powerful governments and their media toadies.

The anti-war movement did not grow fast in Britain and the U.S. Fortunately we can still, as Orwell urged in another passage, 'turn our consciousness to strength' and shake off warmongers 'like horses shaking off flies.' If we don't, we are in for another awful round of victories over our own memories and of doublethink…

We must 'shake off the warmongers' and their Doublespeak New Think host of lies. We must place the media, their running dogs and their 'toadies' in the correct perspective under the heading of 'congenital liars.' If we do not, we are indeed doomed to live under a regime as terrifying as the regime described in Orwell's '1984.' Of that we may be absolutely certain. Go back to 1991 and relive the lies, the deception and the Doublespeak New Think of George Bush, the elder, April Glaspie, Margaret Thatcher and her cronies and place your memories of these events, side-by-side with your consciousness of events today and see the striking similarity. Then, let your voices of protest be heard.

Let us turn our consciousness to the war of genocide still being waged against the ancient, small nation of Iraq, a people and a nation that has never done the U.S. any harm, although, au contraire, we in the United States have a long history of trying to harm them. Since the 1920s, there are hundreds of pages of historical records that testify to this truth. Secret governments, the petroleum industry and the running dogs of the media in complicity with Oceania have already done dreadful harm to an innocent people.

The British effort to rob Iraq is even worse than those of the U.S. although Oceania must bear full equal responsibility for their brutal barbarity toward this small, virtually defenseless nation. British efforts crystallized in slicing off part of Iraq and calling it

'Kuwait.' Through force of arms they created a new 'State' they called Kuwait, a puppet of Westminster, placing in charge some of the worst tyrants in Middle East history, the Al Sabah family.

Yet, when Iraq tried to reclaim that which is rightfully theirs, Bush of Oceania sent Glaspie to blatantly lie to Hussein and people of the United States by giving the green light for Iraqi forces to go into Kuwait and disband it. Glaspie's double speak told Hussein:

'We do not interfere in border disputes between Arab states.'

Worse yet, when in later years she was brought before the Senate (before her disappearing act), Glaspie deliberately lied and has thus far escaped the consequences of her treasonous conduct. She deceived the people of Oceania. This woman, this mistress of the oil junta is directly responsible for the deaths of more than one million Iraqis in the imperial fight for oil.

What is the difference between what Germany did which ended in the Nuremberg Tribunals and what Oceania has done to Iraq? There is no difference. The leaders of Oceania, past and present, ought to be dragged kicking and screaming before the bar of justice and tried for their heinous and grievous crimes. Until this is done, there will be no peace in the world.

In the meantime the chief priests of Oceania continue with their Doublespeak New Think jargon. Rumsfeld was one of the best practitioners of this type of misinformation. He claimed that there are scores of 'coalition partners' in the War on Iraq, March 20, 2003 when in fact there were but two; Australia and Britain. So using the word 'coalition' to bolster support for his cause was in fact deceitful. The only true alliance forces are the U.S. Navy, Army and Air Force.

President Bush's categorical demand that people must submit to classification: 'either you are with us or you are against us' is triple Doublespeak, for one can be for the United States while being thoroughly against the cruel barbarity being practiced against the people of Iraq. Bush expects the majority to acquiesce to his Doublespeak, but in our consciousness we must resist him. This war is not about being 'patriotic' and 'supporting the troops.' This war is about truth and the truth is that twice an imperial U.S. has attacked a small, weak nation without reason and without just cause, but it now attempts to Doublespeak its way out of the horrendous crime it has committed.

The only possible way, in which we can stand up and be counted, is to bring the truth to the streets. We are not going to go anywhere with the U.S. Congress. It has tangoed its way through this terrible crisis, locked in the arms of the oil junta, its ears deaf and stopped to the worldwide protests going on, deathly afraid of the multinational corporations. We have to reclassify ourselves as opponents of the oil junta, which is marching the nation to perdition, and we must oppose those who are marching under the banner of the Petroleum Industry.

George Orwell:

> "Turn your consciousness into strength. Shake off the war mongers like flies."

It is only in this way that we can defeat their drive toward the New World Order. If we fail then the warmongers from Oceania will overwhelm us, and we cannot allow that to happen. If we want a future for our children and ourselves, Oceania must be defeated. Unfortunately, the American people did not respond to the challenge of being swept into war by a warmongering Republican Party that in the aftermath of 9/11 threw all restraints (including the checks imposed by the U.S. Constitution) to the four winds, and thus there was no holding back the imperial U.S.-British military assault on Iraq on the flimsy pretext of finding non-existent 'Weapons of Mass Destruction' (Tavistock English), but in reality, in an attempt to snatch Iraq's oil from them.

The success of the vast propaganda machine used without restraint against the American people is one of the major developments in the history of the science, which has come long distances since the days of Wellington House, Bernays and Lipmann. With the attention span of the average American being only two weeks, the lies and distortions about the so-called "Weapons of Mass Destruction" will soon be forgotten, and the British and American governments of Blair and Bush will be forgiven. The issue is just too great to be swept under the carpet, but it will fade as the passing of time crowds it off the front pages of the news media.

In his State of the Union message to the United States Congress on January 28, 2003, President Bush told the whole world that there was no time to lose, no time to wait. Being held back by the UN or by the mass protests around the world against attacking Iraq, Bush said, would expose the United States and Britain to 'Saddam's weapons of mass destruction.'

Bush stated categorically that Iraq needed to account for... 25,000 liters of anthrax, 38,000 liters of botulinum toxin, 500 tons of Sarin, mustard gas, VX nerve agent and several mobile biological weapons laboratories, and advanced nuclear weapons developments.

On the basis of this claim, repeated at the United Nations by Secretary of State Powell and in the British Parliament by Prime Minister Blair, fifty-one percent of the American people were persuaded to give their consent to an immediate all-out military assault on Iraq, notwithstanding that it was forbidden by the U.S. Constitution, and notwithstanding that the UN Security Council had refused to sanction a war against Iraq. We do not speak here of how international law was grossly violated by the U.S. and British governments, but suffice to say that the invasion of Iraq by U.S. military forces violated every one of the four Geneva

Conventions, the 1922 Hague Rules of Aerial Warfare, and the Nuremberg Protocols. In the British Parliament, Blair gave an impassioned speech to sway the wavering members of his own party, declaring most empathically that Iraq could mount an attack on Britain in 45 minutes, using chemical and biological weapons of mass destruction. He told the House of Commons that intelligence agencies had provided proof that Iraq had weapons of mass destruction and was ready to use them. But for the persuasive powers of Blair coupled with what he said was intelligence reports to back his assertions, Parliament would not have given its assent to the rush to war against Iraq. It now turns out that the road to war was paved with lies. As the *Independent* newspaper stated:

> The case for invading Iraq to remove its weapons of mass destruction was based on selective use of intelligence, exaggeration, use of sources known to be discredited and outright fabrication etc.

With the end of the Iraqi President rule, we expected that such weapons would be found, especially as Prime Minister Blair told the Parliament, that they could be got ready and operational within 45 minutes. It is very difficult to hide rockets on a launch pad or vehicle all fueled up and ready to fire. Yet, by May 15, 2008, no such weapons had been discovered, in spite of a series of the most intensive searches conducted by teams of 6000 American and British 'inspectors.' President Bush emphatically refused to permit the return of UN weapons inspectors to Iraq as requested by Chief Weapons Inspector Hans Blix, notwithstanding the UN Security Council's resolution which was still in effect. An obdurate Bush set his face against the leader of the UN search team. There would be no return of the UN search teams to Iraq. Just as emphatically Bush declared that the weapons would be found. Coming under attack for lack of progress in this regard, 'coalition partner' Jack Straw, who had backed Blair with at least 35 positive statements that Iraq was a danger to the whole world because of its weapons of mass destruction, was forced to back peddle furiously in Parliament on

May 15, 2004.

According to a report filed by Nicholas Watt, political correspondent in London, on proceedings in the House of Parliament (Britain back- tracked on 'Contentious Issue of Iraqi Weapons') Britain had to retreat on the all important issues of weapons of mass destruction. Taking his cue for a change of tune from U.S. Secretary of State Powell and National Security Advisor Rice, who attempted to spin their way out of the dilemma of failing to find the fabled Iraqi weapons, Jack Straw added his own spin:

> "Britain backtracked on the issue of Iraq's weapons of mass destruction when foreign secretary Jack Straw was forced to concede that hard evidence might never be uncovered. He said it was 'not crucially important' to find them because the evidence of Iraqi wrongdoing was overwhelming. He dismissed the significance of the failure to find banned weapons on the grounds that Hans Blix, the chief UN weapons inspector, had uncovered a 'phenomenal amount of evidence' before the war. This 'phenomenal amount of evidence' consisted of 10,000 liters of anthrax, which only partly-filled a petrol tanker. 'Whether or not we are able to find one third of one petrol tanker in a country twice the size if France remains to be seen,' Straw said. 'We did not go to war on a contingent basis. We went to war on the basis of evidence which was fully available to the international community."

His comment, seized on by critics of the war, was a dramatic retreat from the ministers' claim that Saddam Hussein could launch a chemical and biological attack within 45 minutes. Mr. Straw may also find himself in trouble with Dr. Blix who may take exception to the claim that he produced 'overwhelming evidence' of banned weapons. The ever-cautious Dr. Blix only ever said there was a 'strong presumption' that Iraq had 10,000 liters of anthrax.

As a lawyer, Mr. Straw was careful to say that Dr. Blix had only 'suggested' that Iraq possessed anthrax, but he tried to show the existence of anthrax could be accepted when he described the discovery of chemical and biological suits as 'further evidence.'

Alice Mahon, the Labor MP for Halifax, who has been one of the government's strongest critics said;

> "the whole basis of the war is based on an untruth. The whole world can see that ministers are backing away from their claims. People genuinely believed what the Prime Minister said about Iraq's weapons program and its ability to launch an attack in 45 minutes. This is making the war even more illegal."

Labor dissidents, led by the former defense minister Peter Kilfoyle, will step up pressure on the government by tabling a commons motion demanding evidence of mass destruction, They feel particularly strongly about the issue because a series of ministers, led by Tony Blair, won the support of wavering MPs before the war by issuing dire warnings about the threat posed by Saddam Hussein. As criticism for the failure to find banned weapons has increased, ministers have struggled to offer a plausible explanation. But thus far their explanations have been bogus.

CHAPTER 8

Phantom WMD's

The team searching for weapons of mass destruction in Iraq is ending its operation without having found proof that Saddam Hussein had stocks of chemical, biological or nuclear weapons. It investigated numerous sites identified by U.S. intelligence as those likely to harbor weapons of mass destruction (WMD) but has now all but accepted that it is unlikely to find any weapons.

Operations are being wound up and a scaled-down unit called the Iraq Survey Group will take over. The leader of the U.S. Army's 75th Exploitation Task Force, Colonel Richard McPhee, said his team of biologists, chemists, computer experts and documents specialists arrived in Iraq believing the intelligence community's warning that Saddam had given 'release authority' to those in charge of a chemical arsenal. 'We didn't have all those people in protective suits for nothing,' he told The Washington Post. But if they planned to use those weapons there had to have been something to use and we haven't found it. Books will be written on that in the intelligence community for a long time.

Saddam's alleged possession of such weapons was one of the central pretexts given by Washington and London for the war against Iraq. In a February 2000 presentation to the UN, Colin Powell, then U.S. Secretary of State, identified sites he said were producing WMD. When George Bush made his declaration of victory aboard the USS Abraham Lincoln on 1 May, he said:

"We've begun the search for hidden chemical and biological weapons and already know of hundreds of sites that will be investigated."

Some progress has been made. It was reported that a team of experts searching for WMD had concluded that a trailer found near the city of Mosul in northern Iraq was a mobile biological weapons laboratory. The team agreed, however other experts did not share their views. Some officials claim, that up to three such laboratories have been discovered although no biological or chemical agents have been found at any of them. (It turned out that the 'mobile labs' were vehicles equipped to fill artillery spotter balloons with hydrogen gas, although this information was buried in the back pages of British and American newspapers.)

On May 11th General Richard Myers, the chairman of the U.S. Joint Chiefs of Staff, said WMD might still be in the hands of Iraqi special units. Were they fully deployed and could they have been brought to bear on us, or are they still perhaps out there somewhere in some sort of bunker and could have been used? he said at the U.S. regional headquarters in Qatar: We are trying to run that one to the ground. But those on the ground were more skeptical. U.S. central command started the war with a list of 19 priority suspected weapons sites. All but two were searched without uncovering any evidence. A further 69 were identified as sites that might offer clues to the whereabouts of WMD. Of these, 45 were searched without success.

Some experts believed that one of the problems was that WMD search teams were held back for too long, allowing Iraqi forces to dismantle or destroy equipment. Others believe that the assessment that such weapons existed was wrong. One Defense Intelligence Agency official said:

"We came to bear country and we came loaded for bear and we found that the bear was not there. The question was "where are Saddam Hussein's chemical and biological weapons?" What is the question now? That is what we are trying to sort out."

In 2008 it is clear that the whole concoction of Hussein's possession of WMD's was nothing, but a disgusting lie of immense proportions and this has been borne out by the Senate Committee Report, led by Sen. Jay Rockefeller. He denounced both Bush and Cheney by name and accused them of deliberately going to the American people and Congress. The search for WMD continued under the auspices of the Iraq Survey Group, which also hunted for information about President Hussein's government. The White House claimed this was a bigger unit than the task force. But officials admitted that the number of staff hunting for weapons was scaled back. For weeks, we heard breathless media reports of possible discoveries of chemical and biological weapons by U.S. and British troops in Iraq. Within hours or days, if one scours the back pages of the newspaper, one finds that it was merely another false alarm. But what was never mentioned was that these weapons, even if they ever existed, were made five, ten or fifteen years ago, and would almost certainly have been unusable, having long since passed their stable shelf-life, according to the Department of Defense's own documents based on a decade of international inspections, electronic surveillance and information supplied by 'spies and defectors.'

There was never any question Iraq had once possessed weapons of mass destruction programs, but no actual weapons, nor was the world naive enough to trust Saddam Hussein not to try and hide such weapons from UN inspectors.

The rationale for the U.S. invasion, however, was that after a decade of sanctions, war, U.S. bombing runs, and UN inspections, Iraq still posed as a viable nuclear, chemical and biological threat. The Bush administration said they could be deployed beyond Iraq's borders or could be supplied to terrorist groups.

Unfortunately for Bush, there is absolutely no basis for this argument, so forcefully made by then Secretary of State Colin Powell at the United Nations, when he claimed to possess clear evidence that huge stocks of everything from Sarin gas, also known by its NATO designation GB, to anthrax, to sanction-violating missiles, were stored in Iraq, ready for use.

Never mind that the same Iraqi defector who told Powell about the stores of chemical and bio weapons also said they had been completely destroyed, which Powell neglected to tell the United Nations and the world. It didn't matter, even if true -- which it was not — because those stores would almost certainly have become useless and perished after all those years on the shelf.

Strangely, the U.S. media have, with almost no exceptions, failed to mention that most bio/chemical agents have a rather limited shelf life. The few who did usually quoted Scott Ritter, former UN Iraqi weapons inspector and controversial opponent of the war. According to Ritter, the chemical weapons Iraq has been known to possess nerve agents like Sarin and Tabun - have a shelf life of five years, with VX just a bit longer. Saddam's major bio weapons are hardly any better; botulinum toxin is potent for about three years, and liquid anthrax about the same (under the right conditions). And Ritter added that since all chemical weapons were made in Iraq's only chemical weapons complex - the Muthanna State establishment, which was blown up during the first Gulf War in 1991 - and all biological weapons plants and research papers were clearly destroyed by 1998, any remaining bio/chemical weapons stores were now 'harmless, useless goo.'

However, others have questioned Ritter's credibility. A former hawk keen on an Iraq invasion after the first Gulf War, as recently as 1998 he wrote in an article for the New Republic that Saddam may have successfully hidden everything from potent biological and chemical agents to his entire nuclear weapons infrastructure from UN inspectors.

But the truth of the matter is that Iraq's WMD may have even less of a shelf life than Ritter had claimed - and the U.S. government knows it. The U.S. Defense Department's 'Militarily Critical Technologies List' (MCTL) is a detailed compendium of technologies that the department advocates as 'critical to maintaining superior U.S. military capabilities.' It applies to all mission areas, especially counter- proliferation.

So what was the MCTL's opinion of Iraq's chemical weapons program?

In making its chemical nerve agents the Iraqis produced a mixture which was inherently unstable. When the Iraqis produced chemical munitions they appeared to adhere to a 'make and use' regimen. Judging by the information Iraq gave the United Nations, later verified by on-site inspections, Iraq had poor product quality for their nerve agents. This low quality was likely due to a lack of purification. They had to get the agent to the front promptly or have it degrade in the munitions.

Defense Department report said:

> "Furthermore the chemical munitions found in Iraq after the (first) Gulf War contained badly deteriorated agents and a significant proportion was visibly leaking."

The shelf life of these poorly made agents were said to be a few weeks at best - hardly the stuff of vast chemical weapons stores. There was some talk shortly before the first Gulf War that the Iraqis had been creating binary chemical weapons in which the relatively non-toxic ingredients of the agent remain unmixed until just before the weapon is used; this allows the user to bypass any worry about shelf life or toxicity. But according to the MCTL; 'The Iraqis had a small number of bastardized binary munitions in which some unfortunate individual was to pour one ingredient into the other from a Jerry can prior to use' - an action few soldiers were willing to perform.

Iraq did produce mustard gas that was somewhat more stable than the nerve agents. It may have a longer shelf life; perhaps potent forms of this agent could still be found. But one must wonder how worried we should be about Iraq's poorly made agents, several years after their production. And, as Ritter now insists, any chemical weapons facilities operating in recent years could, like their nuclear counterpart have given off vented gases; and any new biological weapons programs would had to start again from scratch. Both activities would have been easily detected by Western intelligence, but no such evidence was ever produced because no such evidence was ever found, for the simple reason that it did not exist.

The argument for Iraq as a nuclear threat was built on even shakier ground, but this didn't keep hawks from exploiting non-evidence to frighten any reticent politicians.

As Congress was preparing to vote on the resolution authorizing the use of force in Iraq, Tony Blair's government picked that moment to publicly release an apparent bombshell: British intelligence had obtained documents showing that between 1999 and 2001, Iraq had attempted to buy 'significant quantities of uranium' from an unnamed African country 'despite having no active civil nuclear power program that could require it.'

The New Yorker's Senior reporter, Seymour Hersh wrote, that the very same day Blair unveiled this alleged 'smoking gun,' CIA Director George Tenet discussed the documents between Iraq and Niger, the African country in question, during a closed-session Senate Foreign Relations Committee hearing on the Iraq WMD issue. Blair had handed the papers over to American intelligence, and at just the right time; Tenet's evidence was instrumental in getting Congress to back the war resolution, which, as we have said before is not a power contained in the U.S. Constitution. The Constitution mandates that a declaration of war be passed by a joint session of the House and Senate. Anything less is unconstitutional and the 'resolution' was just that, unconstitutional and of no effect; as it did not meet the criteria of a declaration of war.

The International Atomic Energy Agency (IAEA) was to verify the authenticity of these important documents for the UN Security Council, but only obtained them from the U.S. government after months of pleading - a strange delay, considering the Bush White House was so eager to prove Saddam's nuclear intentions to a skeptical world. As we now know, Mohamed El Baradei, director- general of the IAEA, told the UN Security Council that the Niger documents regarding the uranium sales were clear fakes. These documents are so bad that I cannot imagine they came from a serious intelligence agency. When asked about the forgeries at a later House hearing, Secretary of State Colin Powell said:

> 'It came from other sources. It was provided in good faith to the inspectors.'

Fingers pointed to Britain's MI6 as the perpetrators; Arab sources pointed to Israel's Mossad. Indeed, this administration often obscured the fact that the UN destroyed all of Iraq's nuclear weapons program infrastructure and facilities by the time inspectors left in 1998. Even if Hussein had somehow secretly imported the materials necessary to rebuild them within the past five years, even as UN sanctions, no-fly zones and vigorous spying by Western forces remained firmly in place, Iraq could not hide the gases, heat, and gamma radiation which centrifuge facilities emit - and which our intelligence capacities would have identified by now. A week after the IAEA's bombshell Sen. Jay Rockefeller (D-WV) formally asked for an FBI investigation into the matter, stating that, and

> 'the fabrication of these documents may be part of a larger deception aimed at manipulating public opinion ... regarding Iraq.'

Nothing has ever come from the FBI about this important matter. With White House insiders and media boosters admitting they no longer expect to find much, if any, in the way of weapons of mass destruction in Iraq, different unconvincing storylines were floated: the weapons went to Syria; they were efficiently destroyed just hours before the U.S. invasion, etc. The truth, however, appears to be that Iraq was a paper tiger, with little or no ability to threaten the United States or Israel.

The Bush administration has changed its tune on Iraqi weapons of mass destruction, the reason it went to war. Instead of looking for vast stocks of banned materials, it is now pinning its hopes on finding documentary evidence. The change in rhetoric, apparently designed, in part to dampen public expectations, has unfolded gradually in the past as special U.S. military teams found little to justify the Bush administration's claim that Iraq was concealing vast stocks of chemical and biological agents and was actively working on a covert nuclear weapons program.

The Bush administration seems to be hoping that inconvenient facts will disappear from the public discourse. 'It's happening to a large degree,' said Phyllis Bennis of the Institute for Policy Studies (IPS), a liberal think-tank, which opposed the war. Few politicians have raised the issue, not wishing to question a popular military victory.

However, California Rep. Jane Harman, ranking Democrat on the House of Representatives Intelligence Committee, said she was concerned:

> "Though I was convinced of the case made prior to the war, I am increasingly concerned about the lack of progress in uncovering the Iraqi weapons. We need a thorough accounting of what intelligence was available to Congress and war planners before and during the conflict."

In a *New York Times/CBS* poll 49 percent of their readers said the administration overestimated the amount of banned weapons in Iraq, while 29 percent said its estimates were accurate and 12 percent said they were low.

Earlier, in a speech Oct. 7, 2005, Bush said:

> "The Iraqi regime... possesses and produces chemical and biological weapons. It is seeking nuclear weapons. We know that the regime has produced thousands of tons of chemical agents, including mustard gas, Sarin nerve gas, VX nerve gas... And surveillance photos reveal that the regime is rebuilding facilities that it had used to produce chemical and biological weapons."

In his State of the Union address January, 2006, Bush accused Iraq of having enough material... to produce over 25,000 liters of anthrax — enough doses to kill several million people... more than 38,000 liters of botulinum toxin — enough to subject millions of people to death by respiratory failure... as much as 500 tons of Sarin mustard and VX nerve agent.

In his presentation to the U.N. Security Council on Feb. 6, Secretary of State Colin Powell said Washington 'knew' that Baghdad had dispersed rocket launchers and warheads containing biological warfare agents to locations in western Iraq:

> "We also have satellite photos that indicate that banned materials have recently been moved from a number of Iraqi weapons of mass destruction facilities. There can be no doubt that Saddam Hussein has biological weapons and the capability to rapidly produce more, many more."

In Congressional testimony in April, Powell said weapons will be found. He said of his U.N speech everything we had there had backup and double sourcing and triple sourcing.

An Army general in Iraq said that Saddam Hussein's government might have destroyed stocks of chemical weapons some time before the United States attacked Iraq to topple President Hussein. But Maj. Gen. David H. Petraeus, commander of the 101st Airborne Division, said it was still too early to determine definitively the location or status of Iraq's suspected arsenal of unconventional weapons. General Petraeus, speaking to reporters at the Pentagon by videophone from Mosul, said:

> "… There is no question that there were chemical weapons years ago, I just don't know whether it was all destroyed years ago… whether they were destroyed right before the war, or whether they're still hidden. Our own chemical section looked at the trailer and confirmed that it was very close to identical to the first trailer that was found by Special Forces southeast of here last week."

Military teams scoured dozens of suspected weapons sites, but did not find any illicit weapons. As it turned out the trailer was part of an artillery spotter force that used gas-filled balloons to get the measure of the accuracy of artillery fire and had nothing whatever to do with nuclear weapons. General Tommy R. Franks, the commander of U.S. forces in Iraq said teams may ultimately have to search several thousand sites to find evidence of such weapons. General Petraeus, however, did offer new details about a suspected mobile biological weapons laboratory that he said was found May 9 at Al Kindi, a military research center near Mosul.

American teams have now located parts of three mobile labs, military and civilian officials say. General Petraeus said, however, that the trailer found at Al Kindi was not completed. Certainly, it would have been reasonable to assume that if Saddam Hussein believed his final hour was approaching he would be more likely to green-light a hand-off of WMD to al-Qaeda. Yet the Bush White House and the Pentagon seem not to have planned for such contingencies. They have been geared more toward finding evidence of WMD (which would help Bush justify the war) rather than thwarting the threat supposedly posed by Iraq's weapons of mass destruction.

Why was the Iraq Survey Team not assembled by the start of the war and ready to rush in as soon as possible in an attempt to locate and secure these items that menaced the United States? The war, after all, came as no surprise. And the news from Iraq has not been encouraging. Looters cleaned out Iraq's nuclear facilities long before U.S. investigators reached them. Were they only scavengers who unknowingly grabbed radioactive material posing health and environmental dangers? Or were they some terrorists looking for dirty bomb material? In either event, a fair question for Bush, Secretary of Defense Donald Rumsfeld and other administration and Pentagon officials, is why didn't you try to secure these sites immediately?

On May 4, Barton Gellman in *The Washington Post* reported that a specially trained Defense Department team was not dispatched to the Baghdad Nuclear Research facility until May 3, after a month of official indecision:

> The unit found the site — which was the home to the remains of the nuclear reactor bombed by Israel in 1981 and which stored radioactive waste that would be quite attractive to a dirty-bomb maker -- ransacked., Gellman reported: 'The survey conducted by the team appeared to offer fresh evidence that the war has dispersed the country's most dangerous technologies beyond anyone's knowledge or control.'

Bush was not forced to explain the slow pace of the WMD search or the lack of prewar planning on this crucial front. Fortunately for him, the Democrats spent more time criticizing his photo-op speech on an aircraft carrier (which caused the news channels to show the 'Top Gun' footage over and over). But at the May 7 White House briefing, press secretary Ari Fleischer was pressed on whether the United States failed to act to prevent weapons of mass destruction (if they existed) from being dispersed. The exchange was illuminating.

Question:

'I know that, but you're making these pronouncements without answering the direct question, which is, what does this administration know about not only what has been found ~ you're still checking - but what weapons materials or actual weapons may have been taken out of the country?'

Fleischer:

'Well, we don't have anything concrete to report on that.'

Precisely, and the White House has not had much to report on its efforts to prevent WMD-related material from being given to or snatched by terrorists. The risk identified by the White House before the war was not, as Fleischer suggested, that Saddam Hussein would use WMD against the United States, but that he would slip them to terrorists who would do so. But can he claim that such transfers have not occurred during or after the war? He definitely could not honestly state that the U.S. military has acted assiduously to prevent this sort of nightmare scenario. In fact, the destruction of the command-and- control structure for whatever WMD material might have been in Iraq only increased the likelihood that this dangerous material could end up in the hands of terrorists.

Next Fleischer remarked:

'As I said earlier, we have high confidence that they have weapons of mass destruction. This is what this war was about and is about.'

With more than 110 sites checked inspectors have found nothing conclusive. It has been an exercise in false alarms. Suspect white powder at Latifiyah was only explosive powder. Barrels of what was thought to be Sarin and Tabun nerve agents were pesticides. When a dozen U.S. soldiers checked a suspect site and fell ill, it was because they had inhaled fertilizer fumes.

Each setback ratcheted up the political pressure. In-fighting between government departments and intelligence agencies became vicious on both sides of the Atlantic. Having fought a war to disarm Iraq of its terrible weapons, neither the U.S. nor Britain dared to admit that Iraq never had any such weapons in the first place. The search for weapons of mass destruction was a fiasco that ended in complete failure.

The search was especially vital for the Neo-Bolshevik Cabal. In the brave new world of post-9/11 America, this tight group of analysts deep in the heart of the Pentagon was the driving force behind the war in Iraq. Numbering no more than a dozen, the Cabal is part of the Office of Special Plans, a new intelligence agency that has taken on the CIA and won. Where the CIA dithered over Iraq, the Office of Special Investigation (OSP) pressed on.

Where the CIA doubted, the OSP was firm. It fought a battle royal over Iraq and came down on the side of being weighed in the balance and found wanting. The OSP was the brainchild of Defense Secretary Donald Rumsfeld, who established it up after the 2001 terrorist attacks. It was charged with going over old ground on Iraq and showing that the CIA had overlooked the threat posed. But its rise caused massive ructions in the normally secretive world of intelligence gathering.

The OSP reported directly to Paul Wolfowitz, a leading Neo-Bolshevik warmonger in the administration. The OSP bypassed the CIA and the Pentagon's own Defense Intelligence Agency (DIA) when it came to whispering in the President's ear. They argued a forceful case for war against Saddam before his weapons programs came to fruition.

More moderate voices in the CIA and Defense Intelligence Agency were drowned out. There was a flurry of leaks to the media. One CIA official described the Cabal's members as 'crazed,' on a 'mission from God.' But the Cabal and Rumsfeld's

Pentagon won and Powell's dovish State Department lost. Tensions between the two were now in the open.

"Rumsfeld set up his own intelligence agency because he didn't like the intelligence he was getting," said Larry Korb, director of national security studies at the Council on Foreign Relations. 'He doesn't like Powell's approach, a typical diplomat, too cautious.' Former CIA officials are caustic about the OSP. Unreliable and politically motivated, they say it has undermined decades of work by the CIA's trained spies and ignored the truth when it has contradicted its worldview.

> "Their methods were vicious,' said Vince Cannistraro, former CIA chief of counter-terrorism. 'The politicization of intelligence was pandemic, and deliberate disinformation was being promoted. They choose the worst-case scenario on everything and so much of the information was fallacious."

But Cannistraro is retired. His attacks did not bother The Cabal, firmly 'in the loop' of Washington's movers and shakers. Yet, even among them, continued failure to find any weapons of mass destruction in Iraq was a growing fear. The fallout from the war could bring them down. The warning was there in black and white. Citing 'intelligence' sources, Tony Blair produced an official dossier that concluded Iraq could fire its chemical or biological weapons within 45 minutes of an order to do so. It was a terrifying prospect and ramped up the pro-war argument when the dossier was produced. But cold analysis told a different story. Iraq was abandoned by the UN weapons inspectors, then bombed, invaded and finally brought under imperial U.S. and British military control. During that entire time the 'button' was never pressed on its weapons of mass destruction. Now both the pro-war party and the anti-war lobby wanted to know why. Could this mysterious lapse be explained or did the weapons never exist?

Months before the United States military rained bombs and missiles on Iraq, the Department of Defense was secretly working with Vice President Dick Cheney's old company, Halliburton Corp., on a deal that would give the world's second largest oil services company total control over Iraq's oil fields, according to Halliburton's most senior executives. Moreover, classified Halliburton documents prove that the war in Iraq was about controlling the world's second largest oil reserves rather than overthrowing the regime of Iraq's President Saddam Hussein.

The contract between the Department of Defense and the Halliburton unit of Kellogg, Brown & Root to operate Iraq's oil industry was hatched as early as October 2002, according to the documents, and could ultimately be valued at $7 billion, a boon to Halliburton.

Back in October 2003, Halliburton was saddled with a multi billion dollar asbestos liability and the company was also suffering through a slowdown in domestic oil production. Halliburton's stock price responded swiftly, plummeting to $12.62 in October 2002, from a high of $22 the year before, and rumors began to swirl that the company would be forced to file for bankruptcy. All things considered and given the history of an imperial U.S. government directed and controlled in its foreign policy by the Petroleum industry, it is reasonable to conclude that even without the 'contrived situation' of weapons of mass destruction, Iraq would have been invaded for the sole purpose of gaining control of its vast oil resources.

CHAPTER 9

Naked imperialism at work

The Petroleum Industry has turned the United States from a benign republic with peace and justice for all, to an imperialist global empire that has destroyed the hope offered to the world by the Republic of the Founding Fathers. The creed of the republic was based on a moral philosophy that was distinctly non-materialistic. But the great corporations and banking institutions set themselves up in opposition to the U.S. Republic and America became greedy, materialistic warlike and dedicated to total mercantilism.

Mainly responsible for the vast change and greatly vilified as such, the petroleum industry has richly deserved every known epithet hurled against it by a wide variety of critics, government and private.

The purpose of the following chapters is to explore an ultra-secret group and establish whether the petroleum industry deserves the bad name it undoubtedly has. This is an industry which has survived all attempts to breach its walls. It survived numerous Senate investigations, anti-trust suits and the personal vendettas exhibited by two experienced and determined U.S. senators, the late Henry Jackson and the late Frank Church.

Only one man, Colonel Khaddafi, was able to upset the 'majors;' a lonely Bedouin from the deserts of Libya, the man who upended the 'Seven Sisters' cartel, much to the chagrin - and astonishment - of the 'government within government,' the directors and board members of the most powerful oil companies in the world. But in the wake of the 2003 war against Iraq, Libya was persuaded to 'see the light' and is now under the control of the major oil companies. This was the turning point when the United States went openly from a republic to an imperial empire began with the Reagan presidency. Ronald Reagan packed his cabinet with multinational corporate executives; Secretary of State George Schultz of Bechtel, Secretary of Defense Casper Weinberger, president of the same company, among others. Whereas President Carter had tried to keep the peace, Reagan launched on a campaign of belligerency that was to set the tone for future U.S. administrations.

The petroleum industry cannot be mentioned without the name of John D. Rockefeller (1839-1937) coming to the forefront. John D. Rockefeller and Standard Oil of New Jersey became synonymous with the imperial American petroleum industry.

Rockefeller and Standard Oil became synonymous with treachery, hatred and greed. Unbridled hatred was the hallmark of John D. and his sons were at pains to keep the legend alive, rather than take steps to ameliorate the bad image left behind by their father; this in spite of old John D. having been raised in a strict Baptist faith on a farm near Cleveland, Ohio. In his formative years he became known for exceptional greediness - he would buy candies and resell them to other children at a profit.

John D. was always industrious. He worked at a grocery store as an accountant at the tender age of sixteen and his employer expressed the greatest satisfaction with his diligence. He proved to be very observant, seeing everything and missing nothing. Even at that age he never expressed any emotion. He rose to become the sole owner of a Cleveland trading company and founded Standard Oil in 1870.

What is noteworthy is that the rise of the Rockefeller Standard Oil Trust can be verified by certifiable documentary evidence which in a sense compares to a note in history of foreign policy-making. Almost from its inception in 1870 the Rockefeller Standard Oil Trust came under attack from various State legislatures and the United States Congress because of its shady dealings.

Trust executives were hauled before Congressional committees in 1872 and again in 1876. The Commonwealth of Pennsylvania tried to upend the Trust in 1879, and two years before that, it was forced to appear before the Interstate Commerce Commission. A virtual state of war between the Standard Oil Trust and the State of Ohio existed in 1882. A commission of industrial inquiry was appointed by President McKinley with 19 volumes of testimony taken. Through it all, the Standard Oil Trust stood like a rock that could not be moved. Civil suits proliferated but to no avail.

In doing the research for this work, I was truly astounded to find just how many millions of people all over the world, hated the Rockefeller name, and the family's flagship company, Standard Oil. This abiding hatred is as fierce today in 2008 as it was when the 'Big Hand' of Rockefeller first surfaced in the Pennsylvania oil fields. This is especially true among the descendants of the pioneer drillers who flocked to Titusville and Pithead in 1865 when the 'black gold rush' was at its height. I am indebted to Ida Tarbell, whose fine book exposing John D. Rockefeller's 'pioneering efforts' was a source of endless inside information about the person and character of the head of the Rockefeller clan.

John D's ability to effortlessly rob drillers and prospectors of their claims appears to be strikingly similar of the methods used by Cecil John Rhodes to rob and steal diamond claims from hard working prospectors in the Kimberly fields in South Africa. Both men were ruthless and without any finer feelings about the rights of others and both men never expressed emotion.

If Rockefeller and his sons were self-advertisers, what they were advertising was not in the interests of free men everywhere. Nelson Rockefeller once said that his family's huge fortune was an accident, but history records otherwise.

The taciturn character and dishonesty of John D. were no doubt handed down to his sons, along with his paranoid secrecy and total lack of feeling. The paranoia of secrecy inherited from Standard Oil Trust by the majors is evident in the barriers these companies erected around themselves to keep prying 'outsiders' at bay. They trust their affairs only to petroleum industry banks like the Committee of 300's Morgan Guarantee, Trust Bank and Chase Manhattan Bank, while their accounts and affairs are closeted behind the thick walls of Price, Waterhouse, the Committee of 300's official accountants and auditors. Many a Senate committee has got itself enmeshed in the sticky web woven by that great accounting company. Even the finest investigators and auditors that government could muster became totally confused by Price, Waterhouse accountants. It is said of old John D. that he could count faster than today's calculators, a feat he learned from his father when calculating the price of his 'cancer cure' at fairs and such places. Actually, the 'cure' was simply crude oil, straight from the oil wells, packed in little bottles.

Just as the business was going well, John D. had to flee for his life, because police wanted to arrest him for forced sex with a sixteen year- old. Old John D. didn't believe in friendships and warned his sons to stay clear of what he called, 'letting good fellowship get a hold of you.' He also cheated his sons, 'to keep them sharp,' as he put it. His favorite doggerel was about the wise old owl that said nothing, but heard much. An early portrait shows a man with a long, gaunt, grim face, small eyes without a trace of human quality.

His job as a bookkeeper led him to say little, but keep his accounts in order. It is all the more a source of great wonder that a man with such a dour and sour visage, taciturn and unfriendly, was able to persuade the Clark Brothers, at the Clark Brothers Refinery, to sell him a share in their oil refinery, where he was employed.

The Clark brothers were not long in finding out that they had made a dreadful mistake in letting Rockefeller into their business. Quick with figures and calculations, John D. was able to work the two brothers out of their share of the refinery. He always claimed that he had 'bought them out,' but the Clarks responded by saying they were 'cheated out.'

Some writers attribute John D's penchant for getting rid of partners to his heritage, and it is true that his father used to tell him, 'be as quick as a Jew.' Although he claimed Baptist heritage and attended a Baptist church, this is hardly likely to be true, since his parents came from Eastern Europe. John D. did not care about people; he would stomp over them and discard former partners no longer of any use to him. He was interested in only one person, and that was himself. This resulted in Standard Oil becoming the most secretive major corporation in the U.S., a tradition followed by EXXON. It was said of Standard that it was bolted down and barred, like a fortress. John D's character was so tarnished and he was so universally hated that he hired a public relations man to try and burnish his image, helped along by generous 'philanthropic' tax deductible gifts. But in spite of the best efforts by Ivy Lee, said to be the first P.R. man in American history, the legacy of hatred, which John D. had earned, stuck to him, and remains with the Rockefeller name and EXXON, to this day.

Rockefeller's 'Big Hand' reached out and ruined hundreds of thousands of drillers, prospectors and leaseholders in Titusville and Pithead. These were by and large, young men of another generation who believed they could solve the riddle of price fluctuations - the very thing Rockefeller did not want. Although the life around Titusville and Pithead was pretty tempestuous, it was never rancorous, and everybody dealt fairly with each other, that is, up until the Rockefeller 'Big Hand' was raised against all 'competitors.'

At the age of 26 and buoyed up by his success of robbing the Clark brothers of their refinery and with Oil City near Cleveland under his control, Rockefeller began to cast around for new conquests.

His son, David Rockefeller, inherited his father's cold-blooded nature and became a law unto himself. Very early on in his career, David moved the bulk of the family assets 'off-shore' to tax-free havens, where bank secrecy was virtually unbreakable. David Rockefeller continued to run the oil industry like a government within a government, and by a stroke of luck, he also bought INTERPOL, the world police/intelligence system.

All the major oil companies interface with banks, mining companies, railroads, shipping, insurance companies and investment houses; and in the course of business, they exchange information, but it was the host of 'spies' he employed, that kept old John D. and his sons completely informed about everything that went on.

His most efficient network grew in size and scope, and today, there is not one country that escapes Rockefeller's intelligence network, which quite often, surpasses official intelligence services in both size and budget. There is a great deal of work to be done. There must never come a time when we simply throw in the towel and say, 'they are too big, too powerful for any single person to be able to do anything worthwhile about them.' Each of us, can, and must, make an effort.

Tax avoidance was high on old John D. Rockefeller's list, and his spies were soon able to provide the best information on how to circumvent tax laws in foreign countries, usually through their 'personal' (bribed) sources. If the tax laws were tough, the Rockefellers simply got those laws altered to suit their purposes of tax avoidance. It was this bacillus, planted in the oil business that brought about the curse of American dependence upon foreign imported oil, which in turn, sent American producers at home down the road to oblivion.

It is also the main reason why the United States has become an imperial power seeking to dominate those countries having known, proven sources of oil. It also benefited the Rockefellers in another way - it eliminated competitors outside of the vicious circle of 'the majors' without having to resort to the use of dynamite, as old John D. had quite frequently done in his early days.

What has been the end result? Surely it is ever higher prices for the American consumer and increased profits for the major oil companies. EXXON (Standard) made, and still makes, huge profits. For example, in 1972 - and we have chosen this year because it is the average (median) year for profits made by the oil industry, and we did not take an isolated year to drive home the point, that we, the consumers, are being grossly exploited by the petroleum industry - EXXON made $3,700 billion in that year, but paid only 6.5 percent in U.S. taxes. Is this fair to the American consumer? We do not believe it is fair, just or reasonable.

When challenged, EXXON, and indeed, all of the majors come up with the threadbare excuse that they plow back most of their profits into oil exploration, but when we look at a single year of Exxon profits, and let's take 1972 as an example, EXXON made a profit of $2500 billion, just in the third quarter alone and it is not at all clear that a large part of this enormous profit was 'plowed back' into the business, or that the American people profited from it in any way. 1973 was the year of the Kissinger-Rockefeller instigated the Arab Israeli War, and in the light of what we now know about this event, and how Kissinger worked to bring it about through his close relationship with David Rockefeller, one would have thought that the Congress would long ago have investigated this arrangement. Kissinger and David Rockefeller have been like Siamese twins ever since the discovery in Germany of the Bamburg Files by Kissinger and Helmut Sonnenfeldt, Kissinger's right hand man and trusted aide.

The question begs to be asked; did EXXON know that an Arab-Israeli war was coming, and just how much did it profit from this knowledge? This kind of 'insider information' would have been provided by Rockefeller's private army of intelligence agents from around the world, controlled out of the petroleum industry's headquarters which goes by the name of Logistics, Information and Communication Systems, closeted in EXXON's New York headquarters.

Not the least of Rockefeller's intelligence assets is INTERPOL, which operates illegally out of Federal Government property in Washington, D.C. in total defiance of the U.S. Constitution and violates the highest law of the land, our Constitution and the Bill of Rights. INTERPOL should not be operating in the United States, but Congress is afraid to tackle so large and powerful a monster as the Rockefeller family. This is a disturbing condition, which is not being addressed, leaving one to wonder whether any money changes hands to keep INTERPOL in Washington?

Congress needs a committee of inquiry to look into the so-called "Bankers Faction" embedded inside the CIA. These kinds of operations unlawfully influence our foreign policy, touching often upon our daily lives, and when these organizations and groups want a war, they send our sons and daughters to fight. The Bush Gulf Wars are a particularly good example of what goes on. The Rockefeller dynasty forms the backbone of the imperial oil policy making group. The tares sown among the wheat by John D. Rockefeller, grown to maturity, are now choking the wheat, the life of the people of this once great nation. Old John D. quickly and early on in his career, learned the value of the spy business, which he was instructed in by Charles Pratt, one of his earlier associates. The present upper-level parallel secret government that runs the United States, the so-called Council on Foreign Relations (CFR), is the brainchild of Pratt.

The Pratt mansion in New York later became the home of the CFR and this was not due to happenstance. So all-pervading did the presence of John D. become, and so widely admired were his ruthless methods that they were largely adopted by all of the majors, starting with EXXON, so much so that today, the U.S. petroleum industry is in a position to dictate to every government in the world, including the U.S. The petroleum industry has become a government within a government.

There is ample evidence that the major oil companies operating abroad, dictate and run U.S. foreign policy, and that these companies have combined to form a de facto government inside our U.S. government. EXXON is the undisputed leader of this imperialist onslaught for control of all petroleum resources and nowhere more so than in Iran.

CHAPTER 10

Dr. Mossadegh battles the cartel

B eginning in 1950, the U.S. and Britain's Anglo Persian Oil company had a stranglehold on Iran oil following the First World War, during which the conduct of the 'Allies' smelled to high heaven. The invasion and occupation of Iran during the war on the shakiest grounds needs to be examined a lot more closely. Shortly after the 'Allies' marched into Iran, the Shah was forced to abdicate in favor of his son, Mohammed Reza Pahlevi who was more agreeable to the dictates imposed by the Iranian Consortium, the Iraqi Petroleum Company and ARAMCO. One of the most shameful episodes in the history of supposedly 'Christian,' Britain and 'Christian' United States was the deaths of scores of thousands of Iranians from starvation during this period.

The Allied Occupation Army consisting of 100,000 Russian troops (there by invitation of Winston Churchill) and 70,000 U.S. and British troops, did nothing to stop the requisitioning of food by the occupation army at the cost of the Iranians who were dying like flies from starvation. Typhoid fever spread and killed thousands more while U.S. and British forces stood idly by. Those who did not die of starvation or sickness froze to death in the bitter winter as there was no heating oil available to the general populace.

The occupiers engaged in creating and fostering strife between the various factions in the country, and utterly oppressed and suppressed the Iranian government. Still believing that the U.S.

was a Christian nation given to humanitarian considerations, the Iranian government lodged a desperate appeal for help with Washington. In 1942 Washington sent General M. Norman Schwarzkopf to Iran to report on the situation. (In 1991, his son was sent to wage war against Iraq as the commander of 'Desert Storm.') He remained in Iran until 1948, mainly to acquire first-hand knowledge of how Iran ran its various government departments and intelligence services. Far from helping the Iranians, Schwarzkopf's mission was to acquire as much information about Iran's infrastructure for future use, which came when the move to topple the Shah was launched. During all the years of depravation suffered by the Iranian people, no helping hand was stretched out to them, but in December of 1944, an astute, well- educated and experienced politician by the name of Dr. Mohammed Mossadegh introduced a bill in the Parliament that prohibited all oil negotiations with foreign countries -- that spelled the end to the shocking theft of Iran's oil by the U.S., Britain and Russia.

Born on May 19, 1882, to a Bakhtiari finance minister and a Gujar princess, Mossadegh studied sciences in Paris and received a PhD degree from the prestigious Neuchtal University in Switzerland. Dr. Mossadegh entered politics in 1920 when he was appointed Governor General of the province of Fars by Sheik Ahmad Shah Qajar and received the title 'Mossadegh os-Saltanch' from the Shah. He was appointed finance minister in 1921 and then elected to the Iranian parliament where he voted against the selection of Reza Khan as Reza Sha Pahlavi. In 1944 Mossadegh was again appointed to parliament where he ran as a member of the National Front of Iran, a very patriotic and nationalistic movement of which he was the founder. The aim of the organization was to end all foreign presences in Iran in the wake of the Second World War, and to bring an end to the exploitation of Iranian oil. In garnering support for his bill which sought higher prices for Iranian oil, Mossadegh disclosed a proposal by the occupying powers to divide Iran among them, citing an article in the Times of November 2, 1944, which tended to confirm his bombshell announcement.

With the gloves off, a bitter struggle followed that took the case to the U.N. in 1948 and a fight broke out which led to the withdrawal of all foreign troops from the country. Iran had committed a grave sin in overriding British interests in favor of Iranian national interests. Henceforth Mossadegh would be a public enemy and the Tavistock Institute began a plan to undermine him and have him removed from office. The U.S., British and Russian occupation of Iran was at an end, but that still left the Anglo-Iranian Oil Company (essentially British) in control of Iran's oil which had run the government of Iran since 1919. In 1947 Dr. Mossadegh delivered a proposal to London calling for an increase in Iran's share of revenue of oil sales. The Anglo-Iranian Oil Company made a profit of $320,000,000 in 1948, of which the Iranian received a paltry $38,000,000. Dr. Mossadegh demanded that the terms of the old agreement be re-negotiated. Immediately there followed a most vicious attack on him orchestrated by the Tavistock Institute and the BBC which broadcast a constant stream of propaganda mixed with outright lies against Mossadegh and the Iranian government.. The campaign was aided and abetted by the CIA and U.S. General Huyser. Just two months short of the two years Mossadegh was in office, the British and U.S intelligence agents had done everything to remove the barb in their side by placing a series of obstacles in the way of every move Dr. Mossadegh tried to make.

The British and American cartels were not used to meeting with opposition having easily installed puppet governments in Kuwait, Saudi Arabia, Qatar, the United Arab Emirates, Bahrain and Oman under the watchful eye of the CIA and to a lesser extent, MI6. I am reminded of the striking similarity between the East India Company (forerunner of the Committee of 300) and the Seven Sisters oil cartel. Granted a charter in 1600 during the reign of Elizabeth I, the East India Company received a second charter from Charles II, the Stuart king, giving it the right to wage wars, make peace and conduct commerce with all nations. In 1662 King James I, the Stuart king, granted the company permission to change into a limited stock company. The petroleum industry, although not as formalized, is structured along similar lines. The British dragged their feet all through 1948 without the slightest concession from London. In the meantime British and American intelligence agencies, with General Schwarzkopf's information to help them, spread dissension and discontent among rank and file Iranians in an effort to weaken the government in preparation for the 1949 national election. The small National Front headed by Dr. Mossadegh had entered the elections with what the British and Americans thought would be little chance of winning any seats, but he surprised them by taking six seats and a forum in the Parliament. Worse yet, their enemy was appointed to head a Parliamentary Commission to investigate British-U.S. oil dealings. Mossadegh immediately demanded an equal share for Anglo-Iranian Oil Company and the Iranian Government with full participation of Iran in the affairs of the company.

Backed by the United States, the British refused all proposals causing Iran to fall into disarray, that is, until April 1951, when Dr. Mossadegh was democratically elected to the position of Prime Minister and was asked to form a Government. Now, the mudslinging accusations flew thick and fast, the main being that Mossadegh was a Communist bent upon securing Iranian oil for Russia. British newspapers characterized him as a 'sly lunatic' among other things. Of course there was not the slightest truth in such wild accusations. Dr. Mossadegh was a true patriot of Iran who sought nothing for himself and whose only aim was to free the Iranian people from the rapacious grip of the Anglo-Iranian Oil Company, which later became British Petroleum (BP). The Iranian Parliament voted to accept Dr. Mossadegh's recommendation to nationalize the Anglo-Iranian Oil Company, with fair compensation to be awarded Britain, which had been exploiting the Iranian people for years. The offer included the same level of oil supplies for Britain hitherto enjoyed and British nationals working in the oil industry in Iran would keep their jobs. On April 28, 1951, the recommendation, absolutely fair to Britain was formally approved.

The British response was to appeal to the U.S. for help and send warships to the waters close to Abadan, the site of the largest oil refinery in the world. In September 1951, Britain and the United States, which had zero right to interfere in Iran's internal affairs, declared total economic sanctions against Iran, and their warships blockaded the waters adjacent to Abadan. With these acts of war, the United States assured Britain of its full support for one imperial power to another and backed it with CIA instigated disruptions.

This was not unexpected given the imperial wars waged by Britain in the past and latterly by the United States, and given that the British Government (the House of Windsor) held 53% of the Anglo-Iranian stock. With Naval units on the way, the next threat was to occupy Abadan with British paratroopers, notwithstanding that under international law, Iran was fully within its legal rights to take the action proposed by the Iranian Government and accepted by the Iranian Parliament. Perhaps the fear of Soviet military intervention on the side of Iran kept Britain and the U.S. from exercising the military option. Through Kermit Roosevelt, the grandson of Teddy Roosevelt, the CIA had been very active inside the country infiltrating many leading banking and economic institutions. Buyers for Iran's oil were crudely threatened with reprisals and frightened off. Thus was the conduct of the two biggest bully nations the world has ever known. The telling effect of the boycott reduced Iran's economy to a shambles with oil revenues falling from $40 million in 1951 to less than $2 million at the start of 1952. Dr. Mossadegh, like Mohammed Reza Pahlavi, the Shah of Iran, had no idea of the power and clout of the American oil cartels and BP. Mossadegh, who came from a wealthy family, was a gifted and talented politician, but he was portrayed all over the world as a silly little man running around Teheran in pajamas, immersed in emotion. The establishment press in the U.S. and England under a Tavistock controlled program systematically smeared and ridiculed Mossadegh, whose only crime was to seek to break the hold of the majors on Iranian oil, and daring to challenge their imperialist oil policies.

In 1953, Dr. Mossadegh made a fruitless trip to Washington to appeal for help. Instead he was stonewalled by President Eisenhower who suggested that W. Averill Harriman lead a team to Teheran 'to report back to him on the situation.' Among Harriman's team were the brothers, Allen Dulles of the CIA and John Foster Dulles, Secretary of State and long time servant of the '300,' and General Schwartzkopf.

In 1951 a joint operation to overthrow the government of Mossadegh was planned under the code name 'AJAX' and was signed by President Eisenhower. We need to pause here and stress that Iran had never done any harm to the United States and was now being rewarded in a manner befitting the worst criminal element of the Mafia. Meanwhile Britain took its sordid case to the World Court for arbitration. Dr. Mossadegh who was educated in France and Switzerland, appeared for his country and successfully argued his case, with the World Court ruling against Britain. This was not the first time that the British tried to bring down the government of Iran. Winston Churchill was an infamous imperialist just like his ruthless predecessor, Lord Alfred Milner, who exiled the honorable Boer leaders, who had fought the British so valiantly in the Anglo-Boer War (1899-1902). Churchill ordered the arrest and exiling of Reza Shah, first to the island of Mauritius, and then to South Africa, where he died in exile.

The sins of Winston Churchill are legion. The Boers had fought a marvelous campaign against the Rothschild oligarchy, bent upon seizing the gold and diamonds that lay beneath the soil of the Transvaal and Orange Free State Republics in South Africa. When British casualties reached unacceptable levels, Milner resorted to torching Boer farms, killing livestock and sending Boer women and children to concentration camps where 27,000 of them perished from untreated dysentery and malnutrition. President Paul Kruger was exiled to Switzerland, where he died. So it is easy to understand Churchill's lack of compunction in violating Iran. There was much in the way of precedent to back up his actions. Determined to secure Iraq's oil for British needs,

Churchill then made one of his public relations declaratory speeches, all bombast, wind and hot air, for which he would become famous:

> "We (meaning the major oil companies, including BP, which was in partnership with the British Government) have chased a dictator into exile and installed a constitutional government pledged to a whole catalog of serious-minded reforms and reparations."

Such naked hypocrisy and brazen falsehoods by the British dictator in smearing Reza Shah for daring to defend his country against British aggression, is hard to equal, but given the huge halo that surrounds Churchill, whose name will be synonymous with the great frauds of history, he was able to get away with it. As in the U.S., British Petroleum was able to get the legitimate government of England to do their bidding, regardless of whether such actions were legal. Usurpation of foreign policy by the majors continues unabated and every U.S. president since President Wilson has been a servant of this coiled cobra. This was the start of an imperial U.S. bent upon taking over all oil deposits, world-wide. Undaunted in the face of international derision and in the wake of his World Court victory, Dr. Mossadegh pressed forward with his plan to nationalize Iranian oil.

Rockefeller said to have been personally deeply offended by Mossadegh and worked closely with other major oil companies in making the oil boycott stick.

When an oil tanker, the Rosemarie, in accordance with international law and trade norms carrying Iranian oil, tried to run the blockade, Churchill ordered RAF planes to attack it and force it to put in at Aden, a British protectorate. There was absolutely no law under which to justify the British action, and Churchill again demonstrated that he was the leader of an imperial power that had no respect for international law. This blatant act of piracy met with the full support of the Seven Sisters and the U.S. State Department.

A colleague in London, who is assigned to watch oil companies world-wide said that parliament restrained Churchill only with great difficulty from ordering the RAF to bomb Iran. A year passed, a year in which the Iranian people suffered greatly from the loss of oil revenues. In 1955, Prime Minister Mossadegh wrote to President Eisenhower, appealing for help in his country's struggle against the petroleum industry. Eisenhower, ever a puppet of the CFR, deliberately kept the Iranian leader waiting for a reply. This planned tactic had the desired effect of frightening Dr. Mossadegh. Finally, when Eisenhower did reply, it was to tell the Iranian government that it must abide by its 'international obligations' and to place Royal Dutch Shell in charge of oil operations! What 'international obligations' Eisenhower was invoking were never made clear.

This should tell us something about of the power of the petroleum industry and the secret upper-level, parallel, CFR government of the imperial United States. Yet, we still dare to think of our government as an honorable one, and ourselves as a free people. In witness thereto, the United States sent Kermit Roosevelt, who worked for the CIA, to Iran to stir up trouble and instigate unrest among the populace. Following the Charter granted to the East India Company -in 1600, that allowed it to make foreign policy and wage wars against nations, the inheritors of the East India Company, the Committee of 300 - covered the CIA by using organizations such as the International Monetary Fund (IMF) and the World Bank to finance Roosevelt's dirty work, so that it could not be directly traceable to the U.S. America's transition from a confederated republic to an imperial empire was now well advanced and there would be no deviation from the crooked path.

At the behest of the banker's faction inside the CIA, the Shah was told that it would be a good thing if he dismissed Mossadegh, so that 'normal relations' with Britain and the U.S. could be resumed. Enlisting the aid of royalist elements in the Iranian

Government, Kermit Roosevelt staged a coup and forced the arrest of Dr. Mossadegh whose influence had been undermined by two years of open economic warfare waged by the imperialist Britain and the United States. The CIA then backed the young Reza Shah Pahlevi and brought him to power and economic sanctions were lifted. Once again the oil politics of the petroleum companies had led the governments of Britain and the United States into an act of warfare against a sovereign state that had done them no harm. They triumphed over Iran nationalism. It was a repeat, a virtual carbon copy of the events of the Anglo-Boer War.

The Shah thereupon tried, and failed, to get rid of Mossadegh, but Roosevelt, the CIA and the State Department then equipped a revolutionary band and sent it to fight the Iranian army. Fearing assassination, the Shah fled the country, and the CIA-led coup was successful. Mossadegh was toppled and placed under house arrest where he remained for the rest of his life.

The Shah was allowed to return to Iran and was told that he was safe, as long as he obeyed his imperial masters. The cost to the American taxpayer of this illegal adventure in 1970 was in excess of $1 billion. The only party who benefited from the underhand treachery was the Seven Sisters oil cartel and their paid puppets that had made it all possible.

Although he did not know it at the time, the Shah was to suffer the same fate as Mossadegh and at the hands of the very same imperialist clique of petroleum companies, British and American government officials and the CIA. Other countries have also, since then, felt the lash of the petroleum cartel government-within-government.

CHAPTER 11

Enrico Mattei takes on the seven sisters cartel

One such country was Italy. Crippled by WWII and the invasion of its territory, Italy lay in virtual ruin. Several state enterprises were formed one being the Alienda Generale Italiana Petrloli 'AGIP,' headed by Enrico Mattei who was given orders to dismantle it. But as the first man to recognize that there was a petroleum dictatorship led by the Seven Sisters (Sette Sorelle), Mattei was in open contention with the cartel. Instead of closing AGIP he reformed and strengthened it, changing its name to the National Fuel Trust Ente Nazionale Idrocarburi, E N I. Mattei rushed through a program of oil exploration and contracts with the USSR that would free Italy from the chokehold of the Seven Sisters and much to the annoyance of the latter, Mattei began to succeed.

Enrico Mattei, born on April 29, 1906, was the son of a carabiniere, the Italian military corps, with police functions. At 24 he went to Milan where he joined the Partisans. In 1945 the political committee of the partisans named him as the head of AGIP, the national oil company, with orders to close it. But Mattei chose to ignore the order and instead, built it up to where it became one of the most outstanding economic successes of post war Italy.

In 1953 Mattei set up a second energy company called ENI, which entered into successful agreements with Egypt and by 1961 was importing 2.5 million tons of crude oil from Egypt. In

1957 Mattei boldly attacked the monopoly on crude out of Iran by making direct approach to the Shah. It was successful and under the terms agreed to by Mattei and the Shah, a partnership between and the National Iranian Oil Company was concluded with 75% going to Iran and 25% for ENI and gave ENI's sister company, Societe Irano-Italienne des Petroles (SIRIP) a 25-year exclusive lease to explore and drill 8,800 square miles of known petroleum vilayets.

Mattei astonished the Seven Sisters when he concluded oil agreements with Tunisia and Morocco in a 50-50 partnership deal. After concluding a deal with China and Iran, Mattei declared that the American oil monopoly was a thing of the past. British and American reaction was swift. A delegation met with the Shah and lodged a strong protest against the Mattei contract. But the delegation's views, although noted, had no effect. In August of 1957, Mattei signed a contract that brought Italian 'outsiders' into Iran. The Italian industrialist made his views known. Henceforth he would strive to make the Middle East part of industrial Europe by building a significant infrastructure in the whole of the Middle East.

Mattei was what would today be called a 'mover and shaker' and in four short years of signing the contract, the first ENI tanker arrived at the port of Bari with 18,000 tons of Iranian crude oil. Bolstered by his success, Mattei proceeded to African and Asian nations with oil reserves to strike similar deals.

One of the things that most upset the oil cartel of Britain and the U.S. was ENI's offer to build refineries in the countries with oil deposits, which would be locally-owned and make them full partners. The return for ENI was in the form of exclusive engineering and technical support contracts and the sole right of ENI to sell both the crude and finished products world wide.

Watching from London and New York, the Seven Sisters were stunned and angry at the success of the ENI interloper.

Matters reached a climax in October 1960, when Mattei journeyed to Moscow to meet with the Russian Government for discussions of mutual oil interests. If the Seven Sisters were stunned before, what came out of the discussions between Russian Foreign Trade Minister Patolitschev and Mattei left them reeling and set trans-Atlantic alarm bells ringing wildly. The worst fears of the oil cartel were realized when on October 11, 1956 an agreement between ENI and Moscow was signed that provided for the following:

> ➤ In exchange for a guaranteed delivery of 2.4 million tons of Russian oil per annum covering the next five years, ENI took a significantly increased share of Russian oil in the European market.

> ➤ Payment of the oil would not be in cash but in kind, in guaranteed deliveries of large diameter oil pipes which would be used to construct a massive oil pipeline network to bring Russian oil from the Volga-Urals to Eastern Europe.

> ➤ On completion, the contract called for 15 tons of crude oil annually where it would be exchanged for a variety of food products, manufacturer goods and services.

> ➤ The large diameter pipes would be built by the Finsider Group under the supervision of the Italian Government at Taranto and shipped to Russia at the rate of 2 millions tons each year. (The factory was built in record time and was producing pipes by September 1962, a truly astonishing achievement.)

The contract with Russia was a major triumph for Mattei because now Italy could buy Russian crude oil at $1.00 per barrel on board ships in Black Sea ports compared with $1.59 per barrel plus shipping of $0.69 from Kuwait, and Standard Oil price of $2.75 per barrel. As has happened many times before, when threats to the monopoly of the Seven Sisters could not be removed by fair means, foul means were resorted to.

Early in 1962 Mattel's plane was sabotaged. However before any damage could be done the interference with the plane was discovered, and the finger of suspicion pointed at the CIA. But Mattei was not so lucky the second time when on October 27, 1962, on a flight from Sicily to Milan, his jet crashed into the small village of Bascape in Lombardy. The pilot, Inerio Bertuzzi, an American journalist by the name of William McHale and Mattei, were killed. Rumors of foul play flew thick and fast, but as the crash investigation was under the responsibility of Defense Minister Giulio Andreotti who was known for his sympathies toward the major oil companies and particularly toward the United States, an official investigation seemed slow in coming.

In 2001 Bernard Pletschinger and Calus Bredenbrock aired a TV documentary in which they claimed that evidence at the site of the Mattei plane crash was immediately destroyed. Flight instruments were melted down in a bath of acid. Following the broadcast the bodies of Mattei and Bertuzzi were exhumed. Pieces of metal caused by an on-board explosion were found lodged in the bones of the two men. The common, if not official verdict, was that a bomb had been planted on board Mattel's jet which was set to go off when the landing gear was activated in the 'down' position.

Although it has never been proved, the strongest of circumstantial and other evidence points the finger directly at the CIA and particularly to the CIA station chief in Rome at the time, one Thomas Karamessines who abruptly left his office on October 17, 1962, the very day of the Mattei plane crash in Lombardy, and never returned. No explanation was offered for his unannounced and abrupt departure. The CIA report has never been made public and remains classified 'in national security interests' to this day. All Freedom of Information requests have been rebuffed.

There is a postscript to this 'Unsolved Mystery.' At the time the plane crashed and ended his life, Mattei was scheduled to meet with U.S. President John F. Kennedy. High on their agenda was the oil cartel which Kennedy was known to mistrust and secretly hate, especially because of its close relations with the CIA that had long disturbed him. It was well known in his inner circle that Kennedy regarded the CIA as a cancer upon the American nation; Kennedy believed that if ever the government of the U.S. was overthrown in a coup, it would be master-minded by the CIA.

A scant year later, Kennedy was to fall victim to the same conspirators in U.S. intelligence. Coupled with the story of Enrico Mattei, the brutal rape of Mexico on behalf of American and British oil interests and the countless wrongs done to Iran and Iraq, together they make up the most tragic stories of avarice, greed and lust for power that stain the pages of the history of the petroleum companies. The power wielded by the petroleum companies transcends all governments and national boundaries; it has toppled governments and undercut their national leaders, and even assassinated them. It has cost the American taxpayers billions of dollars and the end is not yet in sight.

Oil, it seems, is the foundation of the new world economic order, with power in the hands of a few people barely known outside of the oil companies. John D. Rockefeller had been quick to see the potential for profit and power, and seized the moment. It enabled him to wield immense personal power, even though such power was obtained at the cost of ruining thousands of smaller oil companies and thousands of lives.

We have referred to the Seven Sisters a number of times. For those who might not be familiar with this group, it consists of the 7 major oil companies in Britain and the U.S. who are responsible for shaping foreign policy of both countries. The oil companies that go to make up the cartel really began after the so-called "break up" of Standard Oil by the U.S. Supreme Court. It was Enrico Mattei who first coined the name 'Seven Sisters.' Their powerful influence is still felt in 2008.

Standard Oil of New York merged with Vacuum Oil and became Socony Vacuum, which became Mobiloil in 1966 while Standard Oil Indianan joined with Standard Oil Nebraska and Standard Oil of Kansas, and in 1985, became known as AMOCO. In 1972 Standard Oil New Jersey became EXXON.

In 1984 Standard Oil California joined Standard Oil Kentucky and became Chevron, which then bought the Mellon-owned Gulf Oil Company. Standard Oil Ohio was bought out by BP. In 1990 BP bought the old Standard Indiana and turned into BP-AMOCO, and in 1999, EXXON and Mobil were merged in a $75 billion deal that gave birth to EXXON-Mobil. In 2000 Chevron merged with Texaco to become Chevron-Texaco.

EXXON (known as ESSO in Europe), Shell, BP, Gulf Oil, Texaco, Mobil and Chevron form part of the global chain made up of interlocking banks, brokerage houses, intelligence agencies, mining, refining, aerospace, banking and petrochemicals who, together, form the backbone of The Committee of 300 companies, whose members are also known as the 'Olympians.' They control production of crude oil, refineries and shipping, except in Russia and now, Venezuela. It is estimated that as much as 75% of the profits made by the oil cartel comes from 'downstream' companies such as refining, storage, shipping, plastics, petrochemicals and so on.

The second largest refinery in the world owned and controlled by the cartel is located at Pulau Bukom and at Jurong in Singapore. Shell owns the largest refinery complex in the world based on the island of Aruba. The building of this massive facility placed a spotlight on the importance of Venezuelan crude oil. There is also a very large Mobil refinery on Aruba.

In 1991 an estimated 60% of EXXON's profits came from so-called "downstream" operations. In 1990 EXXON acquired the plastics division of Allied Signal, and at the same time, struck a deal with Monsanto and Dow Chemicals in the thermoplastic, elastomer field. The top retailers in gasoline are EXXON and Chevron-Texaco. Royal Dutch Shell has the most tankers with 114 in its fleet. The company employs 133,000 persons world-wide. Shell's assets are valued at an estimated $200 billion.

Another 'downstream' profit-maker is EXXON Mobil, which produces more motor oil, transmission oil and lubricant greases than any of the other 'majors.' It is found in over 200 countries of the world and goes 'solo' in the frigid Beaufort Sea off Alaska. It owns huge tracts of land in Yemen, Oman and Chad said to total in excess of 20 million acres. The investment has to do as always, with the future of oil supplies. EXXON guards its refining secrets like state secrets and indeed, Bahrain, where most of the refining is done is guarded by warships of the U.S. Navy's 5th Fleet. Not even Saudi Arabia is given access to such secrets. Out of the more than 500 refineries in existence, only 16 are in the Persian Gulf States.

CHAPTER 12

ROYAL DUTCH SHELL

B y far the most important of the Committee of 300 flagship petroleum companies is Royal Dutch Shell (Het Koninklijke Nederlandse Shell) of Anglo-Dutch origin. It is one of the largest energy corporations in the world and a flagship company of the Committee of 300. The majority stockholders are the House of Windsor and the House of Orange of the Netherlands. There are said to be only fourteen thousand stockholders, with Queen Elizabeth (representing the House of Windsor), Queen Juliana (representing the House of Orange) and Lord Victor Rothschild being the biggest single stockholder. There are no directors that we know of, but the CEO is Jeroen van der Veer, and Jorma Ollila is Chairman, both Dutch businessmen.

The principal activity of the company is oil and gas exploration, transportation and marketing of hydrocarbons with a significant presence in the petrochemicals arena. Annual revenues in 2005 amounted to U.S. $306 billion, making it the third largest corporation in the world. The company has come a long way since 1901 when William Knox D'Arcy was granted a concession to search for oil in Iran.

Like the Federal Reserve Bank, nobody really knows who the most important shareholders in Shell are. In 1972 the U.S. Senate made a one and only attempt to force the company to divulge a list of its top 30 shareholders. The investigation was in the hands of Senator Lee Metcalf, but his request was flatly rejected. The

message: Do not try to intrude into the affairs of the Committee
of 300. The elitist New World Order-One World Government
who rode to power on the discovery of oil and its usages brooks
no interference from anybody, be it governments, rulers, sheiks
or private citizens, heads of state of nations great and small. The
world has long ago come to the realization that the Seven Sisters
cartel has control of oil firmly grasped in its greedy hands, and
that it continues to control the supply and demand of crude oil,
worldwide.

The supranational oil giants, with expertise and methods of
accounting, flummoxed the best brains in world government, tax
collectors and accountants, placed the Seven Sisters beyond the
reach of ordinary government control. The history of the Seven
Sisters shows that governments were always eager to parcel out
their sovereignty and natural resources, the moment these bandits
came riding into the national camp. John D. would have heartily
approved the closed shop, the international club and its secret
deals and international intrigue, which to this day, the American
public knows nothing about.

In their secret hideaways, in New York, London and Zurich,
these all- powerful leaders meet to plot and plan wars around the
globe. They are much more powerful in 2008 than at any time
since they began operations in the 19th century. The same '300'
members, most of whom are also members of the Illuminati, the
old and the famous, unbelievably rich families, revel in their
power. It is they who decide which governments have to go and
which political leaders must fall.

When real trouble knocked on their secret doors - such as Dr.
Mossadegh nationalizing Iranian oil ~ they were always ready to
hit back and 'neutralize' troublemakers, if they could not be
bought off. When the Mossadegh crisis arose, it became a matter
of calling on the right parties in the troubled countries, to show
their power and frighten off those who could not be bought. It
was only a matter of calling for the right army, navy, air force

and government officials to get rid of the nuisance. It was no more trouble than swatting a fly. The Seven Sisters became a government within governments, very much after the lines of the East India Company, and nobody tried to dislodge them for a considerable time.

If one wanted to know Britain's Arab policy, it was only necessary to consult BP and Shell. If one wanted to find out about U.S. Middle East policy, likewise, it was only necessary to consult EXXON, ARAMCO, Mobil, etc. ARAMCO became synonymous with U.S. policy toward Saudi Arabia. Indeed, who would have imagined that Standard Oil of New Jersey would one day call the shots at the State Department? Can we imagine any other company or group receiving huge, special tax concessions running into billions of dollars? Has there ever been a group so favored as the members of the petroleum industry cartel?

I have often been asked why it is that the U.S. domestic oil industry, once full of promise and a guarantor to keep cheap gas flowing at the pumps, went into such a steep decline and why gas prices rose out of all proportion to the overall supply and demand. The answer is the greed of the petroleum cartel, the Seven Sisters. There is no organization or corporation to equal the greed of the Seven Sisters.

One of the group, EXXON, even while making record profits of $8.4 billion in the first quarter of 2008 demanded and got even bigger tax concessions and tax breaks. Not one cent of this was ever passed on to the consumer in the form of a reduction in price of gasoline at the pumps.

Did the American people benefit from Mobil, EXXON and Gulf Oil obscene profits? There is no evidence of it. Thanks to the wheeling and dealing that goes on in Washington, where, because of the 17 Amendment, it is now possible to buy and sell senators and representatives, the oil companies never, ever plowed back any part of their obscene profits to lower the domestic price of gas, nor to explore and drill for oil in the continental United States. It is not a pretty story, and Congress is to blame.

The 17th Amendment changed Section 3 and 4 of Article 1, which had to do with the people of the States no longer being able to choose their Senators. It now meant that senators were voted into office and with the possibility of abuse of campaign donations, it opened up a veritable Pandora's Box.

We, the People are also to blame for allowing this state of affairs to continue. The American consumer continually faces rising gas prices at the pumps while the coffers of the Seven Sisters grow fatter and fatter, and while price gouging and every manner of deceit is engaged in by the petroleum industry, to rob the American people blind and the American people lie down and let the petroleum industry roll over them. Which ever way we care to look at it - and there are those apologists who try to confuse the issues by comparing gas prices in the U.S. with gas prices in Europe (not a valid comparison) - we can only arrive at the conclusion that the petroleum industry has never strayed very far from the tenets and precepts of old John D. Rockefeller. It was then, and is now, a law unto itself. Greed and more profit motivated and ruled the life of old John D. and not much has changed since his hey-days. Profits made 'upstream' in places like Aruba and Bahrain are kept out of sight of the American consumer.

John D. counseled his sons never to make friends or 'fellowship' with others, in this manner he was able to flout the aspiring independents and prevent them getting a toehold in the oil markets. However, he did not mind breaking his 'no friends' rule where he saw it to his advantage.

For instance, he curried favor with Henry Flagler, the railroad magnate who opened up Florida. Being a born businessman, John D. very early on in the game realized that his point of entry into the oil business was through refining and distribution of the finished product. His friendship with Flagler was to this end, secure control of refining and distribution, and he would come out on top. Secretive to the point of paranoia John D. entered into a confidential arrangement with Flagler, whereby special reduced transportation rebates would be granted to his enterprises. In this manner Rockefeller was able to undercut 'the competition' and put several of his business rivals out of business.

'Free enterprise' was not something that John D. cared about and he cared still less about the people he ruined through his unfair practices. Utter ruthlessness when dealing with rivals was the credo by which Rockefeller lived. Secrecy was another of his principles and he lived by these two 'guides' all of his life. It took only 7 years of ruthless practices to eliminate most of the competition and allow John D. to establish the Standard Oil Company of California.

By 1870, Standard already controlled 10 percent of the American oil business, an amazing feat. In choosing to go along with Rockefeller's sneaky way of doing business, the railroads in effect sold out the public and put themselves in John D's pocket. The Central Association controlled railroad tariffs, and other oil companies who joined it had to pay through the nose to get in, but they did enjoy rebates on rail tariffs. Those who would not play the game went to the wall.

Author/teacher/journalist Ida Tarbell's book, 'The History of the Standard Oil Company,' gives a clear and concise account of just how highly questionable were the tactics that John D. employed, and it was his base conduct, that earned him the hatred and enmity of most of the independents, a hatred Standard Oil was able to brush aside and ignore because back in 1970, John D. had established markets for his oil products in Europe, which amounted to a staggering 70 percent of Standard's business. Having a virtual monopoly meant that public opinion counted for little.

In order to freeze out his rivals, Rockefeller established a private army of spies, which in sheer numbers — not to mention capabilities — far exceeded anything, the governments in whose countries Standard operated, could muster. It is said in intelligence circles, 'not even a sparrow sneezes without John D. knowing about it.' Although supposedly a strict Baptist, this was a parody of the Bible, where it is written that not a single sparrow falls to the ground without God seeing it, and was meant to mock the Bible, something John D. enjoyed doing.

But Rockefeller's march across the North American continent into the foreign markets did not go unnoticed, in spite of John D's secret ways. Public hatred of Standard Oil had reached new heights ~ thanks to revelations by Tarbell and H.D. Lloyd, that here was a company, seemingly above local, state and federal government and the laws of the United States, a corporation which 'has declared peace, negotiated war, reduced courts, legislatures and sovereign states to an unequaled level that no government agency could curb. Thousands of angry letters poured into the Senate, which resulted in the enactment of the Sherman Anti-Trust Act was passed. But so vague were its terms (probably deliberately so) that compliance was easy to avoid, especially with a slippery customer like John D. It was quickly apparent that John D. wielded enormous influence in the U.S. Senate. The Sherman Anti-Trust Act turned out to be little more than a public relations exercise, full of rules, but with no teeth. Finally, things changed in 1907 when the Act was invoked in a U.S. Justice Department suit filed by prosecutor Frank Kellogg.

During the trial Rockefeller took the stand and testified as to his public-spiritedness, portraying himself as a benign benefactor of humanity and especially of the citizens of America. When pressed by Kellogg to explain his many irregular deals, John D. took the tack that he 'couldn't remember.'

On May 11, 1911, Chief Justice Whyte handed down his decision: Standard was to shed itself of all its subsidiaries within 6 months. Rockefeller, as was his custom, then hired a veritable army of lawyers and writers to explain that the petroleum business could not be run like other businesses. In short, it was to be treated as a special entity in the grand manner of the Rockefellers.

To dilute the effect of Judge Whyte's ruling, Rockefeller set up a patronage system modeled on the royal courts of England and Europe, interfaced with philanthropic foundations that were intended to shield Rockefeller's empire and his fortune from the coming Income Tax Act, which his army of spies and bought-and-paid-for senators assured him was coming, and which, in fact, did get enacted in 1913 in a manner so devious as to defy logic and reason.

CHAPTER 13

John D. Rockefeller the Nobel brothers Russia

I n this manner was the secret, permanent upper-level government established in the United States which secured and paved the way for The Council on Foreign Relations (CFR) to come into being as the United States representatives of the Committee of 300. That the CFR owes its existence to John D. and Harold Pratt is beyond question. This is a formidable evil, and forms part of the case against the petroleum industry who with billions of dollars, and with the help of the CFR, was able to take control of this nation which it has ruled ever since.

Others who followed the Rockefeller plan were Occidental Petroleum, Armand Hammer's company, which was mainly responsible for passage of the Intermediate Range Nuclear Forces Treaty, negotiated by Kissinger, David Rockefeller's 'Siamese twin,' whose permanent attachment to his mentor came after the discovery of the Bamberg Files mentioned earlier herein. The INF Treaty was one the most outrageous betrayals of U.S. interests. No doubt there are other treasonable treaties, but in my opinion, the INF treaty topped them all.

The mendacity of John D. continues to be felt in U.S. policy toward a number of nations, and the pernicious influence of his oil corporations, remain with us until this day. In 1914, there was reference to 'Rockefeller's secret government' in the Congressional Records. It was the same year that the 'Great Man' (Winston Churchill) suffered the mortification of seeing his offer to do a 'whitewash job' on John D. rejected, because the asking price of $50,000 was considered 'too high.' Churchill thereupon spitefully announced, 'Two gigantic corporations virtually control the world's oil industry.' He was, of course, referring to Shell and Standard oil. The former company was founded by Marcus Samuel, who used to make decorative boxes for royalty out of seashells, from whence came the name, 'Shell Oil Company.' Samuel had begun his career by shipping coal to Japan, but then, seeing the light, switched to oil. It was a change that was to prove enormously beneficial.

In 1873, the Tsar of Russia, being badly advised by a group of traitors who had infiltrated his inner circle, gave a concession to the Nobel Dynamite Company to explore for oil in the Caucasus. Nobel's sons, Albert, Ludwig and Robert, swarmed all over the landscape, financed by the French Rothschild banks, a move which eventually gave Rothschild a strangle-hold over the finances of Russia and led to the Bolshevik Revolution.

Nobel, Rockefeller, Rothschild and their companies and banks, raped Russia, bled it dry of its resources and then turned it over to the Bolshevik hordes to complete the destruction of what had always been a beautiful, noble, Christian country.

The participation of the petroleum industry in the rape of Christian Russia by the Bolsheviks and its downfall into the Dark Ages of slavery is a significant accusation against this government within government, and not one which can lightly be put aside. It is a charge that the petroleum industry has never been called upon to answer.

Following their success in Russia with Standard having virtually seized the Rumanian fields, John D. turned his attention to the Middle East. First to be undermined was the old Turkish Petroleum Company. The British offered John D. a stake in its partnership with Turkey of 20 percent, which Exxon took up. Next, the greedy multinationals began to eye Iraq, and Mobil,

Exxon and Texaco soon set up shop in that country. The agreement called for an equal partnership deal, but the Iraqis were cheated from the very beginning of the operations. In terms of the San Remo Agreement, Iraq was supposed to have a 20 percent share of the consortium, but in actual fact, got nothing. Thus began the deep dislike and fear of the British and American petroleum companies that spread throughout the world. Exxon routed money through a Swiss front company, to disguise its participation. As for the Soviets who were very busy in Iraq and Iran, they welcomed the arrival of the American companies. Years later, Henri Deterding, the CEO of Shell, accused EXXON of close collaboration with the Bolsheviks, a fact which was amply supported by MI6 intelligence papers in the possession of Lord Alfred Milner. Deterding said that EXXON had supported the Bolsheviks all along, many of its programs being designed specifically to favor the Communist government. EXXON, in true John D. style, battened down the hatches and survived the storm of criticism that the charges evoked in the U.S. As for Deterding, because of his revelations, which hurt the petroleum industry, he was blacklisted and fell from favor.

In documents on the White Russian campaign to defeat the Red Army, in the archives of Whitehall, it is revealed that White Russian Generals, Wrangle and Deniken, were promised by Standard Oil that if they could push the Red Army out of the rich Baku oil fields, they would be substantially supported by the United States government.

The task was accomplished by the military forces of the White Russians. In fact they rolled up the Red Army, pushing it back to the very gates of Moscow. But instead of being supplied with money and weapons as was promised, Lloyd George, a personal representative of the U.S. State Department and William Bullit, Prime Minister of Britain, acting on the instructions of the Committee of 300 through its Council on Foreign Relations (CFR), pulled the rug out from under the White Russian Armies, and left them without money and arms, and with no option but to disband.

The boycott on ammunition going to the White Russian forces was a CFR conspiracy, carried out by Lloyd George, and it ensured the collapse of the only military force capable of destroying the Red Army and bringing Bolshevik rule to an end in Russia, but this was not what imperial Britain and an imperial U.S. partner had in mind.

Why did Bullit and Lloyd George stab the White Russian Armies in the back? Why, when the Red Army was staring defeat in the face, when the Bolshevik Revolution was in imminent danger of collapse, did the U.S. and British governments act so treacherously? In the documents I have already referred to, which are to be found in the War Office in Whitehall, London, it is revealed that the CFR wanted to do a deal to keep Lenin in power, in exchange for a sole concession for oil from the vast Russian fields. They thought Lenin was more likely to deliver a deal than the White Russian generals. This skullduggery, this betrayal, was what helped the Bolsheviks to come back from the very edge of defeat to become a powerful force able to subdue Russia at a cost of the lives of untold millions of its citizens.

When Britain officially recognized the Bolshevik government in 1924, it was on condition that an official sign an agreement with British Petroleum (BP), securing huge tracts of oil lands for exploration by British interests. The groundwork for this had been laid by Sydney Reilly, British MI6 operative, during the Bolshevik Revolution. Reilly had seven passports with different official MI6 names and represented Lord Alfred Milner, who was largely responsible for financing the Bolshevik Revolution, more directly than he did the British Government.

Likewise, Standard Oil for the United States signed similar agreements with imperialist Lenin. To make it look as if the United States and Britain were really fighting against the rise of the Bolsheviks, an allied expeditionary force was dispatched to Archangel in the far north of Russia. All its troops did was lounge around their barracks, except once, when they made a ceremonial march through the streets of Archangel, after which the so-called expeditionary force boarded ship and sailed for home.

The only man with any principle in the consortium was Deterding, who steadfastly refused to work with the Bolsheviks. Of the betrayal of the White Russians and the Bolshevik oil deal, Deterding said:

> "I feel that someday, everybody will regret that we have had anything to do with these robbers."

It is no wonder that Deterding was relegated to obscurity! How prophetic his words turned out to be will be judged by history, and we don't mean the history written by the so-called historians who were Rockefeller's paid writers. In order to forestall competition in the future, which Rockefeller said he was sure would happen; on August 18, 1928, a secret meeting was held at Achnacarry Castle in Scotland, on the preserves of the Earl of Achnaccary. The meeting was arranged by the Anglo-Iranian Oil Company (later called British Petroleum-BP) and was attended by executives from Standard, Shell, Anglo-Iranian Oil Company and Mobil. Deterding was in attendance as Royal Dutch Shell's representative, but his life was made a hell by Rockefeller, who made no secret of his hatred of the man who had publicly opposed his oil agreement arrangements made with the Bolsheviks.

The Anglo-Iranian Oil Company drafted the agenda that was signed by all parties on September 17, 1928. The single aim of the Achnacarry imperialists was to divide world oil business into 'spheres of interest,' which the majors would control, in real terms meaning everything, was to be left 'as is.'

The Yalta agreement that followed in 1945 was patterned on the Achnacarry agreement, and the 'Big Three' were able to enforce this arrangement, right up until 1952. The Achnacarry agreement violated the Sherman anti-trust, anti-monopoly laws of the

United States, and more than that it showed that the giants of the petroleum industry were strong enough to fix prices and allocate supplies, regardless what the legitimate governments of the world might say to the contrary.

Did the American consumer benefit from the Achnacarry Agreement that lasted for 28 years? The answer is, no. In fact, the American consumers were the victims of higher prices at a time when prices could have been considerably lowered. In truth, the Achnacarry agreement was a giant conspiracy against the anti-trust laws of the U.S. with intention to defraud consumers worldwide, but the U.S. consumer bore the brunt of the price fixing.

If ever there was a most blatant criminal case waiting to be prosecuted, this was the one. But, apparently there were only a small number of brave men in the U.S. Justice Department willing to take on the giants of the industry who have gone on 'shafting' the American consumer throughout their long history. To its credit, 'the few' at the Justice Department did try to prosecute the cartel, but their efforts were blocked by Eisenhower and Truman.

The fact that the 'Big Three' were obtaining cheap oil from all over the world, just added insult to injury. The 'big hand' of old John D. was everywhere, and with the passage of time, honest men in the petroleum industry became harder and harder to find.

But worse was to come. Not satisfied with their bloated profits, the Big Three now sought and obtained U.S. tax concessions with the help of the top hands at the State Department. The oil companies argued that their special status was justified because

> "we are carrying on the policy of the United States toward these countries."

Their claim goes even further:

'We help to keep trouble-spots cool, whereas, direct U.S. intervention in these hot spots, would only make matters come to the boil,'

as one executive told a Senate Foreign Affairs Committee in 1985. We shall see just how little water this argument holds as we proceed.

The main thrust of EXXON after Baku was into Saudi Arabia. Everette Lee De Goyler had said in 1943:

'This oil in this region (Saudi Arabia) is the greatest single prize in all history.'

Under the guise of helping the ruling Abdul Azziz clan to counter the Israeli threat, EXXON was able to entrench its position by ensuring that Saudi Arabia's interests were not downplayed by the formidable, menacing Israeli lobby in Washington.

The State Department played its role by telling King Ibn Saud that the U.S. would keep an evenhanded policy toward the Middle East, if the Saudis would work through EXXON. Of course the king agreed to this nefarious deal. As a 'consideration,' EXXON paid a mere $500,000 to secure the sole rights to Saudi oil! However, neither EXXON nor the State Department was able to adhere to their promise to keep Washington's Middle East Policy evenhanded, because of the uproar from the Israeli lobby. This did not sit well with the Saudis who had bitterly opposed the establishment of Israel as a state in 1946. Senator Fulbright had always practiced an evenhanded approach, and was generally able to stick to his guns, even when the going got rough in Washington. However, when Fulbright was nominated for the job of Secretary of State, the Zionist Lobby joined with Exxon to quash the nomination, which went instead, to Dean Rusk, a hater of the Arab nations and an imperialist of the worst stripe. As a result, U.S. foreign policy toward Middle East Arab/Muslim, countries, always woefully lopsided and totally biased in favor of Israel, became a great deal more pro-Israel.

The Saudi royal family then demanded annual tribute from Exxon to keep the concession going, which tribute reached $50 million in the first year it was implemented. With production of cheap Saudi oil reaching dizzying heights, the so-called "tax concessions golden gimmick" grew in proportion, and it remains to this day, one of the greatest frauds of monumental dimensions. Under an agreement with the State Department, EXXON (ARAMCO) is allowed to deduct the bribe payments from its taxes in the United States, on the grounds that the bribe is a legitimate payment of 'Saudi income tax'!

What it really amounted to was a huge foreign aid payment to Saudi Arabia -- although not registered as such -- so that EXXON could go on producing and exporting cheap Saudi oil. Six years after this tax dodge was resorted to, Israel began demanding its share of the loot, and wound up getting around $13 million dollars, courtesy of the U.S. taxpayers. Israel's total foreign aid income from the U.S. is currently running at about $50 billion per annum. Do the American taxpayers, who foot the bill, get any benefits from the arrangement, any benefit such as lower gas prices at the pumps? After all, with Saudi oil so cheap, shouldn't the benefit have been passed on to the customer? The answer is - 'not as far as ARAMCO was concerned.'

American consumers got no benefit from paying the bills, worse yet, domestic oil prices suffered an enormous increase, from which it never recovered, due to the fact that cheap crude oil from the Middle East killed all local efforts to make the U.S. energy-independent by producing more gas and oil from U.S. sources, such as the Arctic fields.

CHAPTER 14

Nixon closes gold window

A large number of independent 'wildcatter,' small oil prospecting companies, were forced out of business, by higher taxes pitched against them, and a maze of new and more stringent measures aimed at curbing their activities. The opportunity to hike domestic gas prices at the pumps came with the 1970 mini-recession during the end of President Nixon's term. The U.S. economy was suffering a recession and interest rates were sharply reduced, which triggered an alarming outflow of foreign capital. President Nixon, on the advice of Sir Sigmund Warburg, Edmond de Rothschild and other City of London '300' bankers decided to close the gold window at the Federal Reserve Banks.

On August 15, 1971, Nixon announced that henceforth, U.S. dollars would no longer be exchanged for gold. The central provision of the Bretton Woods Conference was ripped into small pieces. The demonetization of the dollar sent gas prices at the pumps up steeply.

According to evidence presented to the Multinational Hearings commission in 1975, the major U.S. oil companies made close to 70 percent of their profits abroad, profits on which they were not required to pay any income tax in the United States. With the bulk of their business being done "upstream" (in foreign countries), the U.S. majors were not about to make a major capital investment in local drilling and exploration, on which they would have to pay taxes.

Why spend money looking for and exploiting oilfields in the U.S. when the product could be had, tax free, and at a cheaper price, in Saudi Arabia? Why allow small, independent, "wildcatters" to explore for oil and possibly strike significant vilayets that would inevitably eat into the Seven Sisters' profits? EXXON did what it knows best. It turned to the tame members of the Congress and demanded (and got) a heavy tax imposed on oil prospecting in the continental United States.

American consumers went right on subsidizing the imperialist majors in foreign countries, all the while paying artificially high gasoline prices at the pumps, which when the cost of all of the hidden taxes is added, makes U.S. gasoline one of the most expensive in the world, a shocking and artificially-contrived situation, which ought to have been stamped upon decades ago. The immorality of this arrangement was that had the majors not been so greedy, they could have produced and sold more gas in the U.S. because of a very much-reduced price. In our opinion, the way the petroleum industry fostered an illegal practice leaves it open to criminal charges of conspiracy to defraud the U.S. consumer.

In 1949 the U.S. Justice Department filed criminal charges against the 'International Petroleum Cartel,' which included the major U.S. oil companies, but before the case went very far, Truman and Eisenhower stepped in and forced the Justice Department to downgrade the prosecution to a civil case.

When floating exchange rates hit the economic world, the Arab oil producing states demanded and got a promise of a fixed price for oil, so that they would not unexpectedly suffer a sharp decline in their oil revenues due to currency fluctuations. The majors complied by rigging gasoline prices. Thus, the oil companies paid taxes on an artificial price, which was not the real market price, but was offset by the lower taxes they paid in the U.S., a benefit which no other industry in the U.S. ever enjoyed. That made it possible for EXXON and Mobil, plus the rest of the majors, to pay on average a tax of no more than 5 percent, in spite of the huge profits they were making. It is clear from the foregoing that not only were the major oil companies gouging the American taxpayer - and they are still gouging consumers for all they are worth - they were carrying out U.S. imperialist foreign policy by acting as bankrollers of the foreign countries, whose oil they were acquiring at bargain-basement prices. The arrangement placed the major oil companies above the law, giving them a position from where they could constantly dictate to the elected governments. How was this stunning victory over the American consumer achieved? For answers we must go to the secret meeting held at the island of Saltsjoebaden owned by the Swedish Wallenberg members of the Committee of 300, where in May 1973, the Bilderberg Group held a secret meeting attended by Sir Eric Roll of Warburg, Giani Agnelli, of the Fiat conglomerate, Henry Kissinger, Robert O. Anderson of Atlantic Richfield Oil Company, George Ball of Lehman Brothers, Zbigniew Brzezinski, Otto Wolf von Armerongen and David Rockefeller. The thrust of the meeting was how to trigger a global oil embargo as a vehicle to increase oil prices by as much as 400 percent.

The Saltsjobasden meeting must surely have been a high point of achievement for the Committee of 300, for never had so few controlled the economic future of the entire world. What steps they resolved to take to achieve their goal of a 400 percent increase in oil revenues and the resulting enormous boost for the dollar, are not known, except by those who attended the meeting. But the outcome of their deliberations was not long in coming.

A scant six months later, on October 6, 1973, Egypt and Syria launched a war against Israel, the so-called "Yom Kippur" war. Let us leave for the moment all ostensible reasons for the attack on Israel and go behind the scenes. From what we were able to uncover by reading a series of dispatches and reports, it is fairly certain that using diplomatic back channels, Henry Kissinger orchestrated the outbreak of the war from Washington. It is well-known that Kissinger was very close to the Israeli Ambassador in Washington, one Simcha Dinitz. At the same time, Kissinger was working his Egyptian-Syrian connections. Kissinger used the oldest formula in the world he deliberately misrepresented the facts to both sides.

On October 16, 1972, OPEC held a meeting in Vienna and announced to the world that it was increasing the price of its oil from $1.50 per barrel to $11.00 per barrel, and that it would boycott the U.S. because of its grossly one-sided consistent favoring of Israel. The Netherlands was singled out for special attack because it is where the major oil ports for Europe are located. The Bilderberg plotters achieved their goal. If we look at oil prices from 1949 to 1970 and take note that the price of a barrel of crude oil was increased by only approximately $1.89. By January 1974 the price of crude oil had risen by 400 percent, the Bilderberg Group's Saltsjoebaden target.

There is little room for doubt that Henry Kissinger, on behalf of the Bilderberg Group, orchestrated and carried out the plan hatched at the Wallenberg retreat and at the same time laid the blame for the 400 percent increase in crude oil squarely at the door of the Arab/OPEC producers at a time when global oil consumption had increased 5.5 times since 1949. Senator 'Scoop' Jackson called for an immediate break-up and divesture of the major petroleum companies, calling their profits, 'obscene.'

Next we turn to Mexico again and the much-hated Henri Deterding of Shell, who bought up some of Cowdrey's leases (which John D. had rejected as he felt they were not worth much anyway). This was the start of corrupt practices by the oil companies backed up by a government, some of whose officials were very susceptible to bribes.

Oil was first discovered in Mexico by British construction magnate, Weetman Pearson, who we have already met. Pearson was not really in the oil business, but just happened upon it after a visit to Laredo, Texas, if we are to believe his account of events. Mexican President Porfirio Diaz, gave Weetman the right to prospect (for a private consideration) and the British businessman set up his drilling equipment right on land said to have huge oil reserves, next to where old John D. had filed his claims. John D., always one to harbor hatred, then started dynamiting Weetman's claims and setting fire to his wells. All the dirty tricks behavior taught by William 'Doc' Avery was immediately brought to bear against his rival. But Weetman stuck to his task, and for the first time in his life, Rockefeller was thwarted. Having gained control of every oil resource in the U.S., Rockefeller did not like it. His mask of benign philanthropy, displayed in Judge Whyte's courtroom, slipped, revealing the full ugliness of the character of the man, a face molded in ruthless rapaciousness.

Weetman outsmarted and outfoxed Rockefeller, causing him to miscalculate badly. 'I think the Mexican oilfields are too costly,' he told Avery, but little did he know that his assessment of the Mexican scene was badly flawed. But behind the scenes, Rockefeller's private intelligence service was bent upon making maximum problems for Weetman, as well as turmoil and bloodshed for the Mexican people.

The British Government promoted Weetman to the House of Lords in recognition of his work in the Mexican oilfields for his country, and for building bombers for the Royal Flying Corps (RFC) in the First World War. He was a close friend of Sir Douglas Haig, who initiated the program for the Royal Flying Corps (RFC). Henceforth, he was known as Lord Cowdrey. It was not very long before he became very friendly with the newly elected President Woodrow Wilson.

Angry at being beaten, John D. began putting tremendous pressure on Wilson. Standard Oil wanted back in, and if it took the United States military to do the job, then, so be it. This was imperialism at its worst with the oil companies using the U.S.

military as their own private army as we saw when, in later years, President Bush ordered the invasion of Panama and Iraq.

Inside Mexico, Rockefeller's private intelligence army fomented trouble around the clock, and to add to the looming crisis, Mexico elected General Huerto as its new president. In his election manifesto, Huerto had sworn that he would regain control of Mexican oil for his people. Using Lord Cowdrey, Wilson was approached by the British government to seek American help for getting rid of the fiery Huerto. Britain and the U.S. joined forces 'against the common enemy' as Cowdrey put it, all the while pumping as much crude oil as he could, night and day, before the balloon went up. But it was the United States that hurt Mexico the most, plunging the country into one round of civil war after another, mistakenly called 'revolutions,' shedding needlessly the blood of hundreds of thousands of Mexicans, so that foreign imperialists might retain control of Mexico's natural resources. Mexico was wracked by bitterness and strife; yet, all the while Cowdrey grew richer and richer. His personal empire encompassed Lazard Freres, the international banker-brokerage house, 'Penguin Books,' 'The Economist' and the London 'Financial Times,' all built on the blood and tears of the Mexican people and the blood of millions killed in WWI, which could not have been prosecuted except for Mexican oil. The Mexican people were robbed blind, first by Cowdrey and then by Shell, who bought the billionaire's interests in Mexico in 1919 at the close of WWI, when having been badly hurt by the death of his son in WWI, Cowdrey decided he had made enough money to retire.

Civil war followed (called 'revolution' in the British and American press) - as the Mexican people sought to regain control of their natural resources. While Cowdrey lived in total luxury, Mexican oil workers were worse off than the slaves of the Pharaoh, huddling together in abject misery and squalor in oil 'towns' that beggared description, composed of the vilest of shacks with no sanitation or water.

By 1936 there were 17 foreign countries busily pumping out the oil that rightfully belonged to Mexico. Finally, when the Mexican oil workers were on the edge of a revolt against their employers because of their conditions, Mexico's President Lazaro Cardenas belatedly demanded better conditions and pay for them. In America, the press announced that 'Communism was trying to take over in Mexico.'

The 17 offending companies refused to budge on the just demands of the workers, and Cardenas thereupon nationalized all foreign oil companies, as he had every right to do. As they had done with Iran, when Churchill's naked aggression ruined the economy by instituting a world boycott of Iranian oil, the British and American government announced that they would enforce an embargo against anyone shipping oil out of Mexico. PEMEX, the national company running the oil industry was so disrupted by the boycott that it became totally incompetent, and as the boycott went on, individual PEMEX employees began to succumb to bribery and corruption. All of this mischief was the work of Rockefeller's private army of agents and spies, who were everywhere. In 1966, several prominent writers sought to expose the role played by the British and American imperialists in Mexico. Cowdrey then hired Desmond Young, a prominent writer of the time, to prepare a whitewash of his activities, for which Young was paid the prostitutes' going rate for hire.

To backtrack to Europe, just before WWII. In 1936, the Communists tried to seize control of Spain. It was to be their big prize after capturing Russia. Texaco, seeing a bonanza in the making, sided with General Franco. Its tankers, loaded with Mexican oil, were diverted to ports in Spain controlled by Franco.

Enter Sir William Stephenson, the man who plotted to take over U.S. intelligence agencies in WWII, and who later engineered the assassination of President John F. Kennedy. Stephenson uncovered the Texaco-Franco oil deal and promptly went to

Roosevelt with it. As is the American secret government's custom - and there is a long history to support this statement -- where rightwing governments were engaged in a life-and-death struggle against Communist forces trying to overthrow them (as in Cuba), the CFR either adopted a position of neutrality, all the while secretly undermining the legitimate government and supporting the Communist forces, or else it openly sided with the insurgent forces (as in Spain and later, South Africa).

In the Spanish War against Communism, known as the 'Spanish Civil War,' America was officially 'neutral.' But Roosevelt allowed the CFR to secretly supply money, arms and munitions to the Communists against whom Franco was struggling. When Stephenson came galloping into his office with the 'bad news,' Roosevelt became very angry and indignantly ordered Texaco to obey the neutrality laws and cease shipments of oil to Franco.

However, Roosevelt did not stop the flow of cash, weapons and food to the Communists. Nor did he order the Bolsheviks not to recruit men in the U.S. who were willing to fight for the Communists in Spain.

The Communists promptly began recruiting American volunteers to fight in the 'Abraham Lincoln Brigade' in opposition to Franco. No attempt was made by Roosevelt to prosecute those responsible for it. Franco has never been forgiven for smashing the attempted Communist takeover of Christian Spain. Nor will he ever be by the Socialists who make up the bulk of the U.S. State Department. Although it did not play a major role in the Spanish Civil War, the Federal Reserve Board, the governing body of the 12 Federal Reserve Banks, was a major player in WWI and WWII. Without it, there would have been no World Wars, no Korean and Vietnam wars. The Federal Reserve Banks were set up by Senator Nelson Aldrich, at the behest, and acting as the servant of the Rockefellers. Senator Nelson Aldrich was bought and paid for by the Rothschilds and he became the prime mover of the bill to establish a central bank in the U.S. in violation of his oath to defend and uphold the U.S. Constitution.

It is fair to say that Rothschild and Rockefeller money paid the cost (legitimate, and in bribes) of setting up the Federal Reserve Banks. Senator Aldrich's daughter, Abbey Green Aldrich, married John Rockefeller Jr., and Abbey was always very generous with her grants to leftwing and outright Communist institutions.

Mexico and the Federal Reserve are two more indictments in the case against the petroleum industry. Other indictments against the Rockefellers are that they spread their oil money around in such hotbeds of Communism as the World Council of Churches and the Rockefeller Riverside Church in New York. These two leftwing institutions were on the cutting edge of the drive to wipe the Christian Church off the map in South Africa.

So imperialistic did the petroleum industry become that with the help of an extensive spy network, very little happened without it coming to the Rockefeller's attention. Very shortly after WWII ended, oil began flowing strongly from the Saudi fields as the price of gasoline shot up from $1.02 per gallon to $1.43 per gallon, without any economic reason for the jump. The sheer greed of the petroleum industry cost the American consumer billions of dollars, which did not include the billions of dollars the U.S. taxpayers had to provide to keep the 'Golden Gimmick' going.

EXXON showed no fear of the American people or the government. The secret, upper-level parallel government executive, known as the Council on Foreign Relations, saw to it that nobody dared lay a finger on EXXON and its Saudi company, ARAMCO.

Consequently ARAMCO was able to get away with things like selling oil to France at $0.95 per barrel, while charging the U.S. Navy $1.23 per barrel for the very same oil. This was barefaced, arrogant robbery of the American people. But in spite of the cover-up by the press and radio, in 1948 Senator Brewster decided he had enough information to challenge the petroleum industry.

Brewster charged the majors with acting in bad faith,

> "… with an avaricious desire for enormous profits, while at the same time constantly seeking to cloak themselves with U.S. protection and financial assistance to preserve their vast concessions."

The major oil companies responded with a memo to Brewster, in which they arrogantly stated that they owed no special allegiance to the United States! Rockefeller's 'imperialism' was never more boldly flaunted in the face of America than during the Brewster hearings.

Apart from geopolitical considerations, the major oil companies were also guilty of simple gerrymandering of prices. The cheap Arabian oil, for instance, was fixed at the higher American price when sold to Western Europe and imported into the U.S. The scam was pulled off through what was known as 'phantom freight rates.'

One of the best reports to throw a great deal of light on the conduct of the petroleum industry was the 'International Petroleum Cartel; A report compiled by the staff of the Federal Trade Commission.' This incisive account should be compulsory reading for every member of the U.S. House of Representatives and the Senate.

I am amazed that the report ever saw the light of day, and would suppose it was sufficient reason for Rockefeller and his fellow conspirators to have been highly alarmed. Inspired by the late Senator John Sparkman and carefully put together by Professor M. Blair, the history of the petroleum cartel is traced right back to the conspiracy at Achnacarry Castle in Scotland.

CHAPTER 15

Senator Sparkman lashes out at Rockefeller's oil empire

Senator Sparkman pulled no punches, lashing out at Rockefeller's oil empire in particular. Professor Blair carefully, and convincingly, built up the case against the petroleum industry, inch by inch, finally providing unassailable evidence that the major oil companies had entered into a conspiracy to achieve the following goals:

➢ To control all technology and patents relating to oil production and refining.

➢ To control pipelines and tankers between seven companies, 'The Seven Sisters.'

➢ To share world markets with each other and to allocate spheres of influence.

➢ To control all oil producing foreign countries in so far as production, sale and distribution of oil was concerned.

➢ To act jointly and severally in maintaining artificially high oil prices.

Professor Blair said that specifically ARAMCO had been guilty of keeping oil prices high even when it was pumping oil in Saudi Arabia at incredibly low prices. In view of Senator Sparkman's wide-ranging allegations, the Justice Department began its own probe of ARAMCO'S business practices to see if any U.S. laws were being violated. Standard Oil and the Rockefellers immediately dispatched Dean Acheson, their hireling at the State Department, to blunt the investigation. Acheson, who might have been impeached on charges of treason, is the best, or perhaps the worst example of how the U.S. Government is suborned and turned upside down by the major oil companies. This happened every time there was a move to investigate the conspirators who long ago said they owe no special allegiance to the United States. Appearing before a Senate investigation committee in 1952, Acheson cited the interests of the State Department as being preeminent in protecting America's foreign policy interests in the Middle East (thereby tacitly admitting that the major oil companies ran the foreign policy), Acheson asked the committee and the Justice Department to shelve their investigations into ARAMCO'S dealings, in the interests of not weakening U.S. diplomatic initiatives in the Middle East. Acheson very cleverly used the Mossadegh crisis in Iran to make his point, and the Justice Department duly complied. But the Attorney General was able to get a sharp observation in, before the doors closed on ARAMCO's unsavory business practices:

> The oil business is in the hands of the few. Oil monopolies are not in the best interest of free trade. Free enterprise can only be preserved by safeguarding it from excesses of power, both governmental and private.

But the Attorney General's most stinging rebuke was addressed to the petroleum cartel, which, he said, 'Is profoundly damaging to national security interests.' A furious Rockefeller immediately took damage control measures, using his pet attack dog, Acheson, to accuse the anti-trust prosecutors of being 'police dogs from the anti-trust section of the Justice Department, who want no truck with mammon and the unrighteous.' His tone was belligerent and filled with bombast.

Lining up the Defense and Interior Departments, Acheson declared the imperialist creed:

The companies (the Seven Sisters) play a vital role in supplying the free world's most essential commodity. American oil operations are for all practical intents and purposes, instruments of our foreign policy toward these nations.

Acheson's masterstroke was to drag in the specter of possible Soviet Bolshevik intervention in Saudi Arabia:

We cannot overlook the significance of the role played by oil companies in the struggle to further the ideals of the former Soviet Union, nor can we leave unchallenged the assertion that these companies are engaged in a criminal conspiracy for the purpose of predatory exploration.

Acheson's position was altogether false. The oil cartel was, and still is, engaged in imperial predatory rape of oil-producing countries, and their activities in interfering with, or making foreign policy decisions based on their best interests, is a danger to the good relations of the Arab and Islamic world with the United States, and threatens rather than protects our national security interests. As for Acheson's Soviet red herring, ever since the Bolshevik Revolution, the petroleum industry, and the Rockefellers in particular, has enjoyed very cozy, warm, relations with the Bolshevik leadership. When one of their number, Sir Henri Deterding, derided being in bed with the Bolsheviks, he was shown the door. The Rockefellers had long been in bed with the Bolsheviks in a most blatant illicit relationship, and in any case, wasn't it Churchill, with the full approval of the petroleum industry, who invited the Russians to join in the invasion of Iran and also Iraq? The power of the oil cartel was never in doubt. Truman's Attorney General had warned years before that the world should be free of control of the imperial petroleum industry:

The world petroleum cartel is an authoritarian dominating power over a great and vital world industry, in private hands. A decision to terminate the pending investigation would be regarded by the world as a confession that our abhorrence of monopoly and restrictive cartel activities does not extend to the world's most important single industry.

This, in essence is my case against the petroleum industry. As might have been expected, Rockefeller and his legal team, particularly Acheson, prevailed. Having nothing to lose, as he was about to leave the White House, Truman told the Attorney General to drop the pending charges against the cartel, 'in the interests of national security.'

CHAPTER 16

Kuwait created from stolen Iraqi land

A s a sop to the American people, albeit a meaningless sop, Truman said that civil proceedings would be allowed to continue. But the sop was exposed for what it was, when the oil companies refused to accept subpoenas. The matter was quietly dropped when Eisenhower and Dulles, two of the leading servants of the Committee of 300, the Rockefellers and the CFR, replaced Truman and Acheson. Thus was the stage set for the spread of the cancer of oil imperialism.

Kermit Roosevelt was involved in the plot to topple Prime Minister Mossadegh from the very outset. Even as civil proceeding against his corrupt masters was being readied in April of 1953, Kermit was in Teheran overseeing the upcoming coup against Mossadegh, which broke on April 15, and was successful. Poor Mossadegh, not being aware that Rockefeller and Eisenhower were in cahoots, kept right on appealing to Eisenhower, who, being the pathetic plaything of the Rockefellers and the oil cartel, did nothing to stop the illegal activities of the CIA in Iran.

After Mossadegh was ousted, the Shah returned to Iran, but soon became disillusioned when he discovered ~ thanks to the work of Dr. Mossadegh ~ just how the American oil companies were bleeding Iran's oil reserves dry and making off with big bundles of dollars in profits.

Citing the precedent of Mexico and Venezuela's demands, and

the large bribe given to Saudi Arabia, the Shah thought it time to claim a much larger share of oil revenues than Iran had been getting. What the Shah learned was that Venezuela's oil industry had been corrupted by Juan Vincente Gomez who was bribed to allow an American to write Venezuela's petroleum laws that led to a nasty strike in Maracaibo in 1922. But the information provided by the Shah was to be his undoing. The civil proceedings in Washington against the oil cartel members began to fizzle and even as Kermit Roosevelt was going at it hammer and tongs in Teheran, Eisenhower instructed his Attorney General to work out a face-saving compromise between the courts and the oil cartel, one which, in his words

> "… would protect the interests of the free world in the Near East as a major source of petroleum supplies."

Even more astounding, Eisenhower then instructed the Attorney general to 'henceforth, regard the antitrust laws as secondary to national security interests.' It is no wonder that the Ayatollah Khomeini called the United States, 'the Great Satan.' As far as the petroleum industry is concerned it is a well-deserved epithet. Acting under the flag of an imperialist United States, Eisenhower granted the petroleum cartel carte blanche to act as it saw fit.

Khomeini took pains to say that the 'Great Satan' was not the American people, but their corrupt government. When we consider how the U.S. government has lied to its own people, how it called upon the sons and daughters of this nation to throw their lives away in the interests of the petroleum industry, we can certainly see where Khomeini might be justified in such a characterization.

Throughout the near-farcical civil proceedings against the oil cartel members, the State Department continuously referred to the defendants as 'the so-called petroleum cartel' knowing full well that there was nothing 'so-called' about the Seven Sisters and the participants of the Achnacarry Castle conspiracy. We might add that time, the State Department was densely packed with Rockefeller- Rothschild sympathizers and remains so at the present time.

Acting as an apologist for the members of the cartel, the State Department eventually allowed it to prevail. Thus was justice perverted and raped and the conspirators got clean away with their crimes, even as they do to this very day. The State Department's claim that the Seven Sisters were in the forefront of fending off Soviet penetration into the Saudi and Iran oilfields was a blatant lie in a whole string of lies brought forth by the petroleum industry since the days of John D. Rockefeller.

In 1953, a giant conspiracy was entered into by the major oil companies of imperial Britain and the United States, which called for a unified need to act against what it called, 'the Iranian problem.' (Remember Mexico and the 'common enemy?') Sir William Fraser wrote to Mobil, Texaco, Socol, BP, Shell and Gulf Oil, proposing that a meeting of the minds be held as soon as possible, to settle the difficulties with Iran, for once and for all.

Representatives of the major U.S. oil companies joined their British counterparts in London (a long-time favorite meeting place of those seeking to avoid conspiracy laws in the United States). They were joined by representatives of the French company, Française des Pétroles. It was agreed that a cartel be formed - only it would be called a 'consortium' to take full control of the oil in Iran. Decades later, when the Shah tried to stand up to the cartel, he was put to flight and then to death.

The letter and the subsequent agreement by the cartel was the basis of the conspiracy entered into by the imperial Carter administration to get rid of the Shah, and it was really a carbon copy of the methods used to get rid of Dr. Mossadegh. Some 60 'Banker's Faction' CIA agents were dispatched to Teheran to undermine the Shah. And a further example of the power of the petroleum industry occurred with the Arab-Israeli War of 1967.

On June 4, 1967, the Israeli army invaded Egypt and this resulted in a short-lived boycott of the entire West, by the Arabs. It was later reduced to Israel's chief backers, Britain and the United States. Instead of opening up new domestic oil fields, the petroleum companies increased the price of gas when there was no reason for it. We say no reason for a price increase, because the petroleum companies had on hand, a huge stock of billions of gallons of gasoline refined from cheap Saudi oil. It was suggested by the Egyptian foreign minister, that the

> "... support of the aggressor, Israel who attacked us, cost the American taxpayer billions of dollars, not only through vast arms shipments to the aggressor state of Israel, but also through increased gasoline prices which the America public must now pay."

I believe that I have made out a strong case of criminal conspiracy against the petroleum industry, which embarked on a conspiracy with foreign oil companies to plunder, steal and rob the American people; to undermine the foreign policy of the elected government, and in general, act as a government inside government that has committed hundreds of criminal acts. The United States has become an imperial power in every sense of the word.

The other United States-Kuwait ally, Saudi Arabia, was now at loggerheads with Iran and fearful of its security. Quietly, and behind the scenes, King Fahd was subjected to a lot of pressure by his family members urging him to ask the United States to locate its military bases outside the kingdom. King Fahd, in attempting to put the brakes on rising unrest in the nation, was supposed to institute a number of reforms after the Gulf War. Like Kuwait, the 'democratic' reforms have been long in speech and short in action. The ruling families are not about to loosen their grip on the country, less still will they go up against the Petroleum Cartel.

In March of 1992 King Fahd declared that censorship would be lifted as part of the promised reforms. This followed in the wake of the brutal treatment of a Saudi journalist, Zuhair al-Safwani, who was arrested on January 18, 1992, and sentenced to four years in prison for making a mildly unfavorable remark about the Abdul Aziz family that the House of Saud found uncomfortably close to the truth. In addition to the four-year prison sentence, al-Safwani was given 300 lashes that left him paralyzed down the left side of his body.

Such gruesome torture would have made headlines on CNN, ABC, NBC, FOX and the New York Times, had it taken place in South Africa, Iraq or Malaysia. When an American youth was sentenced to 9 strokes with a cane by a Singapore court after being found guilty of drug smuggling, even President Clinton got into the clemency appeal act.

But this awful brutality having happened in Saudi Arabia, our intrepid media giants who love to tell the truth, the whole truth, maintained a deafeningly silence. Not one word of condemnation of Saudi Arabia came out of CNN, CBS, ABC, NBC and FOX.

The United States government is in bed with the Saudi despots, that is why we rush our military forces over there if there is any threat, real or imaginary, to the Saudi 'democracy.' The fact is that American troops are based in Dhahran, Saudi Arabia, solely to protect and perpetuate one of the most despotic regimes in the world today. The correct thing to do would be to bring U.S. troops home and cancel the 'golden gimmick' payments running into billions of dollars, ever since the program was begun by the Rockefellers. Money paid to the Saudi rulers as an inducement to let United States oil companies pump oil out of their wells, is deducted from United States income taxes, as taxes paid in a foreign country. The people of America unfairly have to bear this cost.

Meanwhile things did not go well for the petroleum industry in

Somalia. As revealed in my monograph, 'What Are We Doing in Somalia,' former President Bush, ever the servant of the petroleum industry, rushed United States armed forces to Somalia, ostensibly to feed the starving Somali population. My monograph ripped that mask from the face of the Bush administration, revealing the true intent and purpose behind the presence of units of U.S. armed forces in Somalia.

World In Review Magazine reported that the United States was engaged in refurbishing the old base at the port city of Berbera, strategically located on the Red Sea, well astride the oil fields of Saudi Arabia. It also revealed that American Armed Forces were in Somalia to protect teams of oil drillers who were drilling for oil in that country, oil that is reputed to be there in abundance. While the newly refurbished Berbera base may be a big help in quelling the fears of Shi'ites about the presence of American troops in Saudi Arabia, the downside is a possible loss of revenue for the kingdom if and when Somalia oil begins to flow, although this is possibly twenty or more years away. Nevertheless, the insistence by religious elements in Riyadh that the United States be given notice to quit the kingdom, did not sit well with King Fahd and some of his sons.

It brought family differences in the palace to the surface in no uncertain manner. With his health failing and demands for a loosening up of the tight grip the Saudi family has on the country, what seemed like an interminable bright future for the Saudi royal family, began to cloud over.

The strength of religious opposition to the continued absolute rule by the Saudis and Wahabis was having a telling effect. Every day brought new provocations from the Shi'ites and other fundamentalists who wanted King Fahd to keep his promise to hold elections in the immediate future, something he was not at all anxious to go ahead with. It used to be that the Abdul Aziz family despotic rulers of Saudi Arabia presented a united front to all outsiders who are opposed to their dictatorial rule.

I learned from intelligence sources that this is no longer the case. Intense family rivalry and the death of King Fahd are threatening the once united front. Added to this is the escalation of Muslim fundamentalist pressure culminating in the arrest of several hundred of their leaders whom Riyadh has described as 'religious radicals,' but who are really a group of mullahs seeking to have some say in the way the country is governed.

The war between Hezbollah and the Israeli military in Lebanon that began in July 2006 had a disquieting effect in Riyadh. The fundamentalists wanted the Saudi regime to openly declare itself on the side of the Hezbollah, which the ruling Abdul Aziz clan hoped to avoid. In its ongoing petroleum wars against Arab and Muslim oil- producing states, the petroleum industry is more and more relying on the U.S. military to get involved and fight its oil battles.

We need reminding that Bush had no constitutional powers to send American troops to fight against Iraq. Only the Congress can declare war. The President has zero authority to send troops anywhere and minus zero authority to keep troops stationed in Saudi Arabia pursuant to guarding BP's assets in Kuwait.

Thus Bush, who has no authority to send U.S. troops anywhere without Congressional approval (in the form of a Declaration of War), literally got away with a serious crime, that of violating his oath of office, for which he should have been prosecuted for failing to uphold the Constitution and for war crimes, among other things.

Representative Henry Gonzales actually drew up a list of crimes committed by G.H.W. Bush and sought to have him impeached, but his efforts were stalled by Democrats and Republicans in the House, who thought it disloyal not to go with the tide running against Pres. Saddam Hussein, but quite in order to shield Bush from charges of treason. It just goes to show that on vital issues, there is little difference between the two U.S. political parties. As a result, the foreign policy of the United States has deteriorated into an imperialist power. Since 1991, the Congress has been passing all sorts of unconstitutional legislation under the guise of combating 'terrorism.' The U.S. Congress needs to give Bush and the Department of Defense a sharp rap over the knuckles. Any attempt by the United States to interfere in the sovereign affairs of other nations could only be seen by the world — and the majority of Americans — as an act of extreme violence, far outstripping in terrorism and utter depravity, any marginal benefit that might accrue.

One of the things that chill the most, is that there has been no public outcry against the George Bush for even proposing to use nuclear weapons against small nations, and shows just how far the U.S. is on the road to a One World Government. For thirty years the United States has been saying that the use of nuclear weapons must be banned. Yet, here we have someone who was not elected by the voters, setting a dangerous precedent that it is fine to attack nations as long as those nations are so-called "rouge states" sitting on top of valuable oil reserves. Our military must not be allowed to become the attack dogs of the petroleum industry. Surely, we learned something from the Gulf War?

If we study the work of the great constitutional scholar Judge Joseph Story, Volume III, Commentaries on the Constitution of the United States, and particularly chapter five, there is no mention of the Secretary of Defense and the Pentagon having the power to make and carry out the foreign policy of the United States. Every member of Congress should be obliged to read this work, so that they will be in a position to put an end to such flagrant abuses of power as Bush has engaged in, in the Middle East. This, the petroleum industry thought, would be a good way to weaken both nations who are major oil producers, and set them up for a quick knock-down. President Bush, without the slightest authority from Congress, created a climate of hatred against Iraq, thinking the U.S. military would have an excuse to engage in an imperialist war of attrition against the people of Iraq, all for the sole benefit of the petroleum industry. When will this nation learn that the petroleum industry is run by Globalists of the One World Government whose greed knows no bounds? The petroleum industry cannot be trusted - their leaders are real troublemakers, who will plunge this nation into all sorts of quagmires if it is to their sole benefit.

The latest casualties among U.S. servicemen in Iraq are a national disgrace. Our servicemen are not over there fighting for the United States. They are in Baghdad to secure Iraq's oil reserves for the petroleum cartel. And our troops are in Saudi Arabia to keep the Abdul Azziz dynasty in place, because theirs is a regime of mountebanks keeping the oil flowing to the U.S.-ARAMCO giant. Not one single American soldier must ever again be sacrificed on the altar of the petroleum industry's greed.

Who put our servicemen in this danger area and by what constitutional authority was this done? The frenetic rush by George Herbert Walker Bush and the Pentagon to defend Kuwait, one of the most baneful dictatorships in the world (next to Saudi Arabia) is indicative of the state of anarchy and chaos that prevails in Washington. American troops and supplies rushed to Kuwait on behalf of the British Petroleum and City of London bankers, exposed to what an advanced level of brainwashing the American public has been brought. Let's get matters in perspective:

Kuwait is not a country. It is an appendage of British Petroleum and City of London bankers. The territory known as Kuwait belonged to Iraq and was recognized as an integral part of Iraq for over 400 years - until the British army marched in, drew a line across the desert sands and declared, 'This is now Kuwait.' Of course the imaginary border just happened to run through the middle of the richest oilfields in the area, the Rumalia oil fields that had belonged to Iraq for 400 years, and still belong to Iraq. Theft of land never transfers ownership.

Quoting from 'Diplomacy by Deception:'[1]

> In 1880, the British Government formed a friendship with an Arab sheik by the name of Emir Abdullah al Salam al Sabah, who was appointed their representative in the area along the southern border of Iraq, where the Rumalia oilfields had been discovered inside Iraqi territory. At the time there was no other country but Iraq - to which all the lands belonged, there being no such entity as Kuwait.

> The Al Sabah family kept an eye on the rich prize ... On behalf of the Committee of 300, on November 25, 1899 - the same year the British went to war against the small Boer Republics in South Africa — the British government made a deal with Emir Al Sabah, whereby the lands encroaching on the Rumalia oilfields belonging to Iraq, would be ceded to the British Government, notwithstanding the fact that the land was an integral part of Iraq, to which neither the Emir Al Sabah nor the British had claim.

The deal was signed by Sheik Mubarak Al Sabah, who traveled to London in style... 'Kuwait' became a de facto British protectorate. The local population and the Iraq government were never consulted and had no say in the matter and the Al Sabahs as absolute dictators, soon showed cruel ruthlessness. In 1915 the British marched into Baghdad and occupied it in what George Bush would have called an act of 'naked aggression.'

The British government set up a self-proclaimed 'mandate' and sent High Commissioner Cox to run it, who named former King Faisal of Syria as head of a puppet regime in Basra. Britain now

---

[1] *Diplomacy By Deception: An account of the treasonous conduct by the governments of Britain and the United States*, Omnia Veritas Ltd, www.omnia-veritas.com.

had a puppet in northern Iraq and another in southern Iraq...

In 1961 Iraqi Premier Hassan Abdul Kassem fiercely attacked Britain over the Kuwait issue, pointing out that the promised negotiations agreed to by the Lausanne Conference had not taken place. Kassem declared that the territory called Kuwait had been an integral part of Iraq and was so recognized for more than 400 years by the Ottoman Empire. Instead, the British government granted Kuwait independence...

There was no actual border between 'Kuwait' and Iraq; the whole thing was a farce. Had Kassem succeeded in taking the land occupied by Kuwait back, the British rulers would have lost billions of dollars in oil revenues. But when Kassem vanished after Kuwait got its independence, (there is little doubt that he was murdered by British MI6 agents) the movement to challenge Britain lost its momentum.

By granting independence to Kuwait in 1961, and ignoring the fact that the land was not theirs to give, Britain was able to fend off the just claims of Iraq. We know that the British government did the same thing in Palestine, India, and later, in South Africa.

For the next 30 years Kuwait continued as the vassal state of Great Britain, pouring billions of dollars derived from the sale of Iraqi oil into British banks, while Iraq got nothing... Britain's seizure of Iraqi land, calling it Kuwait, and granting it independence, must rank as one of the most audacious acts of piracy in modern times, and contributed directly to the Gulf War.

I have gone to some lengths to explain background events that led to the Gulf War in an attempt to show the power of the Committee of 300, and how unjustly the United State acted toward Iraq.

President G.H.W. Bush repeated the same 100 percent illegal tactics practiced by the Petroleum Cartel. It is this sort of behavior that is leading the United States into anarchy and chaos. Since 1991 Iraqi women and children have died by the hundreds of thousands, from diseases, many of them caused by radiation sickness emanating from spent depleted uranium (DU) shell casings, and from malnutrition resulting from the inhuman boycott that went on for 19 years.

Iraq had no money to buy food and medical supplies - which the U.N. embargo magnanimously allowed. How could Iraq buy these essentials when its oil revenues were reduced to below a subsistence level? Meningitis raged among children in Baghdad, while Britain and the United States played games with the lives of a people that have never harmed them. Imperialism against Iraq has reigned supreme for the past 18 years. There is no justification for it, and it is 100 percent unconstitutional for the United States to be doing the bidding of the petroleum cartel. No Scam too Big or too Small or Unsavory for the Petroleum Cartel.

In mid-2008 we are once again witnessing the way in which the imperial petroleum cartel is a law unto itself, a ruthless organization which no government has been able to curb or bring under control. We have seen an altogether astonishing situation where U.S. oil reserves in Alaska, now flow on a regular basis to refineries in China. Will the U.S. and China ever come to blows? That remains to be seen.

In the Middle East we have witnessed the policy of extermination brought about by the petroleum giants, with the Iraqi people as their victims. This ongoing horror story has remained well hidden by the media; for fear that some might have their eyes opened and begin to question what is going on. Remember, always; the United States and Britain are the two most imperialistic and decadent aggressive countries in the world today, and that under their leadership, imperialism has flourished and spread like the plague. The American people tolerate things today that they would not have tolerated just a few short years ago.

Both former President George Bush and President Clinton were guilty of obfuscation. When George Bush Sr. unilaterally, and without any authority under international law and the Constitution of the United States, established two so-called "no fly zones" over Iraq, he acted in violation of the U.S. Constitution, imposing his will on the sovereign nation of Iraq, and on the United States people, without one shred of authority to support his actions.

This deed was done supposedly to protect the Kurdish people who were allegedly in danger of being overrun by Saddam Hussein. Never was a more unilateral dictatorial act perpetrated in the name of the people of the U.S., reinforced by the weight of the U.S. Armed Forces. Here we are, today, in 2008, still putting up with the dubious acts of George Bush as though he were a king, of whom the world stands in fear and trembling. America, what has happened to you?

There is no United Nations secretariat for the Security Council resolution number authorizing the 'no fly zones' and the Security Council did not issue resolutions to cover 'no fly zones.' Mr. Bush took this action unilaterally. The State Department was not able to cite authorization for the 'no fly zones' in established U.S. law or in the highest law, the U.S. Constitution. The unilateral action taken by George Bush the elder was a clear case of an imperialist dictator at work. The long-standing respect for the rule of law, respect for our Constitution, was trampled by an arrogant, imperialistic President Bush. Americans are apparently satisfied to let the moguls of the petroleum industry get away with illegal, unlawful conduct.

George Bush the elder is one of the top men in the petroleum industry; not interested in the welfare of the Kurds. The petroleum industry, this lawless group, has its eye on is the huge, untapped reserves of oil in the vilayets of the Mosul in Iraq. As luck would have it, the Kurds, whom George Bush wanted to 'protect,' just happen to occupy the land in Iraq under which the

Mosul oil pools lie. So the mogul of the petroleum industry, friend of Queen Elizabeth II, George Bush, just went along and declared that no Iraqi planes could fly in the 'no fly zones.'

Bush, the elder said, 'no fly zones' were to protect the Kurds, yet a few short miles away; the kill rate of Kurds by the Turkish army made a strange backdrop. Of course it does make sense when we know that U.S. foreign policy is dictated by the petroleum giants, and it makes even greater sense when we begin to understand that the Mosul oil vilayets are the true reason for the 'no fly zones' and for twice launching multi-million dollar cruise missile attacks on the defenseless citizens of Baghdad.

The American people are the most trusting, most lied-to, connived, cheated, most ruled and regulated people in the world, living in a dense jungle of disinformation and even denser thickets of false propaganda. As a result the American people do not realize that their government is a government under the direction of a secret parallel upper-level body, the Committee of 300 that enables would-be dictators and tyrants to cover their unconstitutional, despotic actions. Anyone who questions Bush foreign policy toward Iraq is labeled unpatriotic, when if the truth be told, the unpatriotic ones are the Bush family and those who support their petroleum cartel policies toward Iraq and indeed, the whole Middle East. These are the people who supported the totally unconstitutional bombing and the illegal (under international law) boycott of Iraq; the unconstitutional bombing of Serbia, and acts of aggression against the Iranian and Lebanese people. No nation is safe from the moguls of the petroleum industry. California has scores of refineries from Los Angeles to Bakersfield to the greater San Francisco area. Oil is found in good supply in the State. Yet, for years the citizens of California have been gouged by the greedy petroleum industry. When gasoline was 79 cents a gallon in Kansas, Californians were paying $1.35 per gallon.

There was never any justification for it, but with the California legislature in their pockets, what was there for the moguls to worry about? And so the price gouging went on and on. Gasoline prices at the pumps rose to a staggering $2.65 for regular and $3.99/10ths per gallon for super grade gas. There is no justification for these shocking price increases. Greed was the motivating factor. Refineries were never short of crude with stocks of gasoline at near normal levels.

The American military are today mercenaries of the gargantuan monster called the petroleum industry. America's armed forces will be led into one regional war after another in the interest of greed and profit for the monsters of the petroleum industry. The American taxpayers will continue to fund the 'golden handshake,' which enables ARAMCO to keep pumping oil in Saudi Arabia. What is needed is a great awakening of the American people. Like some old religious revival, a spirit of law and order, love for the U.S. Constitution is needed to sweep this once great Nation and restore it to a nation of laws, and not of men.

The modern-day robber barons fleece the American people at the pumps in the most brazen and shameless fashion in their long, brazen and shameless history. The oil cartel is ruthless, well-organized and will brook no interference from government, whether it be the Government of the United States or any other nation. The American taxpayers are forced to meet the cost of the bribes paid to the Saudi ruling family through their agents in government whom they have bought and paid for and are still paying for every time you pump gasoline for your car.

Americans need to know about this giant cartel which is flouting the laws of several nations, including their own, and with knowledge will come the desire to take remedial action which a public outcry putting pressure on the lawmakers to break the monopoly. Behind this cartel stands the power of the Central Intelligence Agency (CIA) No one who opposes this all-powerful cartel can be safe. They imposed 'grand theft, gasoline' on the

American people without any opposition worth mentioning from our elected representatives in Washington. The 'Golden Handshake' is a story of corruption which surpasses anything in modern history.

The House and Senate either will not do anything to stop the moguls from consuming our living, or else they are so afraid of its power that they will not make even the feeblest attempt to curb it.

Let the American petroleum industry produce charts and graphs and tell as much as they want; let their economists explain why we have to bear their cost of doing business; dubious deals; why the American people have to pay the salaries of the CIA engaged in upholding their monopoly, but it becomes evident that their efforts amount to the Big Lie when we know the facts!

What are some of the facts? Due to the manner in which the cartel has manipulated tax laws, since 1976 not a single new oil refinery has been built in America, while over in Saudi Arabia, thanks to American tax dollars paid out in bribes to the Saudi royal family, billions of dollars have gone into expanding oil facilities.

In the period 1992 to the present, no less than 36 refineries in America have closed. Between 1990 and the present, the number of American oil rigs has declined from 657 to 153. The number of Americans engaged in oil exploration operations in America has dwindled from 405,000 to 293,000 in a matter of ten years. So where is the oil we are using in increasing quantities coming from? The Middle East! Thus, we are being hit with three sledgehammer blows:

> The tax structure in America is making it impossible for independent oil drillers to stay in the business of oil exploration.

> Refining and distribution of the finished product is a monopoly.

> ➤ The beneficiary of this treachery is ARAMCO which can charge higher prices for gasoline derived from Saudi sources and earn themselves obscene profits at the cost of the American motorist.

Theirs is a racket which makes the wealth of the combined Mafia 'families' in America look like pocket change, and perhaps that makes the oil cartel members racketeers. Why is the RICO statute not being enforced against the Petroleum Industry? Thanks to their agents in the legislature, they have been able to get away with 'grand theft, gasoline' for decades.

Let the legislators take up this deplorable case and let them put an end to the bare-faced robbery at the gasoline pumps, which because of their silence, has become a permanent fixture on the American landscape. Be sure of one thing, the racketeers of the oil cartel will not stop until they have imposed a price of $4.50 per gallon on all of us.

CHAPTER 17

Rockefeller Complains to the state dept. Britain invades Iraq

The history of the lust of Britain and the United States to take possession of Iraq's oil dates back to 1912, when President Saddam Hussein, the great villain, who was hanged by a kangaroo court was not yet born, and when Henri Deterding, founder of the Royal Dutch Shell Company was granted oil concessions in a number of oil- producing states. In 1912, Deterding turned his attention to U.S. oil interests in California by acquiring a number of small and large oil companies, notably the California Oil-Field Company and Roxana Petroleum.

Naturally, John D. Rockefeller's Standard Oil Company lodged complaints against Deterding with the State Department, but Deterding allowed Standard to purchase stock in Shell's California enterprises in order to nullify the complaint. What old John D. did not seem to realize was that by eagerly snapping up Deterding's offers, he was subsidizing Shell's efforts to corner the American market. But all that changed in 1917 when President Wilson, in flagrant abuse of his oath of office, dragged America into WWI.

Suddenly, overnight, Britain, who had been attacking both Standard and particularly, Deterding of Royal Dutch Shell, did an about face. The villain of the piece became Kaiser Wilhelm II and Henri Deterding, suddenly became an important ally.

A short year before that change of heart, the British invaded Iraq in the most blatant and flagrant violation of international law, but failed to reach Mosul when they were deserted by France, its troops failing to back the British invaders. Instead of helping the British, France signed an agreement with Turkey, ceding a part of the Mosul oil fields to Turkey. Imagine the gall of these aggressors! They called Stalin a 'dictator,' yet no one has acted more dictatorially toward Iraq than Britain, France, Turkey and latterly, the United States.

The in-fighting between the would-be robbers of Iraqi oil went on until the San Remo conference of April 24, 1920, at which time it was agreed by Britain, France and Turkey, that the largest part of the Mosul would be ceded to Britain, for certain considerations involving a petroleum conglomerate, which did not include Iraq and from which Iraq derived no benefit. The Iraqi government was never consulted at any time.

In May of 1920, the State Department went to the U.S. Congress to complain about Britain taking the Mosul and several other substantial oil fields. Not that the State Department cared about the rights of the Iraqi people. I repeat, Iraq was never consulted while its lands and oil riches were being parceled off and sold to the highest bidder-members of the petroleum cartel. Rather, what the State Department was concerned about was that John D. Rockefeller and Standard Oil had been completely shut out of the Mosul 'deal.'

The State Department pressured and pushed for a new all-parties conference to be held in Lausanne. Under cover of ostensibly agreeing to meet with the U.S. and other 'interested nations,' the British used the time to launch another invasion of Iraq, and this time, British troops succeeded in reaching and taking over the Mosul. At last, Britain had its hands on the great prize! Of this brazen act of aggression, the world press said nothing.

If ever there was any doubt about the aggression by the British

Imperial Forces in South Africa in their no-holds barred quest to wrest control of the gold away from the Transvaal Republic in South Africa, it was dispelled years later by the actions of British armed forces in Iraq.

The quest for gold begun by Cecil John Rhodes on behalf of his masters, the Rothschild's, was now being repeated in Iraq, this time, for 'black gold.' There was no attempt to invite Iraq to Lausanne to soften the image of 'grand theft, crude oil.' In fact the British press gloated over the success of Whitehall's so-called diplomacy.

Try as it might, Turkey could not dislodge the British from what it saw as its legitimate right to Iraq's oil! Just think about that for a moment. It was not until the April 23, 1921, second Lausanne Conference that Turkey conceded that Britain had what it quaintly described as, 'legal possession' of the Mosul, this without the consent of the people of Iraq, to whom the Mosul belonged. Thus, solely by virtue of its superior armed might, did Britain take over the Mosul and the super-rich Ahwaz and Kirkuk oil pools.

No wonder the British correspondent of the *London Financial Times* crowed:

> "We British shall have the satisfaction of knowing that three enormous fields situated within close proximity of each other, and capable of supplying the oil requirements of the Empire for many years to come, are being almost entirely developed by British enterprise."

Source: *The London Financial Times,*
British Museum London

But the British triumph was short-lived. When the League of Nations was forced to meet again by an irate France, Russia and Turkey, it refused to recognize Britain's armed aggression-acquisition of the Mosul as legitimate, and returned it to its rightful owners, the people of Iraq. Ever since then, Britain and the United States have been trying to steal the Mosul away from Iraq and the fighting with Iraq today is in the hope that their cherished dream will become a reality.

Perhaps we will now have a more balanced view of why George Bush, the elder, ordered U.S. armed forces to attack Iraq, even though he must have been aware that he was without a mandate from the Congress, and therefore, in violation of his oath of office and in defiance of international law. The United States House and Senate failed to halt the illegal action by cutting off funding, which constitutional action it was too frightened to take; frightened of reprisals of the Committee of 300. Fear plays a huge role in the destinies of nations. Fear has not gone away. When the Rothschild's ordered a body of men to frighten the government of France into accepting its terms for financial control of the nation, a large force of cut-throat Communist were rushed to the Paris Communes. Frightened by the show of force, the French government capitulated to the Rothschild demands. It seems the U.S. Congress found itself in the same predicament - too frightened of the Petroleum Cartel to act against it. If the United States of America was not being run by the Committee of 300, the Rothschilds, the Rockefellers and their petroleum cartel, backed by the might of the international bankers and if so many key members of the U.S. House and Senate were not dictated to by the Council on Foreign Relations (CFR), the United States House and Senate would have called a halt to the war of genocide against Iraq. The following partial list that we have is for 2006, but it gives some indication of the control of the CFR, which must have intensified in the last two years:

<table><tr><td>The White House</td><td>5</td></tr></table>

The National Security Council	9
State Department	27
U.S. Ambassadors serving abroad	25
Defense Department	12
Joint Chiefs of Staff	8
Judiciary	6
Senate	15
House	25

Since the United States House and Senate did not declare war on Iraq, nor give proper constitutional consent in the form of a mandated declaration of war, the invasion of Iraq in 1991 and in 2003 were clearly unlawful and illegal, and made the U.S. a nation of bandits under the control of the grandfather of all bandits, the moguls of the petroleum cartel. The men of the petroleum cartel, whose motto is 'We Fight for Oil,' have not neglected other areas: China, Alaska, Venezuela, Indonesia, Malaysia and the Congo. Their turn will come.

CHAPTER 18

Environment loses Alaska to oil

In April 1997, WIR told of a 'deal' with far wider ramifications and much wider in scope than any other that was in the making. In order for Tommy Boggs who was the lobbyist piloting the deal, and Governor Tony Knowles to succeed in turning loose the huge oil reserves beneath Alaska's state parks for the ultimate exploitation by British Petroleum (BP) they needed the fullest cooperation of Interior Secretary Bruce Babbitt.

Knowles cleared Tommy Boggs' game plan with President Clinton during a 'coffee' at the White House, and was invited to sleep over one night in January 1995. The game plan was then spelled out by Alaska's Lieutenant Governor Fran Ulmer, at another of those interminable 'coffees,' this time, rather appropriately, held in the White House Map Room on the morning of February 28, 1996.

Having set the course of action — to sell Alaska's national oil reserves to British Petroleum who would use the oil to supply China's ever- growing need for crude oil, Knowles began with some grandstanding of his own, using his 1996 State of the State message as his forum:

> Just five years ago they said we would be turning off the lights on the industry with one the State's largest payrolls. Now our motto should be that old bumper sticker: 'Dear Lord, please let there be one more oil boom, and I promise

we won't waste it.'

Knowles got an answer to his prayer; on February 7, Interior Secretary Bruce Babbitt stepped up to the batter's plate, right on cue. Enjoying the limelight Babbitt tried to excuse putting the cart before the horse — that an environmental study of the proposed new drilling area should have been completed first, and Babbitt said he would guarantee that the environment would be respected, even though he was now prepared to approve the venture, even before any studies had even begun, much less been completed.

Babbitt announced a new way of doing business with the dictators of the petroleum industry, while at the same time putting the Congress in its place, flouting the National Environmental Policy Act, which clearly spelled out that such studies are to be completed and reported on to Congress before any drilling can commence in national park lands. With his halo positively glowing, Babbitt told the people of Alaska and the Nation:

> We'd like to break the adversarial style and see if we can put together some new way of doing business with the oil industry. I think we've got lots of possibilities.

Again, no mention was made, that the ultimate beneficiary would be British Petroleum (BP). The 'we've' Babbitt was referring to was the giant Shell Oil and a group of multinational oil companies which have always demonstrated their contempt for the laws of the nations which they frequently disobeyed.

The petroleum cartel puts the 'we've' in proper perspective and proves beyond a shadow of a doubt that here is a rapacious group, a cabal, capable of doing very great harm without concern for the consequences of its actions, and always securing their objective, no matter who opposes them, or how they threaten U.S. national security.

Congress has a constitutional obligation to haul the modern-day robber barons before special committees to protect a great asset of the people of the United States and raise serious objections to Alaskan oil going to China, a Communist nation. But Congress has failed in a most lamentable manner to do its duty.

Continuing the masquerade, Babbitt stated:

> I want to get out on the ground this summer and I want to look at every square inch (23 million acres) of the National Petroleum Reserve. My plans now are to fly to Anchorage, change planes at Barrow, and then I want to disappear into the N.P.R. for as much time as I need, to understand every geological structure, every lake, and examine every wildlife issue, so that I will be prepared to be a meaningful participant in this process.

This is a perfect example of how the American people are the most connived, lied-to, people on this planet. We can see just how deceiving this statement of intent by Babbitt was, when we consider how much time it would take to explore 'every inch' of 23 million acres. The National Petroleum Reserve (NPR) is the size of Indiana, but the secretary did not elucidate how he proposed to 'explore every inch of it,' or explain how he could afford to be away from his office for a year at the very least. Would the secretary be accompanied by representatives of British Petroleum and have the entire Prudhoe Bay locked up, from which small oil prospecting companies would be summarily ejected?

The American people were soon to find out: The NPR was to become the private preserve of BP, Shell (two of the largest foreign petroleum companies in the world), Mobil, ARCO and the rest of the Jackson Hole, Wyoming conspirators, for the benefit of the 'Seven Sisters.' Here was a clear case where profit was put ahead of U.S. national security. In other times, it would have been called treason.

Then President Clinton became the personal property of the petroleum cartel, as witness his curtain-raising speech on their behalf:

> "Many Americans do not know it, but a significant percentage of the oil and natural gas produced in the United States comes from federal lands. Until today, regulatory red tape and conflict in court rulings had discouraged many companies of taking full advantage of these resources."

He should also have pointed out that the Alaskan oil deal was oil from our national emergency pool which is not supposed to be touched. It is one of our national strategic reserves! What was to follow was one of the biggest scams in the history of the U.S.; one that positively dwarfed the Tea Pot Dome Scandal, and fittingly, it was ARCO that gulped down Harry Sinclair's old company in 1969. What Clinton was alluding to was the trickery, chicanery, deceptive practices, and knavery, embarked upon in the last days of the 1996 summer session of the 104th Congress, which Congress, without any hindrance from the press, without any outcry from the environmental groups, without outcry from ABC, NBC, CBS, or any of the jackals of the media, slipped through one of the most arrogantly deceptively titled bills ever to sully the halls of power, 'The Federal Oil and Gas Simplification and Fairness Act.' The bill was the work of oil lobbyists who infest Congress.

What the 'Fairness Act' did was to pour money in a never ending stream into the already bulging coffers of the major oil companies. As I said earlier, this is a scandal which dwarfs the Teapot Dome Scandal, a two-bit affair when compared with the 'Federal Oil and Gas Simplification and Fairness Act.'

How the system worked was that a moratorium was declared on Federal audits for a period of seven years covering royalty payments to the Treasury for oil removed from Federal lands. More than this -- and we had to rub our eyes to make sure that what we were reading was actually in the Act — there is a clause which provides for the oil companies to sue the Federal government for 'overpayments' of royalties! And that is not all. The Act allows the robber barons to set their own 'fair market price' for oil drained from Federal lands belonging to the American people. Perhaps, readers won't believe this astounding clause? Neither did I, but after reading the bill several times, I saw that it is states exactly what it says it will do; allow massive benefits to be handed to two of the largest foreign oil companies in the world (BP and Shell) on a Congressional golden plate.

It is the market price of crude oil which determines the amount of royalties the oil companies must pay the Federal government, but a congressionally-sanctioned legal provision allows the oil companies to set their own price, which will, in the years to come, rob the people of billions of dollars in royalty payments. It is scam which is beginning to resemble the 1912 Federal Reserve Act swindle. This was the agenda for the Jackson Hole gathering of the conspirators at which Clinton played the genial host. Thus, for a comparatively small amount of money given away in campaign donations - $350,000 in the case of ARCO, literally billions of dollars were handed to the major oil companies who were to participate in the Alaskan oil for China rip- off. Poor American people, so leaderless in the Congress, without a champion to stand up for what is best for the United States; at the mercy of a group of super-charlatans practicing one thing and preaching another; how could they know just how they were being deceived, when Clinton vowed to veto any bill that would open up the 17 million acre Arctic Wildlife Refuge to drillers, while with his other hand, behind his back, he was opening the door to a far richer prize, the oil beneath the National Park Reserve oil reserves set aside for national emergency fuel.

The meeting at Jackson Hole Wyoming, stamping ground of the Rockefeller family was held to prepare the way for the oil for China deal. President Clinton played the role of a gracious host, and announced his intentions to his honored guests, happy that such esteemed personages had consented to enjoy his hospitality, in a setting much like that of a Mafia don, who brings together 'family' leaders to his estate on the shores of Lake Tahoe, wining and dining them like royalty. Indeed, royalty could not have done a better job had the venue been Balmoral Castle.

Thus, within a few short years of having promised the leaders of China, that they would have oil from our national emergency Alaskan oil reserve, the Clinton administration fulfilled its promise. Don't look to the Republicans to reverse the deal made with BP, Shell, Mobil and ARCO. Oil politics knows no party lines. Big money is mobile. Look what happened during the height of the Vietnam War.

In exchange for oil concessions off the Vietnam coast, Rockefeller Standard Oil flew doctors into Haiphong in North Vietnam to consult with a very sick Ho Chi Min. These were American doctors, who should have been tried for treason. A second source for verification is lacking, but the source said that Kissinger Associates brokered the deal. In any event, there we had Americans trading with the enemy in time of war while our soldiers were dying in the jungles and rice paddies of South Vietnam. Observe the arrogance of the petroleum cartel. They already knew that the U.S. would lose the war! How could this be? Quite simply, Henry Kissinger was to go to Paris to make a 'peace' deal with the North Vietnamese who already knew the date he would be going to Paris, and precisely how he would surrender Vietnam to Communist control.

George Bush, the elder, was in on the deal from the inception, having maintained good relations with Kissinger all through the war. We might call Kissinger a traitor, but he was serving a Republican president. It was no accident that oil man George Bush was sent to China, when there were others better qualified than he to complete the mission. But Bush knew the oil business, and oil was what China needed.

On his return from his visit to China, Bush set the wheels in motion for and on behalf of the Chinese Government, who had been promised a lion's share of Alaskan oil. And so we move now from the Middle East to Alaska, where we find the Petroleum Cartel busy robbing the American people of their Alaskan oil reserves in defiance of the law; proving once again, as if any proof were needed, that the Petroleum Cartel was a law unto themselves, above the reach of any government on this planet.

China has many good, high ranking friends in the rapacious petroleum industry, neither knowing nor respecting national and international boundaries or national sovereignty.

One such friend is ARCO, which holds a place high on the ladder of Committee of 300 companies and who, along with another jewel in the crown of Committee of 300 oil companies BP, began scheming and plotting to ship Alaskan crude oil to the massive Zhenhai refinery on the outskirts of Shanghai, which was ready to start its operations.

Lodwrick Cook was ARCO's former CEO and like old soldiers or political party leaders who never fade away, Cook was active in 1996, stumping for the reelection of his old friend, Bill Clinton, the 'outsider' from Arkansas. In 1994, the same year Cook got Tony Knowles elected as Governor of Alaska, Cook was invited to the White House to celebrate his birthday with Bill Clinton, who presented his friend with a giant birthday cake, and then allowed him to travel with Commerce Secretary Ron Brown to China, where the two told the Chinese government that ARCO would invest billions in the new Zhenhai refinery. In response to questions by the Chinese government delegation, the sources said Cook assured them that crude oil from Alaska would be forthcoming for the Zhenhai refinery in spite of the fact, that in August 1994 there was a permanent prohibition on exporting Alaskan oil. Approximately one year after the Brown-Cook trip to China, Robert Healy, ARCO'S president of governmental affairs, was invited to the White Coffee House to have coffee with Al Gore and Marvin Rosen, then the finance chairman of the Democratic National Committee. To show ARCO's gratitude, Healy left a $32,000 'tip' for the DNC.

Enter Charles Manatt, former chairman of the Democrat Party and head of Manatt, Phelps and Phillips, Mickey Kantor's old alma mater, which lobbying company handles and fronts for major oil companies, EXXON, Mobil, BP, ARCO and Shell. On May 26, 1995, Manatt was invited to yet another White House coffee for a get together with Clinton.

Manatt dished out $117,150 in a show of appreciation, and then, quite independently, of course, Kantor as an insider member of the Clinton cabinet, set up a drumbeat, demanding that the ban on exporting Alaskan oil be lifted. Hitherto, Federal law prohibited export of oil in the National Petroleum Reserve as it was supposed to be a reserve stock in time of national emergency.

In my work of 1987 'Environmentalism: the Second Civil War has Begun,' the major oil companies are exposed as the biggest contributors to the 'Earth First' and 'Greenpeace' ecology movements. Spelled out are the reasons for the seeming contradiction why the ecology movement would be supported for decades with large sums of money donated by the major oil companies. Environmentalism is a ruse when it comes to oil lands.

The major oil companies wanted the national reserve lands, much of which held huge reserves of oil, kept free of 'outsiders' so that when the time came, they would be able to move in and take possession of the oil reserves beneath the national parks lands at bargain prices. As far as national wildlife reserves in Alaska are concerned, that day arrived in 1996. The hypocritical oil majors cared little or nothing about the ecology or protecting the wildlife of the areas; witness what they have done to Prudhoe Bay.

In 1996, famous lobbyist Tommy Boggs was called in to work the oracle of lifting the ban on Alaskan crude oil. Boggs is the son of the late Sen. Hale Boggs, whose mysterious disappearance in the Alaskan wilderness in 1972 has never been solved. Tommy Boggs is the chief Washington lobbyists for the Patton Boggs law firm and his clients included ARCO, EXXON, BP, Mobil and Shell and, just coincidentally, he was a close golfing friend of Bill Clinton.

A formidable lobbyists, Boggs was believed chiefly responsible for getting the 104th Congress to reverse the ban on exporting Alaskan crude oil, and so it was that in 1996, Clinton signed an order lifting the ban, as Ron Brown and Lodwrick Cook had promised the government of China two years earlier, would happen. It would take a blind man not to see that the skullduggery to rob the nation of its Alaskan oil reserves was set in motion in 1994. In 1996, after the 'coffees' at the White House, Pres. Clinton handed the major oil companies involved in China and Alaska, an astonishing bonus. The press should have shouted this sell-out from the housetops, but Dan Rather, Peter Jennings and Tom Brokaw, not to mention Larry King, were as silent as the grave about this momentous event. Quietly, and without fanfare, Clinton ended the ban on exporting our reserve oil stocks beneath the Alaskan wilderness and handed the petroleum giants a free gift of billions of dollars.

While heating oil and petroleum prices were at an all-time high in 1996, Clinton and his controllers were busy selling the United States from out under the feet of We, the People, for substantial cash contributions to his reelection campaign fund.

Foreshadowing this national disaster — only he didn't call it that — Tommy Boggs wrote a memo to his clients forecasting that he would get the ban on the export of Alaskan oil lifted by the 104th Congress.

But that was not the only shock which the American people were handed; on the last day of the 1996 summer session of Congress, Clinton also signed the 'Federal Oil and Gas Simplification and

Fairness Act.' As the name suggests, the bill was intended to mislead, and was more skullduggery on a massive scale. The 'fairness' bit was not intended to benefit the American people. In fact the Act was a wholesale sell-out by the Clinton administration of the American people. Simply put, what the legislation did was to play ducks and drakes with the price of oil the companies were to pay royalties on to the Federal Government.

The gigantic government-sanctioned rip-off of the American people allowed the majors of the petroleum industry to receive billions of dollars absolutely free. The Act is one of the most audacious daylight robberies ever to be carried out by the petroleum industry. And throughout this great robbery, the jackals of the media - print and electronic ~ remained deathly silent.

Enter Tony Knowles the Governor of Alaska. Lest we forget, ARCO doled out $352,000 in contributions during the 1996 elections. In 1994, Knowles got $32,000 and it helped elect him as the first Democrat Party Governor of Alaska, probably also the first governor of any State to sleep over at the White House, all part of the overall conspiracy to rob the American people.

CHAPTER 19

Libyan oil and the bombing of Pan Am 103

This is not the end of the story about the hijacking of Alaskan oil by the major oil companies. It is more like the first chapter in an ongoing saga, which will end with the American people the losers, while China and the Petroleum Cartel walk away with billions in illicit loot.

The next chapter in our saga of the Petroleum Industry shifts to Libya, for the intrepid cartel men who never sleep and are ever on the move, their slogan being, 'We Fight for Oil,' had long eyed Libyan oil as the bonanza, if only they could get their hands on it. Libyan leader Moamar Khaddafi had proved more than a match for the men of the Petroleum Cartel, and all of their efforts to depose him having failed, new methods and new opportunities were constantly sought.

They could not poison him; Khaddafi always had his food tasted. Assassination would be difficult, as he never traveled except in the company of his trusted, bribe-proof guards, and he never used public transport. Then, quite unexpectedly, their opportunity came with the bombing of Pan Am Flight 103, which went down over Lockerbie, Scotland, killing all 270 people on board. Aided (as always) by the CIA, the cartel men went to work.

In their determination to wrest control of Libyan oil from its rightful owners, the men of the Petroleum Cartel jumped on the chance to charge Moamar Khaddafi for the tragic bombing of Pan Am Flight 103. In pursuance of their goal, the men of the

Petroleum Cartel easily convinced President Ronald Reagan that it was desirable and necessary for the U.S. Air Force to bomb the Libyan capital of Tripoli. To this end, U.S. bombers were launched from bases in Britain, and they did indeed bomb Tripoli in flagrant violation of the United States Constitution, the 1848 Neutrality Act, the four Geneva Conventions and The Hague Arial Bombing Convention to which the U.S. is a signatory. Such is the power of the petroleum cartel, that this unconstitutional attack on a country against which the U.S. never declared war; a country which had never engaged in any proven act of belligerency against the United States, was not condemned as an unlawful act, but was welcomed by the American people, long the victims of the infernal Tavistock Institute brainwashing machine, and the jackals of the press. Khaddafi lost a member of his family in this attack which broke his resolve to retain Libyan independence. Total accounting for the tragedy of Pan Am 103 will never be made, because of the vast propaganda machine available to the U.S. and British governments will see to it that the truth will never come out about this crime committed against the American people. The observation made by Benjamin Disraeli in 1859, agent for Lionel Rothschild is worth quoting:

> "All great events have been distorted, most of the important causes concealed, some of the principal players, never appear, and all who figure are so misunderstood and misrepresented that the result is a complete mystification. If the history of England is ever written by one who has the knowledge and the courage, the world would be astounded."

The British and American governments have demonstrated their uncommon ability to prevaricate and obfuscate in the most convincing manner. This is not a new talent, but it was considerably sharpened by the staffers of Wellington House of which Bernays, a Rothschild relative were the chief propagandists. This major propaganda mill was developed in the early stages of WWI, to counter the lack of enthusiasm of the British people for the war against Germany.

The story of the bombing of Pan Am 103 began on July 3, when an Iranian Airways Airbus, filled with 290 passengers en route to Haj in Mecca, was shot down by the U.S.S. Vincennes. The Airbus having taking off from the civilian airport of Bandar Abbas in Iran was just reaching its cruising altitude when an Aegis missiles fired by the USS Vincennes slammed into it. The Airbus went down killing all on board. Did the crew of the Vincennes know that their target was a civilian airliner? Without exception, all those who were consulted about the attack confirmed that the Airbus could not have been mistaken for anything but a civilian airliner. An outraged Khomeini kept a relatively calm composure, but secretly he had commanded the chief of the Pasdarans (Secret Service) to select four U.S. Flag carrier airlines to be targeted for a revenge attack. The head of the Pasdarans reported back to Ali Akbar Mohtashemi that he had chosen Pan American Airways as the target.

The plan was presented to Mohtashemi in Teheran on July 9, 1988, and endorsed by him for immediate action. It was then given to a former Syrian Army officer, Col. Ahmed Jabril, in command of the Popular Front for the Liberation of Palestine (PFLP), which was headquartered in Damascus under the protection of the late President Hafez al Assad.

The die was cast when Jabril targeted Pan Am Flight 103, starting in Frankfurt, Germany, with a stopover in London - with its final destination, New York. Although subsequently denied by Britain and the United States, Jibril himself said he was paid $10 million to carry out his mission, and there were reports that alleged the CIA actually traced wire transfers amounting to $10 million, to a numbered Swiss account held by Jibril.

There can be no dispute about the expertise of Jibril who was known to be a master-bomber who had chalked up a string of bombings against British, Swiss and American planes, dating back to 1970. Moreover, Jibril was very vain about his bomb-switches, which bore their own trademark and method of triggering, which intelligence experts confirmed, stamped Jibril's 'work' as unmistakable.

Two Libyan nationals, Abdel Basset Ali al-Megrahi and Lamen Khalifa Fhimah, were charged with the bombing, yet they had no such expert bomb-making experience, nor did they have the needed facilities to make such a sophisticated bomb. There has never been any proof positive, any evidence that would link the bomb that brought down Pan Am 103 to the two accused men. On the contrary, there was a large body of evidence that stamped the outrage as the work of Jibril and the PFLP. Clear evidence existed that working on Jibril's team was expert bomb-maker Hafez Kassem Dalkamoni and Abdel Fattah Ghadanfare, both living in Frankfurt, Germany. On October 13, Dalkamoni was joined by another expert bomb-maker, one Marwan Abdel Khreesat, whose residence was in Amman, Jordan. Khreesat was known among Syrian officers and the PFLP as the best 'explosives man' in the business. More than that, Khreesat had lately begun to work both sides of the streets - he was also an informant for the German intelligence service, BKA. I published the full story under the title 'PANAM 103, A Trail of Deadly Trail of Deception,' in 1994.

An international campaign of calumny and slander was launched against Libya for being responsible for the bombing. No basis in fact was ever provided, other than the names of the two Libyans accused of the crime. When Libya refused to surrender the 'accused' to a Scottish court, an international boycott against the sale of Libyan crude oil was instituted, accompanied by a war of words against Libya, the like of which had not been seen since World War II.

As already stated, an impressionable President Reagan was easily induced to agree to a bombing raid on Tripoli. All Libyan assets in foreign banks, where traceable, were frozen. In fact, an all-out war was launched against the country. A Libyan civilian plane en-route to Tripoli from Sudan was shot down by 'forces unknown' in the mistaken belief that Khaddafi was on board. All commerce between Libya and the West was halted.

Libya was falsely accused of making 'weapons of mass destruction' and placed on the State Department's list of countries officially sponsoring international terrorism. All the while an international clamor for Libya to turn over the two 'suspects' to Britain or Scotland was kept up and increased in intensity. Wild unsubstantiated accusations against Libya flew thick and fast. In the meantime, Libya was still selling oil to Western Europe and Russia, but some countries, like France and Italy, began chafing under restrictions and were privately negotiating for the boycott to end. But Britain and the U.S. would have none of it, and Robin Cook (British Foreign Minister) told European Union ministers that Khaddafi was agreeable to handing over the two 'suspects,' provided they were tried in a Scottish court, an announcement which Khaddafi at first labeled 'a lie.' Russia began to increase its purchases of Libyan crude to the point where Britain and the U.S. realized that the boycott wasn't going to be effective for very much longer.

A team of American negotiators was flown to Tripoli to secure an agreement with Khaddafi that would be face-saving for the two major powers and allow Libya to get off the hook, while seeming to comply with demands that the two 'suspects' be handed over to a Scottish court established on neutral territory. This would satisfy Moslem law that citizens of Libya never be extradited to stand trial in foreign countries accusing them of a crime, which is a solution one would expect from devious minds.

The venue for the 'Scottish court' was Camp Zeist in Holland, since Holland was not one of the accusing countries seeking to prosecute the two Libyans. That took care of the Moslem law part of things. Camp Zeist was declared 'Scottish territory' in a magic show that would have done Las Vegas proud. The two 'suspects' then 'volunteered' to stand trial and a date was set for proceedings against them to get under way.

Why was the jurisdiction under Scottish law? The answer is that in addition to the cause of action having arisen in Scotland, Scottish law allows a special third verdict; that of 'not proven,' which is somewhere between guilty and not guilty. Khaddafi was assured that the evidence presented by the prosecution would not be enough to convict the Libyans. Thus while 'justice' would be seen to be done, the Libyans would walk free. But the promise was not kept.

This was the background to the trial which began amid a great deal of fanfare. The prosecutor's case against al Megrahi and Khalifa was weak. The defense lawyer waited until the trial got under way, before announcing their defense. They would submit evidence that Jabril and the PFLP had done the bombing and call 32 witnesses to back up their defense. The experts I spoke with are of the opinion, that if the trial got to a point where it looked as if the PFLP witnesses would actually appear, the trial would be halted on the grounds of 'not proven.' The very last thing Britain and the United States wanted was for the full facts to come out in an open court. In exchange for his 'cooperation' Khaddafi was given a guarantee that the boycott against Libya would be lifted and the spigot of Libyan crude oil again be turned on.

The principal beneficiaries would of course be members of the Petroleum Cartel. The real villain responsible for the dastardly Pan Am crime was never charged. What about the USS Vincennes and the Iranian Airbus it destroyed? That too was part of the agreement made by the government within a government. It would be officially declared that the crew of the Vincennes mistakenly believed that it was under attack by a military plane.

The only ones to benefit were the Petroleum Cartel who almost immediately began making huge profits out of the sale of Libyan crude. As for the relatives of those who died at the hands of Jabril's PFLP, the closure they have sought for twelve years eluded them, no matter that the official verdict pronounced two innocent men guilty of the dastardly bombing.

One note needs to be added, and that is the role played by George Bush and Margaret Thatcher in ensuring that a blanket would be thrown over any full investigation of the bombing of Pan Am 103 that might be called for at a later date. Member of Parliament for Scotland, Tom Dalyell stated in the House that,

> 'British and American authorities are not interested in finding the truth because it would be uncomfortable for them.'

Dalyell was the MP who single-handedly pursued Thatcher for her criminal act of ordering a British submarine to torpedo and sink the Argentinean cruise ship 'Belgrano' in international waters, in gross violation of the Geneva Convention.

Because of Dalyell's relentless pursuit, Thatcher lost the confidence of her controllers and was forced out of office in disgrace and prematurely retired from public life. There is no doubt that the two people who would suffer the most embarrassment if the truth ever came out would be George Bush and Margaret Thatcher. Terrorism of another kind was then staged on the border of Kuwait and Iraq. The corrupt dictatorial regime of the Al Sabahs scored a major triumph in persuading George Bush to issue a by-proxy order to a civilized Christian nation to once again rain cruise missiles down on an already suffering Iraq as collective punishment for an alleged attempt on the life of Bush the elder. Not everybody accepts the word of the ruthless Al Sabah dictators that the alleged plot to assassinate Bush was genuine. Many countries expressed grave doubts about the validity of the Al Sabah claim. An intelligence source had this to say:

> … The 'evidence' supposedly held by the Al Sabahs would be thrown out of any U.S. or British court. The 'evidence' is so faked; that it is no wonder the U.S. government will not dare to reveal it in an open forum. This thing (the alleged attempt to assassinate George Bush by Iraqi nationals) is so

trumped-up and outrageous that one wonders about the depth of depravity into which the United States has descended. If there were any senators in the least bit independent they should demand that Clinton present his evidence to them in open committee session, but of course, Clinton has no evidence that would stand up to scrutiny in an open court where witnesses would be under oath, so the senators were able to duck their duty.

An observer who attended the trial said:

> The Iraqis who were charged were ordinary smugglers with no experience in intelligence or explosives. A more unlikely bunch would be hard to find-not the kind of people the Iraqi government would employ if they wanted to kill George Bush. The truck allegedly containing explosives was actually packed full of contraband goods and 'found' miles away from the Kuwait University, the place where the 'Iraqi intelligence agents' were alleged to be heading to carry out the 'plot' to assassinate George Bush.

The case against the two Iraqi smugglers is so full of holes, and so shrouded in double-talk, obfuscation, manufactured 'evidence' that it would be a good plot for a Laurel and Hardy comedy if it were not so tragic. U.S. investigators interviewed the two men who confessed to the charge of attempting an attack on George Bush, but any confession obtained while the accused were in the hands of the Al Sabah 's had to be treated with the utmost skepticism. Kuwait has a vile record of torture, lynching, and hatred of foreigners-especially Iraqis, skillful propaganda and outright lying. The Al Sabah family is as cruel, vindictive, dictatorial and barbaric as any in the world today. One cannot trust their word. The whole episode smells of a clumsy, hastily-contrived set-up to make Bush look as if he was in danger.

In any event, let us suppose for one minute that the inept would-be terrorists had come to Kuwait with the intention of assassinating George Bush. Why then was Iraq not brought before the United Nations and or the International Court of Justice at The Hague?

If Bush and the Al Sabahs were so anxious to wrap their acts in the mantle of the United Nations, why didn't the U.S. and Kuwait go to The Hague and the U.N. Security Council to present their case? The United States should not have been a party to this cruel charade. Not one shred of verifiable evidence was produced at the 'trial' of these two poor, convenient scapegoats. The whole affair was a disgrace, a political act, which had nothing to do with judicial punishment of a crime.

The U.S. has now started punishing any nation that dares to disagree with it, and we are operating under the dubious premise that might is right. We are fast becoming the world's Number One Bully Boy. It is public knowledge, the Petroleum Cartel moguls paid a number of countries large sums of bribe money to join in the illegal war against Iraq. Countries that were paid a bribe were enumerated in reports, including the amounts paid.

One report dealt with the Al Sabah deal done with Hill and Knowlton, the celebrated advertising agency, for which this firm was paid the sum of $10 million to convince the American people that they needed to rescue the Al Sabah dictators.

The outright well-coached, well-rehearsed lying of Nayira Al Sabah before a Senate committee was the way Hill and Knowlton sold their crooked deal to America, backed all the way by the kept prostitutes of the controlled media. Then from an altogether reliable source, the London Financial Times, there was confirmation of the allegations made against the Al Sabah dictators and their American henchmen back in 1990 and 1991. According to the Financial Times of July 7, the Al Sabahs used the Kuwait Investment Office (KIO) in London to parcel out cash to countries willing to be bribed to get out and bat for Kuwait in the Gulf War. The Financial Times said, '$300 million was used in the United Nations to buy votes in favor of Kuwait,' which was reported at the height of the Gulf War fever. 'This (the United Nations votes) provided the legal basis for Kuwait's liberation by multinational forces.'

The Al Sabahs, caught in the act, launched a furious counter-attack on the 'Financial Times' article. Finance Minister Nasser Abdullah al- Rodhan declared:

> "Kuwait has never resorted to these means at any time, either in the past, or at present. The charge was aimed at tarnishing the country's image and its right to restore its sovereignty following the 1990 Iraqi invasion."

The finance minister went on to say that the $300 million was stolen from the KIO, and that the perpetrators of the crime were merely trying to cover their tracks by accusing Kuwait of buying votes. Responsible Senate committees had a duty to investigate the charges and an even greater duty to find out why the United States went along with the despots in Kuwait and twice dropped cruise missiles on Baghdad, when we had no such constitutional right, legal or moral, to take such action. There is a crying need, even at this late hour, for the truth about Kuwait and Iraq to be brought before the American people, something the moguls of the Petroleum industry are determined to prevent. They will move heaven and earth to see that the Al Sabah dictators are protected, and will continue to lie about Iraq for as long as it takes. The remedy lies in the hands of We, the People. The way the Congress has been willing to bow and scrape to the Al Sabah dictators is nothing short of a national disgrace.

CHAPTER 20

A story that needs telling

A story that needs telling is the story of Venezuela, a country where the disequilibrium between the extreme poor and the extreme rich is more markedly obvious than usual. Venezuela has a history of being shamelessly exploited and sucked dry by the petroleum cartel with no benefits accruing to the country or its people. That was the situation when in 1998 the poor were organized by an ex-paratrooper, Hugo Chavez, and urged to go to the polls in record numbers. Chavez was elected as their president by a landslide that shook the overlords of the petroleum cartel to their foundation.

Once in office Chavez lost no time in keeping his election promises. The Venezuelan Congress, in the pockets of the oil barons for the last 30 years was dissolved. Chavez denounced the United States as the enemy of the poor of the nation. The new president instituted a hydrocarbon law very similar to the law passed by Mexican patriot President Carranza that took control of the oil industry back from the petroleum cartel and placed it squarely in the hands of the people of Venezuela.

Then Chavez hit the petroleum cartel where it hurt the most ~ in its pocket - by introducing a 50 percent increase in royalties to be paid by foreign oil companies. The state company Petroleos de Venezuela underwent a shake-up that left most of the pro-U.S. corporate heads without a job. This was a staggering blow to the United States and indeed to the rest of the world.

Venezuela was no small player in the oil industry. By 2004 it was the fourth-largest oil-exporter in the world and the number three crude oil supplier to the United States. Petroleos de Venezuela employed forty - five thousand people and earned $50 billion in annual sales. The former paratrooper with a booming voice had climbed boldly into the saddle of a wildly bucking bronco. The big question was how long it would be before the moguls of the petroleum cartel unhorsed him? By taking over this large industry, Chavez was suddenly thrust onto the world stage as a man to be reckoned with, somewhat like Dr. Mossadegh.

Maracaibo was the center of Chavez's' power. Oil workers were solidly behind him, and although lacking in money they had the majority when it came to elections. Like the huge oil geyser that burst from the earth on December 14, 1922 (one hundred thousand barrels a day gushed into the air for three days before it could be brought under control) the oil workers needed organizing and control. Chavez would have his work cut out to stop the petrol.

For the next forty years Venezuela grew from a dirt-poor impoverished South American country into the richest country on the continent. The OPEC oil embargo tripled Venezuela's national budget causing unwelcome attention from the predatory sharks cruising its international waters. The agents for the petroleum cartel persuaded the country to overspend. The International Monetary Fund (IMF) flooded the Venezuelan government with huge loans.

The stage was set for economic sabotage and it came with the collapse of world crude oil prices. Venezuela was about to discover that the kindly men in business suits carrying briefcases stamped 'IMF' also carried sharp daggers. The most impossible austerity measures were clamped on Venezuela. As a result, the poor had to repay the loans and the nation's per capita income fell by close to 40 percent.

The classic petroleum cartel take-over pattern was being established. Resentment and anger grew side-by-side until the pressure could no longer be contained. Rioting erupted, in which more than two hundred thousand people were killed. The burgeoning middle class was the hardest hit and most were reduced to being very poor by the next two years. Surprisingly, Chavez hung onto power. Would the U.S. mount another 'Kermit Roosevelt' type operation or would the country simply be invaded by U.S. armed forces mercenaries? But while the petroleum cartel was weighing its options, 9/11 intervened. Venezuela would have to wait. But it did not wait for very long. The first shots were fired by the New York Times painting Chavez as an enemy of freedom. American commentators were predicting massive labor unrest that would lead to the downfall of Chavez. Any analyst worthy of the name could see that the Iranian model was being applied to Venezuela; in fact Washington didn't seem to be inclined to hide it.

As in the case of General Huyser in Teheran, U.S. agitators were urging the oil workers to strike, and they did. The New York Times could barely contain its glee. Screaming headlines declared:

> Hundreds of thousands of Venezuelans filled the streets today declaring their commitment to a national strike, now in its 28th day, to force the ouster of President Hugo Chavez... In recent days the strike has reached a kind of a stalemate, with Mr. Chavez using non-striking workers to try and normalize his operation at the state-owned oil company. His opponents, led by a collation of business and labor leaders, contend that their strike will push the company, and thus the Chavez government, to collapse.

If one were to overlay the Kermit Roosevelt-CIA-General Huyser blueprint (the one that brought down the Shah), on the situation in Caracas, it would be a perfect match. U.S.-trained provocateurs were hard at work. Only this time it was not Kermit Roosevelt but one Otto J. Reich, a veteran rabble rouser with enormous experience in fomenting revolutions in Guatemala, Ecuador, the Philippines, South Africa, Chile, Nicaragua, Panama and Peru. In Washington the Bush administration raised glasses of champagne to toast the success of Reich in Venezuela. But their celebration was short-lived. Rallying his hard-core oil worker supporters, Hugo Chavez, the ex-paratrooper was able to keep the military on his side. All attempts by Reich to turn the officer-corps against their President fell flat. Reich had to tuck his tail between his legs and fly back to Washington post-haste.

Seventy-two hours later President Chavez took firm control of his government and immediately began to weed out traitors and paid hirelings of agent Otto Reich. Oil company executives who had prematurely changed sides were booted out of the country, along with a handful of disloyal army officers. Two of the coup leaders who admitted to complicity with Reich and his Washington bosses, were sentenced to twenty-years in prison. For once, the CIA had to retreat with a black-eye.

In another country under attack by the moguls of the petroleum cartel Iran was locked in combat with the inheritors of the Illuminati. Their carefully laid plans were crowned with seeming success with the coming to power of the Ayatollah Khomeini, fundamentalist leader, and in future it was to be the model for attacks on other selected nation-states with coveted natural resources.

Who the conspirators were, what their motives were and what they gained by destroying the Shah and installing a fanatic fundamentalist in his place will be examined during the course of this book. I shall attempt to throw some light on the mystery of the return of Iran to the Dark Ages from which it was trying so hard to emerge under the Shah's leadership, based on modernizing its oil industry.

The conspirators are the inheritors of the 18th Century secret order with blueprint laid down by Adam Weishaupt and his Order of the Illuminati, the illuminated ones. The list of prominent oil cartel men who are members of the Illuminati has never been made public, but all indications point to it being a substantial number. We will confine this to a brief account of the Illuminati.

The objective of Illuminism is to establish a One World Government by overturning the existing order and destroying all religions, especially Christianity. It calls for a New World Order, the 'Novus Seclorum' printed on the reverse of the $1 Federal Reserve notes. It calls for returning man to the Dark Ages, under a feudal system, where absolute control is exercised over every person in the world. Such a system was operated on a trial basis in the Soviet Union, run by the feudal lords of the Communist Party and was very close to being duplicated by the U.S., Britain and the USSR before it collapsed, and was deemed unworkable. It was this system that George Orwell had warned against.

The conspirators are known by a number of different names; the Venetian Black Nobility, the aristocrats and royal families, the Council on Foreign Relations, the Cini Foundation, the Fondi, and so on. The old families have exercised absolute power for the last five centuries, whether in Europe, Mexico, Britain, Germany or in the U.S. In the Soviet Union, the old families ('raskolniks') were overthrown only to be replaced by a new and far more repressive set of aristocrats. The plan calls for all nations to come under the direction of the 'Committee of 300.'

Most of the old European nobility profess Christianity as their faith, but in reality, they neither believe in it, nor practice its tenets. Instead the majority are cult worshippers. They do not believe that God actually exists. They believe religion is only a tool to be used to manipulate the masses of ordinary people, and through it, retain their iron grip upon the populace.

Karl Marx is mistakenly credited with saying that religion is the opiate of the masses. But the doctrine was formulated and followed hundreds of years earlier, by the very royal families who regularly attended the Christian Church, with an outward show of pomp and ceremony long before Marx was permitted to copy Weishaupt's blueprint and claim it as his own manifesto.

One of the oldest cults the Black Nobility follows closely is the Cult of Dionysus, which teaches that certain people are placed on Earth as the absolute rulers of the planet, and that all wealth and natural resources of earth belong to them. The belief took root some 4000 years ago, and then as now, its adherents call themselves the Olympians.

The Olympians make up part of the Committee of 300. Perpetuating the family line and its rule is the First article of Faith of the Olympians. They hold the belief that there is a scarcity of natural resources, more especially oil, which is reserved for their exclusive ownership. They say oil resources are being consumed and depleted much too rapidly by a burgeoning population, made up of 'useless eaters,' people of little value. The Olympians differ from Weishaupt in that whereas he desired a formalized group, a Novus Seclorum, a body, which would rule the earth openly, the Olympians were satisfied with a loosely knit organization, which is difficult to identify. The Olympians of today took up where Weishaupt left off, and they go by a variety of names: the Club of Rome, Communists, Zionists, Freemasons, the Council on Foreign Relations, the Royal Institute for International Affairs, the Round Table, the Milner Group, the Trilateral, Bilderberg Group and the Mont Pelerin Society, to name but a few of the major ones. There are many other interlocking and overlapping conspiratorial bodies. Selected members make up the Committee of 300 together with the crowned heads of Europe. All these bodies have one thing in common, and that is to control all natural recourses, of witch oil is high on their list.

The Club of Rome is the senior foreign policy organization charged with overseeing all other conspiratorial bodies around the world.

Brainwashing of entire nations is the specialty of the Tavistock Institute, along the lines developed by Brigadier General John Rawlings Reese in 1925, and still used today in 2008. It was one of Reese's trainees who successfully led the American people to believe that a small-time obscure politician from Georgia, James Earl Carter could make a successful leader of the most powerful nation in the world. The belief was that Carter would be the tool of the petroleum companies.

It was a decision taken by the Shah to free his country from the grip which the imperialist British and the United States oil companies, led by leading members of the Illuminati, had upon Iran that led to his downfall - as in the case of Dr. Verwoerd of South Africa and General Somoza of Nicaragua.

As detailed herein, the Shah made a separate oil deal with the Italian company ENI through its president, Enrico Mattei. He did so in the face of orders from Britain to deal only with Philbro, a giant conglomerate, and British Petroleum, part of what Mattei called 'the Seven Sisters' oil companies. The Shah also embarked on a $90 billion dollar nuclear power program in defiance of the orders of the British and the U.S. Illuminati oil leaders, not to do so. Averill Harriman, dean of the diplomatic corps was dispatched to Teheran to give the Shah a personal message from Washington; toe the line, or he would be next. Amongst those rioting in the streets of Teheran was a mullah named Ayatollah Khomeini, only this time he was rioting against the Shah, and not on his own behalf. Just to make sure that the Shah got the message, a strike by teachers in Teheran was organized by Richard Cottam, a university of Pittsburgh professor. Thus did the U.S. interfere in the sovereign affairs of Iran in gross violation of the U.S. Constitution and International Law, all in the name and power of the 'Illuminati leaders' of the petroleum cartel.

In response to such betrayal by the U.S. imperial power, the Shah phoned Kennedy and was invited to the White House in 1962.

An agreement between Kennedy and the Shah was reached. Iran would end independent negotiations with companies like ENI and work only with BP and Philbro; in return, the Shah would be allowed to fire Prime Minister Amini.

But when he returned to Teheran, the Shah did not keep his side of the agreement. He did fire Amini and went right on dealing with ENI besides actively seeking to make oil deals with several other countries. Kennedy was furious at being double-crossed, and he sent for General Bakhtiar who was in exile in Geneva at the time. Bakhtiar arrived in Washington in 1962 and went straight to the White House.

Shortly thereafter, serious riots erupted in Teheran with the Shah denouncing the feudal lords who wanted to return Iran to the Dark Ages of a secular state. In all some 5000 people died as a result of the Bakhtiar-U.S. instigated rioting. But in 1970 Bakhtiar's luck ran out; he strayed too close to the border with Iraq border, and was picked off by a sniper.

The world press said it was a 'hunting accident,' a cover-up for Bakhtiar's activities against the Shah, who in his memoirs 'In Answer to History' wrote:

> "I did not know it then, perhaps I did not want to know - but it is clear to me now, the Americans wanted me out. What was I to make of the sudden appointment of Ball to the While House as an adviser on Iran? I knew that Ball was no friend of Iran. I understood that Ball was working on a special report on Iran. But no one ever informed me what areas the report was to cover, let alone its conclusions. I read them months later when I was in exile, and my worst fears were confirmed. Ball was among those Americans who wanted to abandon me, and ultimately my country."

Too late the Shah saw, that anyone who befriended America was slated for betrayal, as shown by the examples of Vietnam, Korea, Zimbabwe (Rhodesia), Angola, the Philippines, Nicaragua,

Argentina, South Africa, Yugoslavia and then Iraq. At this point it is necessary to mention again the name of U.S. General Huyser. From January 4th until February 4th 1972, General Huyser was in Teheran. What was he doing there? His role has never been explained, either by the general himself, or by anyone else in government but later it came out that he was working with the CIA running 'a spoiler' operation. The Iranian military was without its commander in chief, the Shah, and thus leaderless, while Huyser filled the gap, playing a Judas role.

He persuaded the Shah to leave Teheran for a 'vacation,' which it said would help to cool the temper of the mobs. The Shah accepted what he thought was friendly advice, and left for Egypt. It was at this time that General Huyser was having day-to-day discussions with the Iranian generals. He told them that they were not to attack the street mobs, or the U.S. would cut off military supplies, spare parts and ammunition. At proper time Washington would give the order through the Shah to attack the mobs, Huyser said. But that order never came.

The Iranian army of 350,000 men was effectively sidelined, and the man who accomplished the astonishing feat was General Huyser who has never been called to account, not even by the U.S. Senate. When President Reagan came to the White House in later years, he sincerely wanted to get to the bottom of the Iranian story - he could have ordered General Huyser to appear before a Senate committee to explain his role. But President Reagan did nothing. Behind the scene the puppet-master James Baker III of the firm Baker and Botts was pulling the strings. This old Houston law firm was at the heart of 'protecting' its mighty oil company client's interests in Iran.

James Baker III was to play a decisive role in ramping up the 1991 Gulf War. In 1990 James Baker III let the world know why the U.S coveted Iraq and Iran's oil:

The economic lifeline of the industrial world runs from the

Gulf and we cannot permit a dictator such as this (Saddam Hussein) to sit astride that lifeline. To bring it down to the level of the average American citizen, let me say it means jobs. If you want to sum it up in one word, it is jobs.

The United States Constitution declares that the U.S. cannot meddle in the affairs of a sovereign nation, Baker and Botts through James Baker III believes it does not have to obey the Constitution. The Shah was standing in the way of the major oil companies and he could not be allowed to 'sit astride' that 'economic lifeline.'

Equally disturbing was the role played by the Carter administration in overthrowing the Shah. President Carter knew in advance that the U.S. embassy would be stormed if the Shah was admitted to the U.S., but he did nothing to protect the embassy from seizure. In fact, after Khomeini returned to Iran, the U.S. airlifted arms and spare parts to Iran, using Hercules and 747 cargo planes flying out of New York, with refueling stops in the Azores Islands.

The British government's mouthpiece, the Wall Street Journal, and the Financial Times of London later admitted this. It also disclosed that David Aaron of the CIA had put together a team of sixty agents, who were sent to Iran in January 1979 at the same time General Huyser arrived in Teheran. Particularly it was the Aspen Institute, home of the Committee of 300 in America that betrayed the trust of the Shah. It flattered him as a modern leader, and if the Shah had an Achilles Heel, it was his susceptibility to flattery. As a result of the blandishments of Aspen, he donated several million dollars to that Institute. Aspen promised to hold a symposium in Iran to deal with the subject 'Iran, Past, Present and Future.' Aspen kept its promise and the symposium was held at Persepolis in Iran. It was a gala affair, as the Shah and his wife wined and dined the gathering of distinguished participants. Had the Shah been properly informed he would have sent them packing immediately. But people who tell the truth are penalized; they do not occupy prestigious chairs at famous universities.

The Shah was given a glowing verbal picture of his enlightened rule. But behind the scenes, a very different picture emerged. In attendance at Persepolis were 10 of the top Club of Rome members, including its leader, Aurelio Peccei.

Other notables were Sol Linowitz of the legal firm, Coudet Brothers, and the man who later gave away our Canal at Panama (a member of the Committee of 300) Harlan Cleveland and Robert O. Anderson. Both men were senior members of the Aspen Institute.

Others in the know about the plot were Charles Yost, Catherine Bateson, Richard Gardner, Theo Sommer, John Oakes and Daniel Yankelovitch, the man who makes public opinion through polling activities. This was referred to by MI6 as the beginning of the 'reformation' of the Middle East.

CHAPTER 21

Reformation and a look at history

In the twentieth century, the 'reformation' is being carried on under the auspices of the American Anglophiles - the ruling elites - who were centered on a core group around the Handyside Perkins, Mellon, Delano, Astor, Morgan, Straight, Rockefeller, Brown, Harriman and Morgan family dynasties that made untold fortunes from the opium trade with China. Many of the major petroleum company's spring from this background. The Bush family, beginning with Prescott Bush, has always served as satraps for the cabal.

The 'Committee of 300' lists U.S. imperialists and their servants drawn from obedient British and American ruling cabal decided just prior to WWI that oil would be the bunker fuel of the British Navy and Mercantile Marine. Lord 'Jacky' Fisher was the first to recognize that bunkering for the Royal Navy would have to come from crude oil instead of coal as I detailed earlier herein.

When Winston Churchill became First Lord of the Admiralty, he commissioned MI6 to come up with a plan to take over the vast oil fields of Mesopotamia, with the transparent excuse to 'prevent such vast oil supplies from falling into the hands of the Germans. With WWI having successfully 'made the world safe for democracy,' at the dawn of 1919, the Oil Empire, not hampered by accountability to countries or nations, being in fact a group of fascist private corporations that ruled the world, wanted total and unchallengeable control over the vast oil reserves in the Middle East and southern part of the Soviet Union to pass into its hands.

To this end the '300' financed the nationalist movements rising up Germany, Italy and Japan with the hope that they would invade and control Russia. The Oil Rulers planned the defeat of the German, Italian and Japanese governments and to take control of the oil reserves in the Soviet Union. The Rockefeller circle planned to seize control of Persian Gulf oil from the British-Persian Oil cartel and seize control of Southeast Asian oil from Royal Dutch Shell. In 1939 and 1940, the Germans and Italians did not attack Russia as the 'Big Three' (a Tavistock - created tag) had expected. Instead, the brilliant German General Irwin Rommel smashed his Desert Army across North Africa to grab the Suez Canal and control all oil shipping through it. Rommel did not intend to stop at Suez, but planned to drive on through to Persia and toss the British out from the Persian-Mesopotamian oil fields. Meanwhile, after a failed attack on Russia in 1939, the Japanese swept through Southeast Asia and seized all the oil properties of Royal Dutch Shell. But with the defeat of Japan in 1945, most of those Royal Dutch fields came under the control of Rockefeller's Standard Oil.

Hitler's high command had planned to capture the oil fields in Romania and Baku by the end of 1939 thus assuring Germany its own oil sources. This was accomplished. Then, the brilliant General Irwin Rommel, in command of the army in North Africa, was to have captured the oil fields in Persia by 1941 and the oil fields in Russia in 1942. Only then would Hitler have sufficient fuel for securing Germany's future. But less than a week after the Pearl Harbor attack, the Japanese convinced Hitler to declare war on the United States. This was a strategic gesture as Hitler lacked the resources and manpower to go to war against the U.S.

It was also the worst possible mistake he could have made as it gave Roosevelt the excuse to come into the war on the side of the allies, just as Stimson, Knox and Roosevelt had planned. Hitler agreed only if the Japanese would attack Russia, since German troops were now bogged down in Russia and Hitler would gain strategic advantage if the Russians had to defend themselves from Japan on their eastern flank. When the Japanese failed to attack Russia, the German Army was driven back with very heavy losses and was without enough fuel supplies.

The Romanian oil fields in Ploesti were insufficient for Germany to carry on a war on two fronts, and Germany's war effort began to collapse in the face of the terrible bombing of deliberately targeted German worker housing under Churchill and 'Bomber Harris' of the RAF. The last major German campaign of WWII was the brilliantly planned and executed Battle of the Bulge, in which Field Marshal Gerd von Rundstedt was to attack the invading allies with his armor and drive through to the port of Antwerp and capture the Allied fuel dumps. This would halt the American and British forces and obtain the necessary fuel for Germany to continue its war effort. But General Eisenhower ordered the Allied fuel dumps burned and Germany was defeated by massive bombardment from the air, its fighter planes (including the new twin jet-engine fighter) not able to take to the air because they had no fuel plus a long period of inclement weather.

Turning to Russia, in the early 1950s, Occidental Petroleum's Armand Hammer, a satrap of the Rockefellers, negotiated a deal with Russian leader Joseph Stalin to buy Russian oil, in effect, stealing it from the Russian people just as would happen with 'Yukos' and the 2000 'Wharton School' of Chicago's plan to 'privatize' Russia's national property. Russian oil was then sold on the world market at a much higher price than Stalin would have got by marketing it himself, because few countries were willing to buy oil from Stalin.

Occidental Petroleum and the Russians constructed two large pipelines, from Russia's Siberian oil fields down along both sides of the Caspian Sea, terminating in the old British-Persian - now Standard Oil — oil farm tanks in Iran.

For the next 45 years, Russia secretly sent its oil out through those pipelines and Standard Oil sold the oil on the world market at the 'West Texas Crude' price by claiming it was Iranian oil. For almost fifty years most Americans were using gas refined from Russian by Standard Oil refineries located at large sea ports like San Francisco, Houston and Los Angeles to where most oil from the Persian Gulf was shipped.

Other oil pipelines were constructed through Iraq and Turkey. Russian oil was now called OPEC Arab-Iraq-Middle Eastern oil and began to be marketed as OPEC quotas, and at the even higher 'spot market' price. The huge swindle begun by Kissinger with the 1972 'Oil Crisis' was now fully believed and accepted.

Thus between 1972 and 1979, scores of millions of gulled Americans and Europeans suddenly experienced gasoline shortages and huge price increases which they meekly accepted without dissent. It was one of the most successful large-scale scams ever pulled off and remains so to this very day. In 1979, Russian oil interests tried to secure an alternate, short, safe oil pipeline route from Russia across neighboring Afghanistan. But the CIA got wind of the plan and created out of fresh air an outfit they called the 'Taliban.' One of its leaders was a Saudi by the name of Osama bin Laden, whose family had longstanding and very close ties to the Bush family.

Armed by the CIA, funded by Washington and trained by U.S. Special Forces, the Taliban was unleashed against the Russians who were called by American journalists 'the invaders.' The Taliban proved to be formidable guerillas and checkmated the construction of the pipeline.

But, there was a downside to all this; the Taliban, being very strict Muslims, insisted in shutting down Afghanistan's poppy-heroin trade run out of Britain and by the Eastern Liberal families along the U.S. Eastern seaboard. Thus from the very beginning there was planned obsolescence for the Taliban, who not being deceived, hung onto all of the American supplied arms - and the big stock of U.S. dollars. Several of its leaders visited the U.S and were received like honored guests at the Bush ranch in Texas.

When the new Khomeini-British-controlled regime in Iran came into power, the U.S. Petroleum Industry making U.S. government imperialist foreign policy, immediately threatened to seize $7.9 billion of Iranian assets in U.S. banks and financial institutions. On January 27, 1988 the Wall Street Journal, announced that Standard Oil had merged with British Petroleum.

This actually represented Standard Oil's sellout to British Petroleum, the name of the newly merged company being BP-America. The Wall Street Journal did not see fit to mention worries about the world-wide predatory marketing practices of the deceptively titled Standard Oil, nor did it report on the imperialist policies of Standard Oil. Over the past 13 years, BP-America has merged with, and now controls all of the ex-Standard Oil 'mini-companies,' which existed before the original breakup by the U.S. government in 1911.

Millions of American people have no idea how they have been led astray, gulled, lied to, connived, betrayed and cheated. They go on waving the U.S. flag and declaring their patriotism like the marvelous good, patriotic, trusting citizens they are. They will never know how they were hoodwinked and robbed. It is now possible to understand how President George Bush could again then lead a nation that was ever willing to follow blindly, into a morass in Iraq.

The battle for survival of smaller nations is not just for their survival against a ruthless enemy that will bomb and destroy their civilian infrastructure as the United States and its surrogate Israel, and Britain demonstrated in Iraq, Serbia and Lebanon. Now the desperate struggle of small nations against the United States and Britain is for dominance over the entire earth. Only Russia stands between an imperialist U.S. and the safety of the world. It is not a struggle by individual nations but a struggle against the U.S. imposed New World Order-One World

Government.

Bin Laden and Saddam Hussein became the spokesmen for the new wars against American imperialism, actually a new and much bigger war for Caspian Sea, Iraqi and Iranian oil, the 'open-ended war' promised by Mr. Bush without a murmur from the American Congress or a protest that what Bush proposed was unconstitutional. With 600 legislative heads nodding in assent, Bush received powers to which he was not entitled to under the highest law of the land, the U.S. Constitution.

To return to the Far East oil machinations: With the end of WWII at hand, General Douglas MacArthur was appointed by President Truman as the military Governor of Japan. MacArthur's role was that of assistant to Laurence Rockefeller, a grandson of old 'John D.' During the last six months of the war, preparations were afoot for an invasion of the Japanese home islands. Okinawa was turned into one big munitions dump. Some chroniclers near to MacArthur believe that Truman instructed Laurence Rockefeller to turn over the armaments to North Vietnam's Ho Chi Minh, for the nominal sum of one dollar U.S. in exchange for Ho's 'cooperation and goodwill.' If the 55,000 soldiers, who were to die in Vietnam, could they have but known about the deal, they would have raised the roof. But like all major conspiracies, the stench was carefully concealed beneath tons of 'air-freshener' in the form of 'good relations' with the Communists in diplomatic parlance. Translated it meant 'getting Rockefeller hands on the considerable oil pools in the region.'

What about France? Wasn't it one of the 'Allies?' Wasn't France a colonial power in Vietnam? Isn't it funny how 'our side' is always 'the Allies,' while the opposing bloc is a dark, dank, moldy 'regime.'

There are few answers as to why MacArthur stood aside and let Rockefeller betray the dead of WWII. One man who might have had the answer to that question was Herbert Hoover, who later became President of the United States. He did a study that proved that some of the largest oil vilayets were off the coast of what was then French Indo-China in the South China Sea. It seems that Standard Oil became well aware of that valuable study. This was before off-shore drilling had been devised and in a review of events in the 1920s, a man named George Herbert Walker Bush was to become the CEO of a worldwide offshore drilling company called Zapata Drilling Company.

At the end of WWII in 1945, Vietnam was still occupied by the French. There was not the slightest sign of insurrection on the part of the Vietnamese who seemed to like the French and even adopted their language and many of their customs. But that was to change. Lawrence Rockefeller had orders to turn over an extensive store of U.S. Army weapons stored at Okinawa to Ho Chi Minh, the Vietnamese leader. Thus it came about that the massive, extensive, expensive American arms and armaments was turned over to Ho Chi Minh in the expectation that Vietnam would drive the French out of Indo-China so that Standard Oil would be able to take over the as yet undeveloped offshore fields.

In 1954 Vietnamese General Giap defeated the French at Dien Bien Phu with armaments provided by the U.S. Army courtesy of Lawrence Rockefeller. Desperate appeals by the French for American help went unanswered. Did the Truman administration know about this plan? Of course! Did the gulled American people know about it? Of course not! By now secret deals done behind closed doors had become standard practice for the imperial American government.

However, the imperialist cabal within the gates of Washington had not taken oriental inscrutability into account. Just when the Rockefeller cabal was beginning to congratulate themselves on a job well done, Ho Chi Min reneged on the agreement.

Educated and well informed, Ho Chi Minh somehow knew about the Hoover resource report proving a vast supply of oil off the

Vietnamese coast, and had cleverly used the U.S. to help him get rid of the French before giving Rockefeller the short end of the stick. In the 1950's a method of undersea oil exploration was perfected using small explosions deep in the water and then recording the sound echoes bouncing off the various layers of rock below. The surveyors could then determine the exact location of the arched salt domes which held the accumulated oil beneath them.

But if this method were used off the Vietnam coast on property Standard didn't own or have the rights to, the Vietnamese, the Chinese, the Japanese and probably even the French would quickly run to the United Nations and complain that America was stealing the oil, and that would be sufficient to shut down the operation.

Not willing to relinquish his interest in the offshore oil along the coast of Vietnam, Rockefeller and his minions, including Henry Kissinger, set about dividing Vietnam into two countries; North and South and prevailed on other nations to go along with the division. After Vietnam was artificially split into North and South, the 'contrived situation' formulated by Stimson and Knox, and used to force the United States into WWII at Pearl Harbor, was again pressed into service. The stage was set for the U.S. to drive the North Vietnamese out off the entire area. At President Johnson's instigation, the U.S. staged a false attack on U.S. Navy destroyers in the Gulf of Tonkin by 'phantom' torpedo boats supposedly of the North Korean Navy. President Johnson interrupted regularly scheduled television broadcasts to announce the attack, telling his gulled U.S. audience that 'even as I speak, our sailors are struggling for their lives in the waters of the Gulf of Tonkin.'

It was good theatre, but that was all. There was not a scrap of veracity to Johnson's dramatic announcement. It was all a big lie. The Gulf of Tonkin incident was of course not perceived as a lie by the American people so without any further ado the U.S.

plunged into yet another imperialist oil war, with disastrous results.

U.S. aircraft carriers were anchored offshore of Vietnam in the waters above the oil domes and the struggle by U.S. oil interests to oust the North Vietnamese from the oil rich vilayets below the sand on the sea floor, commenced. Of course it was not called that. Perhaps it need not be mentioned that the war was described in the usual glowing patriotic terms. It was being fought in 'defense of freedom,' 'for democracy,' to 'stop the spread of Communism,' etc.

At regular intervals jet bombers would take off from the carriers and bomb locations in North and South Vietnam. Then using normal military procedure when returning, they would dump their unsafe or unused bombs in the ocean before landing back on the carriers. Safe ordnance drop zones were designated for this purpose away from the carriers, directly over the salt domes beneath which oil lay.

Even close-up observers would only notice many small explosions occurring daily in the waters of the South China Sea and thought it was only part of the war. The U.S. Navy carriers had begun Operation Linebacker One and Standard Oil had begun its ten year oil survey of the seabed off the coast of Vietnam. And the Vietnamese, Chinese and everybody else around, including the Americans, were none the wiser. The oil survey hardly cost Standard Oil a nickel as the U.S. taxpayers paid for it.

Twenty years later and at the cost of 55,000 American lives and half a million Vietnamese dead, Rockefeller and the Standard Oil cabal had collected sufficient data to show exactly where the oil pools lay, and the war in Vietnam could be ended. The Vietnam negotiators were not ready to give up without concessions and so Nelson Rockefeller's personal assistant Henry Kissinger, was dispatched to Paris as 'the U.S. negotiator' (read Rockefeller agent) at the Paris peace talks and won a Nobel Peace Prize in the bargain.

Such hypocrisy, heresy and outright charlatanism, would be impossible to match. After the melancholy echoes of the drawn-out war had receded, Vietnam divided their offshore coastal areas into numerous oil lots, and allowed foreign companies to bid on the lots, with the proviso that Vietnam was to be paid an agreed royalty. Norway's Statoil, British Petroleum, Royal Dutch Shell, Russia, Germany and Australia, all won bids and began drilling within their areas.

How strange, that none of the 'competition' struck oil. However, the lots which Standard Oil bid for and were awarded proved to have vast oil reserves. Their extensive undersea seismic research conducted by U.S. Navy bombers had paid off.

One would have thought that after all the horrible deceptions the American people had endured at the hands of the cabal bent upon betraying them into the slavery of a One World Government, that they would have learned by then in the late 1970's to have not one ounce of trust in their government, and to doubt 100 percent, everything Washington did and said, regardless which party had its leader in the White House.

It was no longer a conflict between individual nations, but a conflict to bring total domination of the whole human race into being through a New World Order in a One World Government.

Common sense would have dictated total mistrust in government, indeed, would have mandated it. But no, the gulling and the culling was to go on at an increased tempo and ferocity and wider in scope than ever before, for another forty-five years. That is where the American people stand today. Thoroughly lost, with nowhere to turn, seemingly with all hope lost. Unfortunately, the Petroleum Industry's appetite and matching greed shows no sign of abating. The Committee of 300's American and British affiliates had developed a strategy by which they fully anticipated would secure total control of the world's energy supplies and the Eurasian continents. It began in 1905 when the Rothschilds set the Japanese against Russia at Port Arthur. Placing Mao in power in China was an integral part of their vision. The 'forward looking' strategy that imperialist Donald Rumsfeld postulated is based on the dialectic approach.

The U.S. begins with selling armaments to a 'friendly' government for example Panama, Iraq, Yugoslavia/Kosovo, Afghanistan, Pakistan, Taliban Mujaheddin, Saudi Arabia, Chile and Argentine, among others. Then, as the Kapellmeister raises his baton, the media symphony orchestra strikes up the overture: The 'friendly' government has a dark secret; it terrorizes its own people, so now we must change its bond rating to 'junk' status.

The percussion section plays a drum roll as the brass section blares forth the truth: This is a 'demon regime,' definitely not nice people. This is a complete about-face, but Americans with notoriously short attention spans fail to notice that this is the very same government we so happily praised and sold armaments to a short while before. Mr. Cheney plays a solo on his oboe to affect that this 'regime' is now a very present danger to the U.S. We must go forthwith and uproot that nation and don't even bother to obey the U.S. Constitution; we don't declare war. Curiously, we don't obey our laws but never mind, the Media Symphony Orchestra plays a full blast rendition of the Gotterdammerung! Panama was invaded on the say of the Emperor, G.W. Bush: Iraq, Afghanistan echo to the sounding of marching U.S. Marines who established bases in the country just defeated, with the stated purpose and intent of bringing 'democracy' to the occupied nations.

A more realistic evaluation quickly shows that the whole operation was nothing but imperialist aggression and the mighty conquerors set up permanent military occupation which has nothing to do with 'democracy,' but has everything to do with the oil that lay beneath the sands of those countries.

Of course we are not told that the military bases are there to control the energy resources of that nation and the surrounding countries. Current U.S. foreign policy is governed by the doctrine of 'full-spectrum dominance;' the U.S. must control military, economic and political developments everywhere, in pursuance of its imperialist role.

This new era of imperial strategy began with the Panama invasion, next, they created the so-called Gulf War, continued with the UN- sanctioned war in the Balkans, and now expands with the new wars against terrorism: Afghanistan, Iraq, and beyond to Iran whose oil it has long coveted. On January 20, 2001, then Defense Secretary Donald Rumsfeld said that he was willing to deploy U.S. military forces in 'another 15 countries' if that is what it takes to 'combat terrorism.'

The UN-sanctioned war in the Balkans was triggered by oil and the pipeline easement for Caspian Sea oil to Western European markets through Kosovo to the Mediterranean Sea. The Chechnya conflict is about the same thing: who shall control the pipeline? When Yugoslavia refused to capitulate and buckle under dictates of the International Monetary Fund (IMF), the U.S. and Germany began a systematic campaign of destabilization, even using some of the veterans of Afghanistan in that 'war.'

Yugoslavia was broken up into compliant mini-states, as planned at the 1972 Bellagio conference, and the former Soviet Union was contained, at least that is what the U.S. thought. The de-facto U.S. occupation of Serbia (where America built its largest military base since the Vietnam War) was up and running.

We turn now to specific areas where control is being sought by the imperialist Empire's Petroleum Industry.

The Caspian Sea area is very much in the sights of an imperial America, because the area has proven oil reserves of fifteen to twenty- eight billion barrels plus has estimated reserves of 40-178 billion, a total of 206 billion barrels -- 16 percent of the earth's potential oil reserves (compared to Saudi's 261 billion barrels of oil and America's own 22 billion barrels). That could add up to $3 trillion in oil.

Thus far no one is in sight and with a new source of oil and gas in the Caucasus, Standard Oil is looking to create a 'democracy' in Saudi Arabia while it develops a new center of operations in Southern Asia. The huge oil and gas reserves in the Caspian Sea must either be moved west to European markets or south to Asian markets. The western route is to move oil from Chechnya, across the Black Sea and through the Bosporus to the Mediterranean, but the narrow Bosporus channel is already clogged with oil tankers from the Black Sea oil fields.

An alternate route would be to move the tankers from the Black Sea, bypassing the Bosporus, up the Danube River and then through a very short pipeline across Kosovo to the Mediterranean at Tirana, Albania. However, that process was halted by China. As one intelligence survey reported:

> The other problem with the western route is that Western Europe is a tough market, characterized by high prices for oil products, an aging population, and increasing competition from natural gas. Furthermore, the region is fiercely competitive, now being serviced by oil from the Middle East, the North Sea, Scandinavia, and Russia.

We know that Russia is about to embark on a program that would eliminate transiting the pipe through Ukraine with it, a world record for stealing Russian gas and oil, that made the 'Orange Revolution Lady,' Julia Timoshenko, a multi-millionaire.

The only other way to get Caspian Sea oil and gas to Asian

markets is through China, which is too long a route, or through Iran, which is politically and economically inimical to U.S.-Standard Oil objectives.

As soon as the Soviets discovered new vast Caspian Sea oil fields in the late 1970's, the government attempted to negotiate with Afghanistan to build a massive north-south pipeline system to transit their oil through Afghanistan and Pakistan to the Indian Ocean. But the United States, with assistance from Saudi Arabia and Pakistan then created the 'Taliban,' an organization that did not exist before U.S. imperialist oil strategies came into being there. The U.S played on the Muslim religion, casting Russia as evil and opposed to Muslims everywhere.

When the Russian Army entered Afghanistan, the CIA armed and trained their 'friends' and sent Osama bin Laden to Kabul to lead the Taliban resistance to the invaders. The Taliban become a potent force that regarded the U.S. as the 'Great Satan.' The result was a protracted war between the Taliban and the Russia invaders in which the Taliban were victorious. The CIA through its former chief, George Bush, the elder, thought they could rely on bin Laden, because of extensive business dealings with the Bush family, but when the U.S. callously abandoned him after the Russians left, bin Laden was embittered and turned on Washington and Riyad to become their worst nightmare.

This was only one of many such imperial 'secret wars' where the imperial petroleum industry set U.S. foreign policy and used the U.S. military to enforce it. Other such wars occurred in Mexico, Iraq, Iran, Italy and Venezuela. We now know that Standard Oil influenced the CIA to draw the attention of U.S. government to the danger of a Russian north-south pipeline crossing Afghanistan, and to provide authority and funding for the CIA to train armed Muslim fundamentalist groups, including Osama bin Laden.

The alternative Russian plan called for control of the flow of oil and gas to Western Europe, through their pipelines that traversed the Southern Asian Republics of the former Soviet Union; Turkmenistan, Kazakhstan, Uzbekistan, Tajikistan and Kyrgyzstan - utterly neglected by the U.S. before, but suddenly the focus of tremendous attention from the CIA who went courting with large bouquets of dollars and promises of more to come.

The CIA wooed these nations like an ardent suitor, and through this ploy was able to persuade its leaders that Russia would not treat them as partners. Thus it was that the former Far Eastern USSR states began to consult the petroleum industry companies of America, and soon found out that here was the real U.S. foreign policy maker. The imperial Petroleum Industry now turned all of its attention to the former Far Eastern Soviet states, just as it had done in the pioneer days with Iraq and Iran. Led by Standard Oil, it drew plans and mapped scenarios for U.S. to thrust through these Southern Asian Republics. The U.S. military had already set up a permanent operations base in Uzbekistan, again at the behest of the petroleum Industry. The Tavistock Institute was called in to cover the true intent with a 'bluff barrier' in which Kissinger's former Italian P2 Masonry chief capo, Michael Ledeen, was involved. It is believed that Ledeen (by now having covered his Trotsky-Bolshevik tracks and turned into a 'Neo-Conservative') called the ploy 'an anti-terrorist measure.'

For such a strategy to work Afghanistan had to be blamed for 9/11, which provided the perfect 'contrived situation' cover. President Bush told the world that 'the Taliban' was responsible for the attack on the Twin Trade Towers, adding that the Taliban world headquarters was in Afghanistan.

Of course 'bringing democracy' to the Afghans while overlooking the absence of democracy next door in Pakistan with a dictator at its head, presented a bit of a challenge, but 'innovative thinking' took care of it. Now the U.S. army was exactly where the Petroleum Industry needed it to be.

CHAPTER 22

NATO violates its charter by going out of theater

Before proceeding to what lay behind the NATO bombing of Serbia, let us add that as smart as Ledeen and his fellow Neo-Bolsheviks, Kristol, Feith, Perle, Wolfowitz, and Cheney think they are, on their very best days they do not even begin to compare with Russian President Vladimir Putin, with a migraine headache. What emerged during the 1999 NATO (read U.S.) attack on Serbia, was that voices were raised expressing strong suspicion that the U.S. and Britain were acting on behalf of the Albanian government that had long sought to wrest control of Kosovo from Serbia. Albania held the trump card in the projected oil pipeline that Britain and the U.S. planned to run from Caspian Sea across Albania.

The pipeline was to run through Bulgaria, Macedonia and Albania, from the Black Sea port of Burgas to Viore in the Adriatic. In full production the pipeline would transit 750,000 barrels a day. The project was approved by the British Government for and on behalf of BP (British Petroleum) and its U.S. partners.

When Robin Cook, then Britain's Foreign Minister was questioned about it, he laughed the 'idea' to scorn, dismissing the enquiry as nonsense. 'There is no oil in Kosovo,' said Cook. Of course this was true, and by making it a matter of oil in Kosovo a very simplistic notion easily dismissed, the enquirers were thrown of the track. The Trans Balkan Pipeline project never saw the light of day in any American or British newspaper.

In May 2005 the U.S. Trade and Development published a paper, which while not confirming the real reason for the war against Yugoslavia, made some significant comments.

> Worthy of note was that... oil coming from the Caspian sea will quickly surpass the safe capacity of the Bosporus as a shipping lane ... the (scheme) will provide a consistent source of crude oil to American refineries and provide American companies with a key role in developing the vital east-west corridor and advance the privatization of the U.S. government in the region, and facilitate rapid integration of the Balkans with western Europe.

The first step in the projected plan was taken in July 1993 with the dispatch of U.S. troops to the Northern border of Macedonia. This might have been regarded as rather strange, to say the least, but the American people did not seem to notice that the 'peacekeeping' American force was not sent to the areas where there was conflict between Serbia and the Albanians. Not known to the American people while all the 'human rights' violations were supposedly going on in Serbia, was that the proposed Trans Balkans pipeline was to pass through Macedonia at Skopje, a mere 15 miles from the Serbian border.

Washington said it wanted to prevent Serb expansion into Macedonia, which was never on the cards. But like the Bush administration's lies during the run-up to the 1991 Gulf War, when Bush warned the Saudis that Saddam Hussein would not stop at invading Kuwait, but once that was accomplished, he would invade Saudi Arabia, the lie worked.

No word leaked out about the true mission of the American military contingent's presence on the Macedonian border, especially not that it was in pursuance of an agreement reached in May 1993 to go ahead with the Trans Balkan pipeline. Although the pipeline would not traverse Serbia, the Albanian

President who attended the meeting that launched it had a message for Britain and the United States that was loud and clear in its implications:

> It is my personal opinion that no solution confined within the Serbian borders will bring lasting peace.

Diplomats attending the meeting were unanimous in concluding that what he was saying was that if the U.S. and Britain wanted Albania's consent for the Trans Balkan pipeline, Kosovo had to be brought under Albania's jurisdiction. With $600 million dollars a month at stake, the United States and Britain launched their cowardly attack on Serbia, which had no oil, under the guise of NATO in the phony cause of ending Serbian's abuse of Albanian nationals in Kosovo. Robin Cook's words ring even more hollowly now than they did when he was asked why Britain was attacking Serbia:

> "We have demonstrated that we are willing to take military action, not to seize territory, not for expansion, not for mineral resources. There is no oil in Kosovo. The Socialist Workers' Party keeps saying we are doing this for oil, which is deeply perplexing, since there is only some dirty lignite, and the sooner we encourage them to use something else other than dirty lignite, the better. This war is a war fought in defense not of territory but in defense of values. So here I can say… foreign policy has been driven by these concerns."

Bukarian would have been proud that Robin Cook could lie so convincingly.

Caspian energy amounting to North Sea reserves (about 3% of world total oil and 1% of gas) is strategically important to Britain and the United States, so important that they decided to instigate war against Yugoslavia to accommodate Albania. The real reason for getting rid of Serbian leader Slobodan Milosevic was his determination to clear Kosovo province of the Albanians. That would have meant continued unrest for years to come, and make lender banks reluctance to commit large-scale financing for the Trans Balkans pipeline.

Since early 1990 British and American petroleum companies like Chevron-Amoco Socar and BP had invested heavily in the Caspian Basin. TRACEA (Transport Corridor Europe-Caucuses-Asia) was established in 1993. IOGATE (Interstate Oil and Gas Transportation to Europe) was set up in 1995. SYNERGY was set up in 1997. AMBO the Albanian Macedonian Bulgarian Oil Pipeline Corp was financed by OPIC (the U.S. Overseas Private Investment Corporation) No wonder U.S. troops were sent to the Macedonian border to act as mercenaries for the petroleum industry.

But the East European Energy Report 20, June 1995 Second Black Sea Oil Pipeline said that 'the fighting in Yugoslavia sits like a massive roadblock across everything' cast a pall over the promising development which the Clinton administration had already committed $30 million in funding through its Southern Balkan Development Initiative (SBDI).

The European Union (EU) Council meeting was held one year before NATO bombing began in which a 'Declaration on Caspian Energy Pipeline' was discussed. It was presided over by Robin Cook and was in effect a declaration that the Serbian fighting had to be resolved. The conclusions drawn from this cannot be overstated.

The propaganda that preceded the bombing was total and all-encompassing. The whole world was led to be believe, and in fact did believe, that the NATO (read U.S.) war on Yugoslavia was to stop the ethnic violence allegedly going on in Serbia, and the human rights violations of Albanians living in Kosovo. Willi Munzenberg would have fully approved of it. In my book, 'The Committee of 300,' 4th Edition and 'the Tavistock Institute for Human Relation,' the career of the greatest master of propaganda who ever lived, Willi Munzenberg is covered.

He had accompanied Lenin in exile in Switzerland, and after Lenin was sent back to Russia via the 'sealed train,' Munzenberg became his Director of Popular Enlightenment. He was responsible for the training of many GRU officers and spies, including the famous Leon Tepper, master spy leader of the Rot Kappell ('Red Orchestra') who fooled every Western intelligence agency, including MI6, for three decades.

John J. Maresca. Vice President of International Relations, Unocal Corporation had this to say about Caspian region oil:

> "Mr. Chairman, the Caspian region contains tremendous untapped hydrocarbon reserves. To give you an idea of the scale proven natural gas reserves is equal to more than 236 trillion cubic feet. The region's oil reserves may well reach more than 60 billion barrels of oil. Some estimates are as high as 200 billion...

> One major problem is yet to be solved; how to get the region's vast energy resources to the markets where they are needed. Central Asia is isolated... Each of the countries faces difficult political challenges. Some have unsettled wars or latent conflicts... In addition, a chief technical obstacle, which we in the industry face in transporting oil is the region's existing pipeline infrastructure. Because the region's oil pipelines we constructed during the Moscow-centered Soviet period, they tend to head north and west to Russia, There are no connections to the south and east. From the outset we have made it clear that the construction of the pipeline we have proposed in Afghanistan could not begin until a recognized government is in place that has the confidence of governments, lenders and our company."

So now we know why the U.S. is engaged in a war in Afghanistan. It has little do with 9/11 and the Taliban, but everything to do with establishing an American puppet government in that country in pursuance of imperial oil geopolitics. We also now know the real reason why NATO attacked Serbia. Its feuding with Albania was unsettling for government involved in the proposed pipeline from the Caspian basin, 'lenders and our company.'

Russia, playing up to the false claim that the U.S. is 'the only super- power,' pretended not to oppose U.S. incursions in Afghanistan, because, Russia was most happy to see America bogged down in Iraq and Afghanistan at the same time. President Putin is a master at 'maskirovka' (deception) and while the Bush Administration in Washington was congratulating itself at having trumped Russia, Putin was negotiating with China and the former Asian territories of the USSR, to form an alliance bloc to curb U.S. imperialist expansionist plans. Led by Putin, China and Russia joined the Shanghai Cooperation Organization (SCO) which included China, Russia, Kazakhstan, Kyrgyzstan, Tajikistan and Uzbekistan. China joined the SCO to align itself with Russia; economically, militarily and politically. The new SCO Pact takes the place of the Rockefeller-Li Family Pact that endured for almost four decades.

Russia's membership in the SCO is an attempt to maintain its traditional hegemony in Central Asia. The underlying rationale of the SCO is the control of its members' enormous reserves of oil and gas. The misgivings of Russia, China, India and other SCO-nations, that Afghanistan and Iraq are slated to become the base of operations in destabilizing, isolating, and establishing control over the South Asian regimes, and the Middle-East proved well-founded, but they rested easier since the SCO was up and running under the leadership of then President Putin.

A glance at a map of the Middle East shows Iran standing between Iraq and Afghanistan, and that was the rationale behind Bush including Iran in the 'Axis of Evil.' The U.S. imperialist strategy is predicated upon Russia standing aside as the U.S. concludes conquest of this area and the permanent military posts are set up without objection from either Russia or China. The next phase is commencement of construction of a pipeline through Turkmenistan, Afghanistan and Pakistan to deliver petroleum to the Eurasian markets.

Spearheading the pipeline project is Unocal for Standard Oil interests. Unocal has been trying to build the north-south pipeline through Afghanistan and Pakistan to the Indian Ocean for several decades. President Karzai, Washington's puppet president of Afghanistan was a former senior executive in Unocal's Afghan adventures. Karzai was in fact the senior in Unocal executive negotiating on behalf of his company, and he is also the leader of the Pushtun Durrani tribe.

A member of Mujaheddin that fought the Soviets during the 1980s, Karzai was a top contact for the CIA, maintaining close relations with CIA Director William Casey, Vice President George Bush and their Pakistani Inter Service Intelligence (ISI) Service go between. After the Soviet Union left Afghanistan, the CIA sponsored the relocation of Karzai and a number of his brothers to the U.S.

According to a *New York Times* report:

> In 1998, the California-based Unocal held 46.5 percent stakes in Central Asia Gas (Cent Gas), a consortium that planned a very long gas pipeline across Afghanistan, withdrew when several fruitless years of trying came up dry. The pipeline was to stretch 7,277 km from Turkmenistan's Dauletabad fields, to Multan in Pakistan a distance of 1,271 kilometers. The cost came in at an estimated $1.9 billion.

What the company did not spell out right away was that firm opposition from bin Laden and the Taliban had sunk the projected pipeline. An additional $600 million could have brought the pipeline to energy-hungry India.

Enter Halliburton, Vice President Dick Cheney's company. Russian military intelligence had been reporting since 1998 that the Americans were planning a major oil venture in Azerbaijan and that Dick Cheney was about to sign a contract with the State Oil Company of Azerbaijan that would build a 6000 square meter marine base to support offshore oil drilling platforms to be constructed in the Caspian Sea.

On May 15, 2001, a statement from Cheney's office said the new Halliburton base would be used to 'assist Halliburton's catamaran crane vessel, the Qurban Abbasov, in upcoming offshore pipe-laying and sub-sea activities.' As mentioned, Unocal's earlier agreement with the Taliban in 1998 was terminated as it had become clear that the Taliban could turn all of the other Afghanistan tribes against the company, thus destabilizing the political environment for a north- south pipeline construction project.

Although I cannot be absolutely sure, there is evidence that suggests it was at this critical juncture that a new 'war against terrorism' ploy was conceived by Unocal-Halliburton and Standard Oil. Dick Cheney carried 'the solution' to the U.S. Government. 9/11 provided the necessary pretext to send in U.S. troops to fight a 'war against terrorism' in Afghanistan.

The propaganda mills churned out a litany of 'reasons' why U.S. troops had to be rushed to Afghanistan. It seems that the Taliban led by bin Laden was planning 'major terrorist attacks around the world and on U.S. installations abroad.' Not one scrap of real evidence was produced to support the contention, but a connived and deceived American people as ever, accepted it as 'gospel.'

By 2006 the transparent motives of the Petroleum Industry's war against Afghanistan were now clear for all to read. On January 2, 2002, the pipeline project took another step forward when U.S. Ambassador to Pakistan, Wendy Chamberlain, acting for Standard Oil, kept a longstanding engagement to meet with Pakistan's oil minister, Usman Aminuddin. The bulk of their meeting centered on plans to forge ahead with the north-south pipeline, and U.S. funding for the construction of Pakistan's Arabian Sea oil terminals for the pipeline.

President Bush has repeatedly said that the U.S. military will remain in Afghanistan. Why should this be when UN forces are supposed to be taking over so that the U.S. Army can go home? The answer is that UN forces will serve as a paramilitary police force, so that U.S. soldiers will be freed to guard the construction of the north-south pipeline. Some reports say that they will also guard the opium poppy fields, but I have not seen any confirmation of poppy field duty. That duty fell on a British force.

The recent appointment by President Bush of Zalmay Khalilzad, an unknown person of Afghan origin, as a member of his National Security team had many scratching their heads. We believe we can explain this seemingly unusual appointment. Khalilzad was a former member of the CentGas project. Khalilzad has recently been named presidential Special Envoy for Afghanistan. He is a Pushtun, and the son of a former government official under King Mohammed Zahir Shah, and he was there to see that the pipeline project went forward in a timely fashion and to report directly to the President, any and every delay or hitch that occurred as the plan unfolded.

His appointment was supported by Condoleezza Rice who was a member of the board of Chevron, although it has never been made clear what exactly her role at Chevron was. Along with being a consultant to the Rand Corporation, Khalizad was a special liaison between Unocol and the Taliban government and he also worked on various risk analyses for the project.

Now that the Afghanistan sector of the 'war on terrorism' is considered 'settled,' although in our understanding of the situation, it is far from that, and permanent U.S. military bases in Uzbekistan and Afghanistan are in place - to what oil rich country may we expect Standard Oil's scouts to infiltrate in their search for more oil? The U.S. Government says it has to keep looking for oil, and ideally, (from this standpoint) most of those places are in countries which have been branded as harboring terrorists: Iraq, Syria, Iran and South America, especially Venezuela and Columbia. Some might say: 'How convenient.'

But the imperial oil warriors also began looking in Russia's backyard in Siberia. EXXON, Mobil, Royal Dutch Shell and the French company Total SA won contracts in the 1990s from what was at that time the USSR to search for oil and natural gas in the Artic region. Bush the elder's undeclared unconstitutional and therefore criminal war, the Gulf War of 1991, resulted in Kuwait stealing even more of the huge Rumalia oil field of southern Iraq than it did the first time around.

It was done by unilaterally expanding the boundaries of Kuwait after the war. The illegal seizure Iraq's property brought a lot of unwelcome retaliation by Iraq. The 'new border' allowed Kuwait, controlled by BP and Standard Oil, to double their prewar oil output. The true and historical account of how the British Army created 'Kuwait' in 1921 came by drawing an arbitrary line through the very middle of the Rumalia Oil Fields, and then calling the stolen land 'Kuwait.'

The following is from an article published in the 'Oil Analyst:'

> Iraq, which recently discovered an oil field in its western desert, is widely regarded as having more oil than Saudi Arabia once its deposits are developed.

Prior to the 2003 U.S. illegal invasion of Iraq, the country was producing 3 million barrels a day, funneling most of it to world markets through a United Nations-monitored program that directed a small part of the proceeds to food and medicine for the Iraqi people, under the so-called "Oil for Food" program. Iraq was still able to export some oil to Syria, which it resold as Syrian oil.

In September of 2001, the Bush regime started threatening Iraq but actually the contingency plan to invade Iraq had been readied several months before that. The threat was intended as a shot across the bows of France and Russia. Both nations had begun to develop an extensive trade with Iraq and Dick Cheney, the new Imperial Oil Prince did not like it one little bit. The reality was that American companies, especially Cheney's Halliburton Oil Company and General Electric (GE) were making billions in Iraq by selling goods and services. No interlopers would be allowed. Prior to the 2003 Iraq war, Iraq was moving to ingratiate itself with the Gulf Arab Cooperation Council (GCC) members: Bahrain, Kuwait, Oman, Qatar, Saudi Arabia and the United Arab Emirates (UAE) to gain support for the lifting of the U.N. sanctions against it.

Alarmed by the unexpected development, Standard Oil foreign policy executives got Big Brother America to threaten GCC members not to allow Iraq to join or face the consequences. Russia began demanding 'a comprehensive settlement' of the sanctions issue, including steps leading to lifting the military embargo against Iraq. On January 24, 2002, Russian Foreign Minister Igor Ivanov came out strongly opposing any U.S. military intervention in Iraq. Russia's Lukoil Oil Company and two Russian government agencies had signed a 23-year contract to develop Iraq's West Qurna oil field.

In terms of the contract, Lukoil was to receive one half, Iraq one-quarter, and the Russian government agencies were to get one-quarter of the oil field's 667 million tons of crude, potentially a $20 billion deal. Iraq still owed Russia at least $8 billion from the old cold war days when Russia armed Iraq, considering it a client state. But Russia opposed 'U.S. imperialism' on other grounds. Sickened by the brutality of the 76 days and nights bombing of Serbia instigated by U.S. Secretary of State Madeline Albright, Russian military brass was determined not to let the U.S. get away with aggression against a small nation for a second time.

Russian Special Forces had dashed to Pristina in Serbia to secure the airport against the arrival of U.S. forces, in the hope that they would be attacked and could then enter the war on the side of Serbia. Only the level-headedness of the British commander on the scene prevented the Third World War from starting. Russia, still smarting over the sack and rape of Serbia, was seeking revenge.

An anxious Washington shuttled back and forth to Moscow seeking to placate Russia, and after still secret negotiations, the situation was defused. In 2001 Russia was awarded $1.3 billion in oil contracts under the United Nations oil-for-food program that allowed Iraq to sell oil to buy supplies to help Iraqi civilians.

In September 2001, the Iraqi oil ministry announced that it intended to award Russian companies another $40 billion in contracts as soon as United Nations sanctions were lifted.

In February 2002, Russia's Foreign Minister, Igor S. Ivanov, said that Russia and Iraq saw eye to eye on questions of extremism and terrorism and that the American-backed sanctions against Iraq were counterproductive and should be lifted. He then emphasized that Russia solidly opposed 'spreading or applying the international anti- terror operation to any arbitrarily chosen state, including Iraq.' By now the rhetoric was getting hotter as Russia sought at the U.N. to use its veto in the Security Council to halt all sanctions against Iraq.

Then in 2003, the imperial Standard Oil-Bush Republican War Party backed by its Neo-Bolshevik allies, grossly violated the U.S. Constitution, international law and the four Geneva Conventions, precipitously launching a bombing raid of Baghdad. The illegal war against Iraq ended all the standing Iraqi agreements with Russia, Germany and France. Unbeknown to the Seven Sisters oil cartel, serious reprisals would follow a scant three years later. The outcry of the European nations against Bush and the Neo-Bolshevik attack on Iraq was immediate.

The puerile excuse given to the world was that Iraq had 'weapons of mass destruction' it was about to use on Britain. The inexperienced, green, unsophisticated Rice added her dire warnings that if not stopped, Americans would see 'mushroom clouds' over its major cities. Six years later we are still waiting for the 'clouds' to appear. The gross Tavistock-generated lie was accepted by about 75 percent of the American people. Although scores of experts came forward to deride and deny the WMD claims of Bush and Blair, both men persisted with the lie until it literally fell to pieces underneath their feet of clay. Not that it mattered. Standard Oil imperial diplomacy had carried the day, U.S. aggression had secured Iraq's oil for them and, in any case, the war was not going to last or so the world was told. American troops were racing across the desert from Kuwait, and would soon overrun Baghdad.

Not taken into account by the Bush planners was China's changed loyalty. Bush considered China still bound by the Rockefeller-Li family pact of 1964. But plans to extend the Standard Oil/Bush oil imperialism were met by China's growing interest in supporting Middle-East nations in their struggle against the U.S. During Jordanian King Abdallah II's January 2002 visit to China, Chinese President Jiang Zemin said that China wanted stronger ties with Arab countries to help promote peace between Israel and the Palestinians. This came as a complete shock to the U.S. State Department. To the dismay of President Bush and Secretary of State Rice, China stood ready to intervene if the Neo-Bolsheviks followed through with their mad plan to attack Iran, no matter that Constitutional authority to commit U.S. Armed Forces to any country, was completely lacking.

China gave notice of its stance by supplying its version of the 'Exocet' deadly shore-to-ship wave skipping cruise missile to Iran, which has the potential to do great damage to the U.S. Navy. The Petroleum Industry's imperialists continue to expand their empire in the Middle East, especially through Iraq. Bolton was installed at the United Nations, courtesy of the White House through an arrogance of power, an abuse of power, in a recess appointment, this in the face of his fitness for office having been rejected by the U.S. Senate. (A few years later he was summarily booted out of office.) It is far from the constitutional authority of the President to make recess appointments save and except when 'necessary and proper' and a matter of urgency. In the case of Bolton it was absolutely not 'necessary' nor 'proper,' because the Senate already had refused to confirm Bolton and the 'recess' appointment was therefore, an abuse of power and of constitutional procedure. But the Standard Oil/Bush imperialists refused to let such concern stop their plans to cope with the threat of China in the Middle East. They only temporarily halted their drive until Bolton could be installed at the U.N. Bolton was needed at the U.N. to harass and bully nations into line to support U.S. actions in Iraq and also, Iran. More than that, he is the law firm Baker and Botts,' special agent-in-place to take back collateral for all the bad loans James Baker III pushed through.

The U.S. imperialist petroleum cartel seized control of Iraq's oil, and now have their eye on Syria and Iranian oil as well. We're now in phase two of the war on terrorism: invading countries that Bush says harbor terrorists, with the real intent to seize those countries' energy sources. Phase three will come when the U.S. goes head-to-head with Russia over Caspian Sea oil and efforts to get it to the European market. That momentous day may not be that far off.

Currently, the Russians have stepped up the pace. On August 28, 2006, President Putin flew to Athens in Greece to move the Caspian pipeline project along which had been stalled for a number of years. In Athens President Putin met with Greek Prime Minister Costas Karamantis and Bulgarian President Gregory Parvanov. The tripartite discussions centered on a quick completion of a pipeline from the Caspian to the Bulgarian port of Burgas and from there by pipeline to the Greek port of Alexandroupolis on the Aegean Sea coast. Once completed the pipeline will be able to carry 35 million tons of oil a year and save at least $8.00 per barrel in transport costs. The pipeline will enable Russia to maintain a hold on Caspian oil destined for the European market by heading off the U.S.-backed pipeline Baku-Tblisi- Ceyhan major pipeline. Thus the U.S. has decided to concentrate for the meanwhile on the north-south Afghanistan pipeline being built there, guarded by U.S. soldiers, who are running into stiff resistance from a resurgent Taliban, stronger and better equipped than before they were driven out by the so-called Northern Alliance. The Taliban leadership is determined to prevent the pipeline from ever coming on line. The renewed fighting, which began in July 2006, reached a high level in August, the battles being characterized in the U.S. jackal media as U.S. efforts to crush the opium trade revenues said to go to the Taliban. This is not the case, but with the massive propaganda machine at the disposal of the Bush administration, it is likely to be seen as such by a gulled American public.

CHAPTER 23

Russia takes on the Seven Sisters

A t this juncture Russia, under the leadership of Vladimir Putin, the most astute geopolitical strategist in the world today, decided to jerk the rug from under the heavy boots of the Seven Sisters. Russia's foreign minister announced that his government was about to curb major Western oil and gas investment projects in Siberia, putting in doubt whether it would honor the agreements reached with the former USSR in 1991.

The U.S. State Department reacted at once with spokesman Tom Casey saying the Bush administration was

> "very concerned about the Russian government's move to revoke environmental permits for $20 million liquefied natural gas projects being developed by Royal Dutch Shell and two Japanese groups on Sakhalin Island."

The Russian government's reply was to announce it was considering canceling an Exxon-Mobil project in Sakhalin. The United States claimed it had rights under an agreement reached with the former USSR in 1991 and 1994. Western Europe and the U.S. began to express fears that Russia under President Putin was making a concerted effort to assert Russian control of the country's vast energy resources.

President Putin made a state visit to France to reassure President Chirac that Total SA was not included in the changes. Observers were quick to point out that during the visit to Paris the two leaders became close.

No doubt Putin was telling the U.S. that France was being rewarded for standing against the war in Iraq and for refusing to join in the proposed UN boycott of Iran. President Chirac awarded Putin with a medal - the Grand Cross of the Legion of Honor in a very public display at the Elysee Palace. During the visit President Putin raised serious concerns Russia had about the situation in Kosovo. An agreement for a French company to build a superhighway between Moscow and St. Petersburg was concluded, as well as a deal committing Russia to buy 22 Airbus A350s. It became apparent on September 24, 2006, that Shell was in danger of having its license suspended to operate the $20 billion oil and gas Sakhalin-2 project, when its environmental permits were revoked by the Ministry of Natural Resources. Sakhalin-2 is about 80 percent complete. Meantime Gazprom the giant state-owned gas company is negotiating to buy into Sakhalin-1. It seems that if this offer is not accepted then Sakhalin-2 is in danger of being stopped. Gazprom is looking to have as much as 25 percent of Sakhalin-2 - which means that the leading company in the Seven Sisters cartel would become a minority stockholder. Skhalin-w2 has reserves of 4.5 billion barrels. Thus it is a rich prize which Russia will certainly claim. It is just a matter of time.

On behalf of Royal Dutch Shell, Prime Minister Blair has expressed deep concern that Shell is going to be shut out of the rich bonanzas of Skahlin-1 and Sakhalin-2. The U.S. State Department continues its lobbying on behalf of Shell and Exxon, but Russia may have other plans. Gazprom sources said it was secretly negotiating with an Indian company, 'The Indian National Oil and Natural Gas Corporation' (ONGG) about buying its 20 percent share in Sakhalin-1. If a deal is struck it will give Gazprom very significant stakes in the most productive oil and gas projects in the world, leaving members of the Seven Sisters cartel in very weak positions.

In the meantime, the hypocrisy of Bush's 'war on terror' is apparent for all to see in Colombia where Bush proposals call for spending $98 million to protect Occidental Petroleum's 480-mile-long pipeline, which runs from Colombia's second-largest oil field to the Caribbean coast.

The $98 million is in addition to the $1.3 billion the U.S. has already given the Colombian Government, ostensibly to fight the FARC 'drug terrorists.' In 2001, the Cano Limon pipeline was closed for 266 days, because the Revolutionary Armed Forces of Colombia (FARC) guerillas kept on blowing it up, to ante up the bribery fee. FARC rebels have closed down the pipeline at regular intervals for the past fifteen years, to emphasize that their threats are not idle and to earn more and more 'protection' money. Meanwhile the resulting 2.5 million barrels of spilled oil running into Colombia's rivers and streams, far exceeds the amount of the 1989 Exxon Valdez oil spill in Alaska.

In spite of distractions in the Balkans, the Caspian Sea and Afghanistan, the petroleum cartel has not given up on its intention to take over Iran's oil. According to sources within the German BDN (Secret Service):

The Bush administration has drawn up plans to hit Iran's nuclear reactors, WMD sites, and military sites with heavy saturation bombing using bunker buster bombs and tactical nuclear weapons. The attack will be coordinated with urban and rural critical infrastructure sabotage carried out element of the People's Mujaheddin (MEK), Pentagon Special Operations units, and other Iranian dissident groups.

Details of the German intelligence information expressing some concern comes from classified briefings provided by elements within the CIA. Apparently the concern is that the Neo-Bolsheviks in the Bush administration will, in attacking Iran, set off a chain of events that will lead to world war.

Intelligence on U.S. plans to attack Iran has also been passed by CIA agents to counterparts in France, Britain, Canada and Australia. U.S. imperialist war plans for Iran also entail quickly seizing Iran's southwestern Khuzestan Province, where most of Iran's oil reserves and refineries are located.

Khuzestan has a majority Shi'ite Arab population that has close links with their ethnic and religious brethren in Iraq. The Bush plans call for a U.S. military strike across the Iraqi border and from naval forces in the Persian Gulf in answer to an appeal for assistance from the Al Ahwaz Popular Democratic Front and Liberation Organization rebel forces in Khuzestan, which will declare an independent Arab state of the Democratic Republic of Ahwaz and receive diplomatic recognition from the United States, Britain and Israel plus a few other close U.S. allies.

After World War I, Khuzestan was annexed by Iran and then called after its ancient historical name, Persia. It is mentioned in the Bible on many occasions by its ancient name. There are also plans to incite rebellions among Iran's other minorities, including Azeris and Turkmen in the oil-rich Caspian Sea region.

Some analysts believe that the 1991 Gulf War was started by the U.S. as a 'curtain-raiser' to the big event, an invasion of Iran by the United States backed by Israel, France and Germany, which is why America gave the green light for Hussein to go war against Iran. The purpose of egging Iraq on to attack Iran must be clear to all; that Iraq and Iran would fight a war that would leave them both desperately weakened. At a minimum, the U.S. signaled Hussein that some aggression was acceptable - that the U.S would not oppose an Iraqi invasion to take back the al-Rumalia oil field, the disputed border strip and the Gulf Islands, including Bubiyan oil fields territories claimed by Iraq as always having been part of Iraq and not of Kuwait or Iran. In later years, a reclusive April Glaspie was cornered by British reporters who pelted her with questions about her role in starting the 1991 war with Iraq, but without a single word Glaspie climbed into a limousine, closed the door behind her and the drove off.

Two years later during the American television network NBC News 'Decision 92' of the third round of the Presidential debates, presidential candidate Ross Perot was quoted as saying:

> "… We told (Saddam) that he could take the northeast part of Kuwait; when he took the whole thing we went nuts. And if we didn't tell him that why won't we even let the Senate Foreign Relations Committee and the Senate Intelligence Committee see the written instructions for Ambassador Glaspie?"

At this point (Perot) is interrupted by then President George Bush Senior who yelled:

> "I've got to reply to that. That goes to national honor. That is absolutely absurd."

Absurd or not, the fact is that April Glaspie left Baghdad in late August 1990 and returned to Washington where she was kept under wraps for eight months, not allowed to talk to the media, and did not surface before the end of the Gulf War (April 11, 1991) when she was called to testify informally (not under oath) before the Senate Foreign Relations Committee about her meeting with President Hussein. Glaspie said she was the victim of "deliberate deception on a major scale" and denounced the transcript of her meeting as "a fabrication" that distorted her position, though she admitted that it contained "a great deal" that was accurate.

Glaspie was thereafter shunted off to Cape Town, South Africa as U.S. Consul General. Nothing has been heard of her since her retirement from the diplomatic service in 2002. It is almost as if Glaspie had become a non-person. Why did the Senate not show more backbone and do its job? Why was the State Department allowed to get away with hiding and withholding information to which the American people were and are, fully entitled?'

Following Glaspie's deception, President George Bush set about cultivating a climate for war, all the while bombing Iraq in the so-called "no fly zones" which apart from violating Iraq's sovereignty were illegal under the U.S. Constitution. At the United Nations Bush had his 'war at any price' crews working the Arab delegation claiming that if the invasion of Kuwait was not dealt with, then they would be next on Hussein's list, a total and palpable untruth without merit.

Bush succeeded in getting an embargo imposed on Iraq. On January 29, 1991, Bush used his State of the Union address as a vehicle to inflame feelings against Iraq. Astonishingly he added the following remarks:

> "The world can therefore seize the opportunity of the present Persian Gulf crisis to fulfill the long-held promise of a New World Order."

The fact that Bush came right out with the true reason for the so-called "Persian Gulf Crisis" was now right out in the open, yet the jackals of the U.S. media failed to report on what the president was talking about. The concept of a New World Order was not new, dating back as it did to King George III, whose plans were interrupted by the American Revolution. Bush's plans to rush the nation into a war in Iraq were quite blatant, so much so that a number of important people in Washington began having serious doubts and began to mount opposition to the drums of war being beaten. One of them, former Navy Secretary James H. Webb, went public with his concerns during a November 12, 1990 television discussion:

> "The purpose of our presence in the Persian Gulf is to further the Bush administration's New World Order, I don't like it."

Another Washington personality to voice strong criticism of the

Bush administration's rush to war was James Atkins, a former ambassador to Saudi Arabia and a genuine expert on Middle East affairs. In a signed article published by the Los Angeles Times of September 17, 1990, he charged that Defense Secretary Richard Cheney had deliberately misled King Fahd to believe that an attack on Saudi Arabia by Iraq was imminent. Atkins also related his experiences with Henry Kissinger who fought Atkins every time he attacked the plans to make war against Iraq.

On the international scene there were some countries, notably France, who were concerned about the systematic daily bombing of Iraq. The former minister of Agriculture under Charles De Gaulle told a German magazine interviewer of his disquiet:

> "I wish it (the bombing) was not so. I am deeply shocked over the fact that a nation is powerful only because it has weapons. The U.S.A. which in its economic affairs has extreme difficulties, has managed to silence Japan and Europe, because they are militarily weak. How long will the world accept that various countries must pay one Gendarme to enforce their own World Order?"

What is troubling to observers is the silence from Russia, which had it stood up to U.S. bullying, would have probably been able to prevent the war against Iraq. At the least Russia could have supplied the Iraq military with its 'Tamara' anti-aircraft state of the art defense system that would have brought British and U.S. planes tumbling down and abruptly ended the reign of terror from the skies that had become a daily occurrence in Iraq. No members of the opposition in the Senate and House were able to stop Bush's rush to war that did damage far beyond the actual invasion of Iraq and which shock waves are still being felt in 2008. Seen in proper perspective the invasion of Iraq, on the orders of the Committee of 300, was to impose a New World Order on the world and in particular, on Europe.

The chaos released by the '300' through the willingness of Tony Blair, George Bush Sr. and his son G.W. Bush to attack Iraq, is yet to be measured. In its total effect, which will not become clear for at least another ten years, we shall see vast changes occurring, all of which can be traced back to the imperial oil policies of the U.S. and Great Britain, which began in earnest with President Wilson sending U.S. marines into Tampico and Vera Cruz in an effort to snatch Mexico's crude oil away from its rightful owners.

That continuation of imperial oil policies was evident in what many thousands of Americans believe was a contrived situation, the 9/11 disaster. If 9/11 was indeed a contrived situation in the manner of Pearl Harbor, then essentially, it was the next phase in the same presentation, a strategy for the U.S. to grab control of the world's oil fields, especially those that lay in the Middle East, Central Asia, South America, Malaysia, Borneo and Afghanistan, while at the same time shifting the United States from a confederate republic to a dictatorship of a New World Order under cover of 'fighting terrorism.'

The United States reached the 'tipping point' in its change from a confederated republic to a One World dictatorship with the attack on the World Trade Center in New York, and the fact that it was achieved with little or no opposition, only serves to underscore just how large a role was played by that event. Since, in the opinion of several astute observers it was all too smooth to have been by chance, this event serves to strengthen the convictions of a good many people that 9/11 was a contrived situation.

CHAPTER 24

Venezuela comes into the equation

What will be the outlook if oil production peaks in about 50 years from now? Will there be even worse jockeying with regional wars all over the globe, or will the opposing forces realize that salvation of the industrialized world lies in absolute cooperation in the area of essential raw materials, especially crude oil. If we are to judge on the basis of U.S. and British behavior over the past 50 years we are bound to conclude that with the stakes being the end of the world's oil reserves, the U.S. foreign policy will be to engage in militarism on the scale of the Roman Empire, while putting down dissent at home. That much we are already seeing. In fact the large number of laws that have been passed since the invasion of Iraq began, bears witness to the course being taken to curb opposition to the oil wars, and at the same time minimizes the highest law of the land in taking away the right of the people to protest.

It is certainly true that restrictive measures introduced by the Bush administration have had a chilling effect on the constitutional rights of the American people. In mid-2008 it has become apparent that the repressive laws passed since the advent of the Gulf Wars are having the desired effect. That might be what has damped down any sign of protest against the Bush administration's policy toward Venezuela and its tough-minded leader, Hugo Chavez.

In view of the marked hostility displayed toward Venezuela by Washington, it is not beyond the realm of possibility that it might be the next target in the imperialist fight for oil. With this in mind, let us take a look at Venezuela in 2008. There have been some changes. I don't think they're dramatic. This is probably the first time in Venezuelan history that there's a government that's making more than gestures towards using its huge resources to help the poorer parts of the population. This is mostly towards health, education, cooperatives and so on. Just how great the impact is it's hard to say. But certainly we know the popular reaction to them, which is after all the most important question. What's important is not what we think about it, but what Venezuelans think about it. And that's very much well known.

There are pretty good polling agencies in Latin America, the main one is Latino barometro, which is in Chile. They monitor attitudes throughout Latin America on all sorts of crucial issues. The most recent one in Chile, found support for democracy, and support for the government has been rising very sharply in Venezuela since 1998. Venezuela is now essentially tied with Uruguay at the top in support for the government and support for democracy.

It's well ahead of the other Latin American countries in support for the economic policies of the government and also well ahead in the belief that the policies help the poor, meaning the huge majority, instead of elites. And there are similar judgments on other issues, and it has been rising rather sharply. Despite the obstacles there has been a degree of progress that has been considered by the population as very meaningful, and that's the best measure. With the announcement of the creation of the United Socialist Party of Venezuela (PSUV) and the acceleration in their attempted appropriation of various services and companies, is there a maturing of this revolution? It's not easy to say. There are conflicting tendencies, and the question for Venezuela is which one will prevail. There are democratizing tendencies, devolution of power, popular assemblies, and communities taking control of their own budgets, workplace cooperatives and so on. All of that is building towards democracy.

There are also authoritarian tendencies: centralization, charismatic figure and so on. These policies in themselves you can't really judge in which direction they'll go. For a country to control its own resources is certainly perfectly reasonable. So if Venezuela takes greater control of its own resources that could be a very positive development. On the other hand, it might not be. So for example, when Saudi Arabia nationalized its oil in the 1970s, it did not mean that they were controlling their own oil instead of foreign corporations - mainly ARAMCO. On the other hand Saudi Arabia is in the hands of a harsh tyranny. Washington's major and most valued ally in the region is a brutal tyranny and the most extreme Islamist fundamentalist state in the world. So the story depends on how the resources are used. Mercosur, the common market of the southern cone, is a group that boasts the largest economies of South America. It is founded on free-market style arrangements, like NAFTA, and does not seem to be leaning towards any alternative to the prevailing neo-liberal doctrine.

Mercosur for the moment is more of a hope than an actuality. Mercosur is part of it, Cochabamba meetings are another step, and there are other steps. Integration is a powerful step towards maintaining sovereignty and independence. When countries are separated from one another they can be picked off, either by force or by economic strangulation. If they are integrated and cooperate, they're much more free from external control, meaning U.S. control in the last half-century - but it goes back much farther than that.

So that's an important step, but there are barriers. One barrier is that there is also a desperate need in Latin America for internal integration. Each of the countries has a very sharp divide between a small wealthy Europeanized, mostly white, elite, and a huge mass of deeply impoverished people, usually Indian, black and mestizos. The race correlation isn't perfect, but it's a correlation. Latin America has some of the worst inequality in the world, and those problems are also beginning to be overcome. There is a long way to go, but there are steps in the right direction in

Venezuela, in Bolivia, to some extent in Brazil, in Argentina and not much elsewhere for the moment. But both the internal integration and the external integration among the countries are quite important steps, and it's the first time since the Spanish colonization 500 years ago, so that's of some significance.

Let's return to some of the criticisms of authoritarianism that have followed term extensions and the recent so-called enabling law. Those laws were passed by the parliament. The parliament happens to be almost completely dominated by Chavez, but the reason for that is that the opposition refuses to take part most probably under U.S. pressure. I don't like those laws myself. How they turn out depends on popular pressures. They could be steps towards authoritarianism. They could be steps towards implementing constructive programs. It's not for us to say, it's for the Venezuelan people to say, and we know their opinion very well.

Oil wealth in Venezuela has given the country the opportunity to extend aid to poor communities in the West, including New York and London, and it has allowed it to buy up the debt of Argentina, Bolivia and Ecuador.

Let's begin with its aid to the West, which is a little ironic. But there's a background to that. It began with a program in Boston. What happened is that a group of Senators approached the 8 major energy corporations and asked if they could provide short-term assistance to poor people in the United States to get through the harsh winter, when they were unable to pay their oil bills because of the high oil prices. They got one response, from CITGO, the Venezuelan owned company, and that one company did indeed provide temporary low- cost oil in Boston, then the Bronx in New York and elsewhere. That's the Western aid. So there's more to it than just Chavez giving aid to America's poor.

As for the rest, yes Chavez did buy up a quarter, or a third of the debt of Argentina. That was an effort to help Argentina rid itself of the IMF, as the President of Argentina put it. The IMF, which is sort of an off-shoot of the U.S. Treasury Department, has had a shattering effect in Latin America. Its programs have been followed more rigorously in Latin America, than in any other part of the world.

Bolivia has been following IMF policies for 25 years and the end result was a per-capita income lower than it was in the beginning. Argentina was the poster-child of the IMF. It was doing all the right things, and urging everyone else to follow the policies, set by the World Bank and the U.S. Treasury Department. Well, what happened is that it led to a total economic catastrophe. Argentina did manage to escape the catastrophe by radically violating IMF rules, and they determined to rid themselves of the IMF, as Kirchner put it, and Venezuela helped them. Brazil was doing the same thing in its own way and now Bolivia is doing it with Venezuelan help. The IMF is in fact in trouble because it's financing came largely from debt collection and if the countries refuse to accept it's borrowing because the policies are too harmful, well it's not clear what it is going to do.

Then there is also Petrocaribe, a program to provide oil on favorable terms, with delayed payment, to many of the Caribbean countries as well to some others. Another program was called Operation Miracle. It uses Venezuelan funding to send Cuban doctors -- Cuban doctors are very highly trained and they have a very advanced medical system, comparable to the first-world systems — to places like Jamaica and other countries of the region. It began by finding people who are blind, have completely lost vision, but could be surgically treated to recover vision, and they are identified by Cuban doctors, brought back to Cuba, and treated with their high-class medical facilities, and returned to their countries able to see. That leaves an impression.

There was some effort apparently by the United States and Mexico to do something similar, but it never got anywhere. In fact, the impact of Chavez's programs can be seen very clearly by George Bush's last trip. The press talked about his new shift of programs towards Latin America, but what actually happened if you look, is that Bush was picking up some of Chavez's rhetoric. That's the wonderful new programs, picking up some of the rhetoric of Chavez, but not implementing it, or barely implementing it.

Any old tale — as long as it advances a cause for war is in vogue. With the exception of Hugo Chavez and Iran's Islamist Mahmoud Ahmadinejad, no other world leader has perfected the role of 'U.S. antagonist' better that leave an eye-opening impression. Along with a close group of confidants that includes some the world's most notorious U.S. antagonists like Cuba's aging dictator Fidel Castro, and Bolivia's nationalist President Evo Morales - Chavez has quickly become one of the leading spokesmen for the global pro-nationalist, anti-American movement. During his several uproarious years in office, Chavez has made his attitude toward the Bush administration a matter of public record.

> 'It's America the most perverse, murderous, genocidal, immoral empire that this planet has known in 100 centuries,' Chavez told an audience at the World Social Forum in Caracas.

In response, Washington has dubbed Chavez's anti-American outbursts and repeated threats to spread a 'Bolivarian Revolution' throughout Latin America, as the ravings of a desperate leader trying to divert public attention away from failed social and economic policies.

Of course Venezuela's policies have not failed, nor does there appear to be any likelihood an American invasion of the country. But recent efforts by Chavez to strengthen energy, defense, nuclear and political relations with Iran may force Washington to revise its thinking. In a passionate speech delivered to supporters in Caracas, Chavez declared:

I had close ties with Mohammad Khatami Iran's President from 1997-2005, whom I consider to be like a brother and now I enjoy close ties with his successor, President Mahmoud Ahmadinejad, whom I also think of as a brother.

Although the statement is not unusual for the enthusiastic and fresh bluntness of Chavez, it does show the direction in which the relationship is headed. After all, any independent sovereign nation has a right to choose its friends and make alliances.

At the 141st Ministerial Meeting of the Organization of the Petroleum Exporting Countries (OPEC) held in Caracas in late May, top officials from Iran and Venezuela discussed several bilateral agreements, most notably, participation by Iranian state oil firm Petropars in oil projects in Venezuela's underdeveloped Orinoco Belt and gas projects in the Gulf of Venezuela. Both countries are expected to undertake exploration of one of the areas in the Orinoco Belt with the ultimate goal of allowing Petropars to export finished fuel to Iran. Iranian experts are scheduled to arrive in Venezuela soon to support government-sponsored engineering projects. Let me hasten to add that both Iran and Venezuela as sovereign independent nations have every right to pursue their own interests even if it does not sit well with other nations. That is the premise of international law. As Venezuela's energy relations with Iran have blossomed, its energy relations with the West have gone the other way. Chavez recently announced that taxes would be raised on foreign oil companies operating in Venezuela from 16.7% to 33%, calling it a 'tax on extraction.' Chavez has accused foreign companies of exploiting his country's petroleum resources without properly compensating the Venezuelan people. This is a very well founded accusation.

Despite the tax increase and Chavez' stance, Venezuela remains an important energy partner for the U.S. According to statistics released by the Energy Information Administration (EIA), Venezuela ranks fourth in total crude exports (1.2 million barrels per day) and third in total petroleum products exported

(1.5 million barrels per day) to the U.S. (Canada is first but we are not quarrelling with Canada). Given America's continued reliance on Venezuelan oil for its everyday survival and the difficulties associated with securing energy resources from other parts of the world, any involvement by Teheran in Venezuela's energy sector should be perceived as a threat to U.S. national security or so says Washington. Firstly, what Venezuela does is none of the business of the Bush administration. Venezuela is not the 51st state of the Union.

In addition to energy cooperation, military and intelligence relations between Caracas and Tehran have intensified. In May, the U.S. State Department accused Venezuela of having an intelligence-sharing relationship with both Iran and Cuba, two countries which the U.S. has identified as sponsors of terrorism. That is only an opinion, not necessarily a fact. In its annual report on international terrorism, the U.S. State Department cited Chavez for sharing an 'ideological affinity' with two leftist guerrilla groups operating in Columbia — the FARC and the National Liberation Army -- both considered terrorist organizations by Washington. That being the case then it poses the question: Why has Washington often worked with these two Colombian groups who are undoubtedly terrorist groups? As a result, all arms and spare parts sales to Caracas, which totaled U.S. $33.9 million in 2005, were halted. Why this act of war? What evidence is there to support the claim that Venezuela is in 'ideological affinity' with terrorist groups? In response, Venezuelan General Alberto Muller Rojas, a senior advisor to Chavez, recommended that his country sell its 21 F-16 fighter jets to Iran. Although the 20 year-old fighter jets are obsolete by today's standards, the proposal aggravated already tense relations between the two countries. What business is it of America if other countries decide who their customers and friends are going to be? Reports that Iran and Venezuela have increased cooperation in the area of nuclear technology, has set off alarms in Washington. We suggest that the entire Bush administration be forced to read George Washington's Farewell Address and as fast as possible at that!

The Argentine newspaper Clarin reported that the Chavez government had asked Buenos Aires to sell it a nuclear reactor. Like the Iranian government, Caracas officials said that discussions took place, but added they involved only ways to explore 'the peaceful scientific uses of the atom.' And why not? Why India, Pakistan, North Korea, Israel, and not Venezuela?

In late 2005 there were reports that Venezuelan uranium deposits were bound for Tehran as part of a $200 million agreement signed between the two countries. Persons, supposedly missionaries, sent news back home that construction had occurred at a small military facility and airstrip close to where uranium deposits are said to be located. Whoever they are, they don't sound much like missionaries.

Iran and Venezuela share an intense dislike of America, and quite naturally so given the huge volume of interference in their internal affairs that has occurred for decades. It is not surprising that they look for ways to retaliate through support for anti-U.S. alliances throughout the Middle East and Latin America.

On an eight-day tour of Latin America, Iranian Majiis Speaker Gholam-Ali Haddad Adel said the strategic unity forged between the two countries is rooted in a response to 'threats by bullying powers such as the U.S.' Iran and Venezuela have concluded that the best way to accomplish their common objective of U.S. global destabilization is to join forces making any targeted response by Washington much more complex and costly.

The Bush administration's efforts would be best spent in restoring New Orleans and fixing the huge gap between poor and extremely rich in America, a condition that has come about following NAFTA, GATT and the World Trade Organization.

With an enthusiastic Iran as his partner, Chavez, the former paratrooper revolutionary has awakened the ghost of Simon Bolivar, with its anti-American ghosts. The Bush administration will just have to live with it or risk a 330-years war in Latin America. Perhaps that is the idea.

In 2007, the first batch out of a total of 100,000 Kalashnikov rifles which Venezuelan President Hugo Chavez has ordered from Moscow began arriving.

Venezuela's military is undergoing a profound transformation, with a major recruitment drive and new technology. The move is likely to worry the U.S., which regards Chavez as a destabilizing influence in the region.

Most defense experts agree that President Chavez needs to overhaul his outdated military hardware. But the United States and Venezuela's neighbor Colombia regard the arrival of 33,000 Kalashnikov rifles as further proof that Chavez is seeking to throw his weight around in the region. The Russian-built AK103 rifles come complete with more than half a million rounds of ammunition, state-of-the-art night vision scopes and bayonets. Another 70,000 rifles are expected to arrive before the end of 2008. But what worries Washington more are Venezuela's plans to build a factory here to assemble and export these Kalashnikov rifles along with bullets.

Chavez's administration is now in talks with the Russian manufacturer which holds the license to make the guns. The U.S., which recently ordered a complete ban on arms sales to Venezuela, has accused President Chavez of trying to destabilize Latin America. But Venezuela insists it has a right to buy arms for defensive purposes. President Chavez has repeatedly warned that the Bush administration was planning to invade Venezuela to get its hands on the country's oil resources.

Sir Maurice Hankey, Britain's First Secretary of the War Cabinet, 1918:

> "Oil in the next war will occupy the place of coal in the

present war, or at least a parallel place to coal. The only big potential supply that we can get under British control is the Persian (now Iran, and Mesopotamian - now Iraq - supply... Control over these oil supplies becomes a first class British war aim."

Alan Greenspan, Federal Reserve Banks Chairman, 1987-2006:

"Whatever their publicized angst over Saddam Hussein's weapons of mass destruction, American and British authorities were also concerned about violence in an area that harbors a resource indispensable for the functioning of the world economy."

We cannot leave Iraq because extremists may be in a position to use oil as a tool to blackmail the West... and they will do so unless we abandon Israel.

George W. Bush, November 1, 2006:

"When there is a regime change in Iraq, you could add 3 million to 5 million barrels of production to world supply."

Lawrence Lindsey, George W. Bush's former chief economic adviser, 2002:

"Secure supplies of energy are essential to our prosperity and security. The concentration of 65 percent of the world's known oil reserves in the Persian Gulf means we must continue to ensure reliable access to competitively priced oil and a prompt, adequate response to any major oil supply disruption."

CHAPTER 25

America cannot go on fighting oil wars indefinitely

When the Bush-Cheney administration took over in January 2001, the international price of oil was about $22 a barrel. Now, nearly eight years later, the price of oil is hovering around $150 a barrel, a more than five hundred percent increase. Thus, as far as oil is concerned, things have not unfolded in Iraq as planned and expected by the Neo- Bolsheviks in the Bush-Cheney administration. First, they thought that gushing Iraqi oil would pay for the invasion and occupation of the country. Instead, the cash outlay for this adventure is likely to reach one trillion dollars, and the total cost to the U.S. economy will likely surpass three trillion dollars.

Second, the price of oil is reaching record levels with no top in sight and this is threatening to tip the U.S. and the world economies into a protracted economic recession. This is partly due to the fact that Iraqi oil output has not increased as planned and is rather below where it was when the United States invaded and occupied Iraq in 2003. From a macroeconomic point of view, this ill-advised and illegal war has been an unmitigated disaster.

Nevertheless, despite sporadic pious declarations about leaving Iraq when asked, the Bush-Cheney administration is planning a 50-year American military occupation of Iraq. They do not want to set a date to end the occupation of Iraq, because they see it as an open-ended military occupation. This is to be expected since the real reasons they invaded Iraq in the first place were to pursue the long range goal of controlling Middle East oil and of protecting the state of Israel from its Muslim neighbors. Indeed, everybody knows that the military invasion of Iraq by American forces had nothing to do with 'democracy' or the wishes of the people. It had everything to do with securing Iraq's oil reserves and with removing one of Israel's enemies in the person of Saddam Hussein.

In May 31, 2007, Secretary of Defense Robert Gates confirmed these long-term plans when he said that the United States was looking for a 'long and enduring presence' in Iraq. That is the reason the U.S. has built the largest embassy in the world, in Baghdad with 21 buildings on a 100-acre site on the banks of the Tigris, which will be capable of housing one thousand employees. That is also why they are consolidating some 100 plus military bases in that Muslim country into 14 permanent super-military bases - all geared to control militarily that part of the world for a very long time.

This is also why the Bush-Cheney administration is pushing the Iraqi Parliament hard to adopt a law that would privatize the Iraqi oil industry. If the current puppet regime now in place in Iraq were to refuse passing such a law, the so-called "Hydrocarbon Act," it would lose over a billion dollars in reconstruction funds that would be blocked by the Bush-Cheney administration. This overt military grab of the oil resources of a Middle East nation is a sure recipe for feeding permanent terrorism in the world and permanent war in the Middle East for as long as one can see.

And if Americans elect a Republican president for a third term in November 2008 by voting for presumptive Republican Presidential nominee, Senator John McCain said that is what will happen since this politician is already committed to a one hundred year war in that part of the world. According to polls, a vast majority of Iraqis is opposed to the privatization of their oil industry. Nevertheless, privatization of Iraqi oil is one of the main 'benchmarks' that the Bush-Cheney administration is imposing on the Iraqi government.

It has installed in occupied Iraq a puppet government of its own that is delivering the merchandise, even though some arm-twisting pressure has been necessary. On July 3, 2007, for instance, the U.S.-controlled al-Maliki's Cabinet approved, with no Sunni ministers present, a U.S. - backed draft oil law that will share Iraqi oil wealth between the three main Iraqi groups, but which will, above all, let American and foreign oil companies into the Iraqi oil sector and enact privatization under so called production sharing agreements. This has been a key political target and even a 'benchmark' set by the Bush-Cheney White House, but so far the Iraqi Parliament has balked in approving the required controversial legislation, because there have been many protests, many Iraqis being very reluctant to adopt a policy of sharing oil production and revenues with foreign oil companies, especially when they have been taken away from them 'at gunpoint.'

The Iraqi oil industry has been nationalized since 1975, some thirty - three years ago. Indeed, before the American-led military invasion and occupation of Iraq, the Iraqi oil fields were controlled by the Iraqi government through a state-owned corporation. This was the foundation for a relatively high standard of living in Iraq, which had one of the best health care systems in the region and was producing more Ph.D.s per capita than the U.S. It is this prosperity and this wealth that are being destroyed by the Bush-Cheney administration. Under their military occupation of Iraq and the contemplated oil arrangements, much of Iraqi oil production and oil revenues would fall under the control of foreign oil companies, mainly American and British EXXON/Mobil, Chevron/Texaco, BP/AMOCO and Royal Dutch/Shell.

One of the two main rationales for launching the illegal invasion of Iraq would have been accomplished, i.e. to keep the flow of oil going, under the surveillance of American troops, the other rationale being the destruction of one of Israel's strategic enemies. Many knowledgeable observers, such as Australian Defense Minister Brendan Nelson, have said it was a paramount reason for the Iraq invasion and occupation when he said that maintaining 'resource security' in the Middle East was a priority. That is the reason why, when the American armies arrived in Baghdad, in early April 2003, their orders were to secure only one kind of public buildings, those of the Iraqi Oil Ministry. All the rest did not matter.

Finally, let us remember that on October 11, 2002, the U.S. Senate voted 77-23 to give George W. Bush and Dick Cheney a blank check authorization to launch a war of aggression against Iraq. Current presidential candidate, John McCain and former presidential candidate, Hillary Clinton, voted for the resolution. Let us remind ourselves also that ten days earlier, the Central Intelligence Agency - CIA - had issued a confidential 90-page classified version of the National Intelligence Estimate, which contained a long list of dire consequences to follow if the USA were to invade Iraq. The report was made available to all 100 senators, but only six of them bothered to avail themselves of the opportunity to read it. Thanks to that knowledge, people have a glimpse now about how decisions were made in Washington D.C. before the onset of this war. Even on questions of life and death, improvisation prevailed on a high scale. And now, the seeds have been sown for permanent military occupations, permanent wars and permanent terrorism in the Middle East and in the world. Truly, we fight for oil.

The price for such a misguided policy will be high and will linger on for years to come. Indeed, many Americans are beginning to see that there is a link between Iraq war spending and deficit, and the ongoing recession and accelerating inflation. Such waste and spending on wars reduces the amount of financial resources available to finance other essential government programs at home, from education to infrastructure. They increase the balance of payments deficit and force the U.S. to borrow abroad. And when the Federal Reserve lowers interest rates to mitigate the banking crisis, the dollar plummets, which feeds inflation further when oil prices and all other prices connected with transportation and world-traded commodities go up. The current stagflation is a direct consequence of excessive U.S. military spending abroad. The sooner a majority of Americans see that, the better.

But in 2008 with gasoline prices at record levels, there is a way out of this mess, which is to stabilize gasoline prices and stabilize the U.S. economy. Let the government open up all strategic oil reserves and start its own refinery to produce gasoline at slightly above cost using a non-profit organization established by an act of Congress. Remove the tax from wild-cat drilling, thus allowing more and more small drillers to come back into the business of oil prospecting in the U.S. This would undercut the rapaciousness of the oil companies and help to put an end to their insatiable appetite for ever greater profits. The U.S cannot go on indefinitely fighting wars for oil, albeit under the guise of 'fighting terrorism.' As powerful as it is, America cannot go on for ever exhausting its treasures in endless war, which is why the Constitution was written to prevent such a thing from happening. But by trampling the Constitution underfoot and ignoring the highest law of the land, the Bush-Cheney administration has launched the U.S. on just such a disastrous course. The end is predictable.

All the while the war in Iraq drags on although opposed by 87% of the American people with Democrats in the House and Senate seemingly powerless to bring it to an immediate halt in accordance with the mandate given to them in the November 2007 elections.

So what then is the future of Iraq? Will the war drag on interminably in violation of the Constitution, or will the new administration slated to take office in 2009 be able to bring this unmitigated disaster to an end? That remains to be seen.

Other titles

All great historical events are planned in secret by men who surround themselves with total discretion.

OMNIA VERITAS LTD PRESENTS:

BEYOND the CONSPIRACY
UNMASKING THE INVISIBLE WORLD GOVERNMENT

by John Coleman

Highly organized groups always have the advantage over citizens

The many tragic and explosive events of the 20th century didn't happen by themselves, but were planned according to a well-established pattern...

OMNIA VERITAS LTD PRESENTS:

THE CLUB OF ROME
THE THINK TANK OF THE NEW WORLD ORDER

BY JOHN COLEMAN

Who were the planners and creators of these major events?

OMNIA VERITAS LTD PRESENTS:

DIPLOMACY BY DECEPTION
AN ACCOUNT OF THE TREASONOUS CONDUCT BY THE GOVERNMENTS OF BRITAIN AND THE UNITED STATES

BY JOHN COLEMAN

The story of the creation of the United Nations is a classic case of diplomacy by deception

The real promoters of this cursed trade are the "elites" of this world.

This book explains what masonry is

Historical events are often caused by a "hidden hand"...

OMNIA VERITAS
OMNIA VERITAS LTD PRESENTS:
ONE WORLD ORDER
SOCIALIST
DICTATORSHIP
All these years, while our attention was focused on the evils of communism in Moscow, the socialists in Washington were busy stealing from America!
BY JOHN COLEMAN
"The enemy in Washington is more to be feared than the enemy in Moscow."

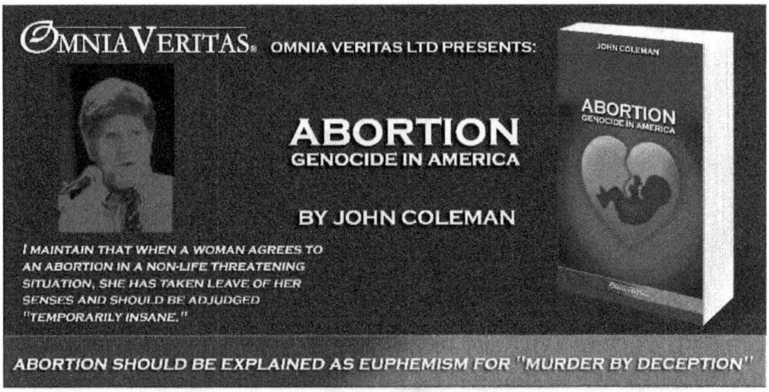
OMNIA VERITAS
OMNIA VERITAS LTD PRESENTS:
JOHN COLEMAN
ABORTION
GENOCIDE IN AMERICA
BY JOHN COLEMAN
I MAINTAIN THAT WHEN A WOMAN AGREES TO AN ABORTION IN A NON-LIFE THREATENING SITUATION, SHE HAS TAKEN LEAVE OF HER SENSES AND SHOULD BE ADJUDGED "TEMPORARILY INSANE."
ABORTION SHOULD BE EXPLAINED AS EUPHEMISM FOR "MURDER BY DECEPTION"

OMNIA VERITAS
Omnia Veritas Ltd presents:
THE SVALI CHRONICLES
BREAKING FREE FROM MIND CONTROL
TESTIMONY OF AN EX-ILLUMINATI
The Illuminati are a group of people who follow a philosophy known as "illuminism" or "enlightenment".
Understanding the programming of the Illuminati sect

OMNIA VERITAS

Omnia Veritas Ltd presents:

THE CURSE
OF CANAAN
A demonology of history

by

EUSTACE MULLINS

Liberalism, more popularly known as secular humanism, can be traced in an unbroken line all the way back to the Biblical "Curse of Canaan."

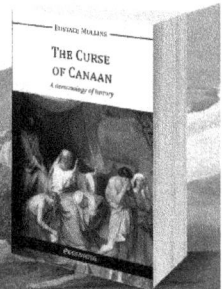

Humanism is the logical result of the demonology of history

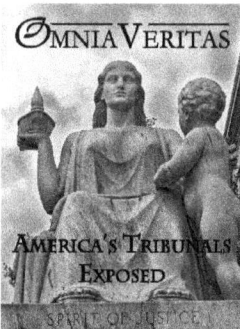

OMNIA VERITAS

Omnia Veritas Ltd presents:

THE RAPE OF
JUSTICE

by

EUSTACE MULLINS

AMERICA'S TRIBUNALS EXPOSED

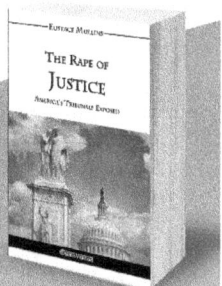

American should know just what is going on in our courts

OMNIA VERITAS

Omnia Veritas Ltd presents:

THE SECRETS OF
THE FEDERAL
RESERVE

by

EUSTACE MULLINS

HERE ARE THE SIMPLE FACTS OF THE GREAT BETRAYAL

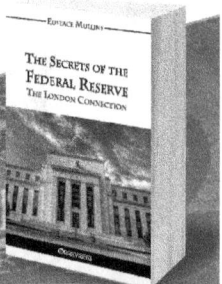

Will we continue to be enslaved by the Babylonian debt money system?

The program of the World Order remains the same; Divide and Conquer

The most concentrated attacks on the White Race are occurring in the United States of America

The Betrayal of America by the Secret Power.

OMNIA VERITAS

Omnia Veritas Ltd presents:

Vladimir Putin & Eurasia

The providential advent of the "predestined man", the "absolute concept" Vladimir Putin, embodying the "New Russia".

by JEAN PARVULESCO

A singularly dangerous book, not to be placed in all hands...

OMNIA VERITAS

Omnia Veritas Ltd presents:

It is no wonder that Wahhabis are now the backbone of terrorism, authorising, financing and planning the shedding of the blood of Muslims and other innocents.

British enmity against Islam

Confessions of a BRITISH SPY

This document reveals the true context of the Wahhabi movement

OMNIA VERITAS

OMNIA VERITAS LTD PRESENTS:

English Freemasonry is wealthy and capitalistic, controlling the money and rulers of the world through banking and commerce. French Freemasonry, on the other hand, is poor and communistic, attempting to control state finances through an all-powerful socialistic government.

SCARLET AND THE BEAST

ENGLISH FREEMASONRY, BANKS, AND THE ILLEGAL DRUG TRADE

The Harlot's abominable cup is in the hands of English Freemasonry

OMNIA VERITAS. Omnia Veritas Ltd presents:

FREDERICK SODDY

WEALTH, VIRTUAL WEALTH AND DEBT

THE SOLUTION OF THE ECONOMIC PARADOX

The most powerful tyranny and the most universal conspiracy against the economic freedom of individuals and the autonomy of nations the world has yet known.

The public are most carefully shielded from any real knowledge...

OMNIA VERITAS

THE MANUFACTURE AND SALE OF ST EINSTEIN

OMNIA VERITAS LTD PRESENTS:

CHRISTOPHER JON BJERKNES

5 volumes to end the illegitimate myth

OMNIA VERITAS. Omnia Veritas Ltd presents:

MYRON FAGAN

THE ILLUMINATI AND THE COUNCIL ON FOREIGN RELATIONS

The objective is to brainwash the people into accepting the phony peace bait to transform the United States into an enslaved unit of the United Nations' one-world government.

They have seized that power on orders from their masters of the great conspiracy

www.ingramcontent.com/pod-product-compliance
Lightning Source LLC
Chambersburg PA
CBHW070800270326
41927CB00010B/2230